WOMEN'S MATTERS

University of Delaware Press
Manuscript Competition Winners

Shakespearean Literature

John W. Blanpied, *Time and the Artist in Shakespeare's English Histories*

Robert Ornstein, *Shakespeare's Comedies: From Roman Farce to Romantic Mystery*

Donald W. Foster, *Elegy by W. S.: A Study in Attribution*

David Hoeniger, *Medicine and Shakespeare in the English Renaissance*

Peggy Muñoz Simonds, *Myth, Emblem, and Music in Shakespeare's Cymbeline*

Marvin Rosenberg, *The Masks of Hamlet*

Frederick Kiefer, *Writing on the Renaissance Stage: Written Words, Printed Pages, Metaphoric Books*

Nina Levine, *Women's Matters: Politics, Gender, and Nation in Shakespeare's Early History Plays*

Early American Culture to 1840

Daniel D. Reiff, *Small Georgian Houses in England and Virginia: Origins and Development through the 1750s*

Military, Naval, and Diplomatic History

Richard J. Hargrove, *General John Burgoyne*

Eighteenth-Century Studies

Donald T. Siebert, *The Moral Animus of David Hume*

Ruben Quintero, *Literate Culture: Pope's Rhetorical Art*

Lois Bueler, *Clarrisa's Plots*

Alexander Pettit, *Illusory Consensus: Bolingbroke and the Polemical Response to Walpole, 1730–1737*

American Art

Rowland, Elzea, *John Sloan's Oil Paintings: A Catalogue Raisonné*

Thomas P. Somma, The Apotheosis of Democracy, *1908–1916: The Pediment for the House Wing of the United States Capitol*

WOMEN'S MATTERS

Politics, Gender, and Nation in Shakespeare's Early History Plays

Nina S. Levine

DELAWARE

Newark: University of Delaware Press
London: Associated University Presses

Associated University Presses
440 Forsgate Drive
Cranbury, NJ 08512

Associated University Presses
16 Barter Street
London WC1A 2AH, England

Associated University Presses
P.O. Box 338, Port Credit
Mississauga, Ontario
Canada L5G 4L8

The paper used in this publication meets the requirements
of the American National Standard for Permanence of Paper
for Printed Library Materials Z39.48–1984.

Library of Congress Cataloging-in-Publication Data

Levine, Nina S., 1950–
    Women's matters : politics, gender, and nation in Shakespeare's early history plays
/ Nina S. Levine.
        p. cm.
    Includes bibliographical references and index.
    ISBN 0–87413–654–7 (alk. paper)
        1. Shakespeare, William, 1564–1616—Histories. 2. Politics and literature—Great
Britain—History—16th century. 3. Shakespeare, William, 1564–1616—political and
social views. 4. Women and literature—Great Britain—History—16th century.
5. Shakespeare, William, 1564–1616—Characters—Women. 6. Historical drama,
English—History and criticism. 7. Political plays, English-English—History and
criticism. 7. Political plays, English—History and criticism. 8. Nationalism in
literature. 9. Sex role in literature. 10. Women in literature. I. Title.
PR2982.L48   1998
822.3'3—dc21   97–41515
                                                                        CIP

PRINTED IN THE UNITED STATES OF AMERICA

For my parents

Contents

Acknowledgments

I wish to express my appreciation to all those who have contributed to the writing of this book. My greatest debt is to J. L. Simmons and Molly Rothenberg, who encouraged this project from the start and who gave generously of their time in reading and commenting on the earlier versions. I am most grateful to colleagues and friends at the University of South Carolina for their help and warm support. My special thanks go to Amittai Aviram, Trevor Howard-Hill, Lawrence Rhu, and Esther Richey. I would also like to express my appreciation to Jay Halio and the University of Delaware Press's anonymous readers for their helpful comments and criticisms.

Shakespeare Studies and *Renaissance Papers* have generously granted me permission to use materials from previously published articles: an earlier version of chapter 2 was published as "The Case of Eleanor Cobham: Authorizing History in *2 Henry VI*," *Shakespeare Studies* 22 (1994): 104–21; and a section of chapter 4 appeared as "'Accursed womb, the bed of death': Women and the Succession in *Richard III*," *Renaissance Papers* (1992): 17–27.

Introduction

For in the book of Numbers is it writ,
When the man dies, let the inheritance
Descend unto the daughter.

— *Henry V,* 1.2.98–100

The Archbishop of Canterbury's refutation of Salic law at the beginning of *Henry V* would seem to constitute a rare moment in Shakespeare's history plays. Arguing against the French practice of prohibiting inheritance through the female line, Canterbury insists on the importance of women in royal lineage and succession. We know, of course, that the archbishop's motives here are suspect, prompted by his interest in protecting church property and revenues, not by his concern for the legitimacy of the king's claim to France, or for women's rights. But what about Shakespeare's motives? In a play that makes explicit reference to England's "gracious Empress,"[1] the defense of female inheritance surely gestures toward both Elizabeth I and her most likely successor, James VI of Scotland, whose claim to the English throne was through his mother's and grandmother's line. Yet how are we to understand this gesture? Does the defense of female inheritance acknowledge, after nearly a half-century of female rule, that women do count in matters of succession and dynastic politics? Or does compliment turn to mockery in the mouth of the self-serving archbishop? In a play that has been described as "devoted to affirming a kind of Salic law of its own,"[2] to minimizing and even suppressing women's roles in royal genealogies, Canterbury's defense is, at the very least, oddly out of place and so prevents us from taking it at face value. And in this sense, the passage may be more representative than it first appears, paradigmatic of the complex relations between politics and gender that characterize Shakespeare's history plays as a whole.

I begin with this passage not simply because it raises questions about women and power that are central to this study but, more importantly,

13

because it demands that we consider these questions in relation to specific political contexts, both on and off Shakespeare's stage. One of my
contentions throughout this book is that representations of women in
power—whether in the plays themselves, in their chronicle sources, or
within Elizabethan society—are shaped not by cultural myths of gender
alone but by the intersection of these myths with specific political situa-
tions. The terms "gender" and "politics" may be commonplace in current
criticism, but nonetheless they remain useful in clarifying the complex
processes of state power and national identity in early modern England.
Drawing on Joan Scott's definition, we may think of gender as both "a
constitutive element of social relationships based on perceived differences between the sexes" and "a primary way of signifying relationships
of power."[3] If we take politics to mean the "discourses and practices of
power in a particular historical moment,"[4] then the interdependence of
gender and politics becomes apparent. When a nation's political practices
overlap with its gendered myths of power, as evidenced by the early
Tudor chronicles, the conjunction appears seamless, a sign of an appar-
ently natural reciprocity between gender and politics. But when political
needs come into conflict with these myths, as they did with the successive reigns of the Tudor queens, the relationship becomes both visible
and contradictory, a sign of instability and even weakness.

This book is a study of Shakespeare's early history plays in relation to
these contradictions, particularly as they play out in the intersections
between past and present, between "history," as defined by the plays'
Tudor sources, and contemporary Elizabethan politics. The plays
participate in these contradictions in part by bringing chronicle history
into the Elizabethan theater—and thereby staging the disjunctions
between the nation's cultural myths and its contemporary realities—but
also, and more precisely, by revising the gendered narratives of the past
in ways that register the concerns of the present. The task of this book is
to attend to the politics of this dialectical interchange—in which the
present shapes the past even as the past gives shape to the present—by
considering the ways in which Shakespeare's representations of women
interpret relations between the Tudor historical record and the concerns
of the Elizabethan nation-state in the 1590s. As it underwrites discourses
of state power and national identity during this period, the category of
gender provides an especially resonant point of entry into these
considerations, underscoring the tensions between past and present and
within Elizabethan culture itself.

Much has been made in recent years of the ideological dissonance of
Elizabeth's rule and the corresponding anxieties experienced by the
queen and her subjects. Indeed, as both new historicists and feminists

have argued, if Elizabeth's rule "incarnated a contradiction at the very center of the Elizabethan sex/gender system,"[5] then we need to understand representations of power during this period in relation to this highly visible contradiction. Elizabethans attempted to address this contradiction in part by, in Louis Montrose's words, "working" the "available terms" of their culture, renegotiating power and privilege within the altered terrain of the political landscape.[6] But if, as Montrose and others have argued, the contradiction of female rule necessitated strategies of accommodation and mediation, it also offered Elizabethans an opportunity to reexamine—and to rewrite—traditional dynastic and national myths. One of the arguments of this book is that for Shakespeare and his contemporaries, the presence of a woman on England's throne also proved liberating, allowing them to challenge, and even to reimagine, orthodox representations of the nation-state as embodied in the figure of the male monarch. In writing women onto history's stage, Shakespeare's plays invite a skepticism about representations of power, both past and present. They call into question the efficacy of patriarchal fictions of state power and national identity and, at the same time, interrogate the politics of the present. In the process, they give shape to a "drama of nation"[7] that is more inclusive, and more iconoclastic, than either the dynastic histories set forth in the Tudor chronicles or the celebrations of power produced by the Elizabethan court.

In considering the ways in which Shakespeare's histories engender the nation, this study shifts the focus away from the more canonical plays of the second tetralogy, where female characters stand on the sidelines, and turns instead to Shakespeare's beginnings, to the *Henry VI* plays, *Richard III*, and *King John*, because it is in these early plays that women rule and questions of power and national identity are framed again and again in gendered terms. Typified by Joan of Arc, whose bold actions "exceed [her] sex" (*1 Henry VI*, 1.2.90), women take center stage in these plays, not only refusing to play the "woman's part" but, in the absence of a strong monarch, actively taking on the roles of men. In the *Henry VI* plays, Joan of Arc and Margaret of Anjou both dress in armor and engage in battle with "manly" courage, and Eleanor Cobham, though she does not assume a man's arms, tries to assume his place on the throne. Queen Elinor likewise plays the soldier in *King John*, riding into battle beside her son, while other women "like Amazons come tripping after drums, / Their thimbles into armed gauntlets change" (5.2.155–56). Even in *Richard III*, where misogyny reigns, women put up a fight, battling with wits and words if not with swords.

That Shakespeare should launch his career on the Elizabethan stage with an unbroken succession of powerful women surely invites consideration, which makes it all the more surprising that questions about gender and politics in these plays have only recently begun to attract critical attention.[8] To be sure, the *Henry VI* plays have long been marginalized in Shakespeare studies, dismissed by the nineteenth-century Disintegrators as the work of multiple authors and by twentieth-century formalists for their inferior artistry, their lack of tightly organized, unified plots and dominant central characters.[9] But even today, in spite of a renewed interest in the history plays as cultural and political texts, these early plays, and the *Henry VI* plays especially, continue to be subordinated to Shakespeare's second cycle of English history. Part of the problem may be that the plays fall between the territories marked out by recent critical practices. New historicists, for instance, more concerned with power than gender, have shown a preference for Shakespeare's later histories in which women recede into the background and the struggle for the Crown is played out between men, whereas feminist scholars have tended to privilege the comedies and tragedies over the histories. But is there also a problem with the plays themselves? Although I will argue otherwise, it is not difficult to see why these plays, centered on conflicts between "patriarchy" and "subversive women," might seem particularly resistant to the kinds of questions critics have been asking over the last decade.

Those who have written about the politics of gender in these early plays generally agree that they are patriarchal in structure. As David Bevington succinctly observed of *1 Henry VI*: "The theme of feminine supremacy echoes the larger theme of discord and division"[10] throughout the play and the tetralogy. There is much to warrant this conclusion, to be sure, as Shakespeare rounds up all the usual suspects in these plays— witches, prophetesses, adulteresses, domineering wives, murderous mothers, cross-dressed Amazons, treacherous French women—drawing on stereotypes befitting a moral history designed to reinforce orthodox notions about female subservience. The plays themselves sound multiple warnings about the dangers of unruly women. As the "good Duke" Humphrey bluntly puts it, censuring Queen Margaret's foray into court politics in *2 Henry VI*: "These are no women's matters" (1.3.117). Those who step out of their place in these plays—and nearly all of the women do—are seen as a threat to order and stability and as such must be brought under control for the good of the nation. Moral history thus provides structure and authority for a patriarchal drama that casts women as England's enemy. As David Kastan concludes of the women in the first tetralogy, "'The monstruous regiment of women,' in John Knox's phrase, must be defeated, and women returned to their usual sphere, merely adjunct to power."[11]

But if these plays are so insistently patriarchal, what were the politics of their performance on the Elizabethan stage in the 1590s? How did Elizabeth's subjects, or the queen herself, reconcile these gendered narratives with the political realities of England, a nation-state that had been ruled by women for nearly fifty years? Until recently, the tendency was to assume that there was no problem at all: the plays simply reflected the dominant patriarchal culture, of which Elizabeth was assumed to be a part, their portraits of "domineering females" consistent with a long tradition of antifeminist literature.[12] Accordingly, the queen was identified with the male rulers of the plays, not with the unruly women, an assumption authorized in part by Elizabeth's own practice of comparing herself with her male predecessors. In this view, the conjunction between gender and politics on Shakespeare's stage, as in chronicle history, appears natural and seamless, unchallenged by the presence of a woman on England's throne. But with new historicists and cultural materialists arguing against the notion of a stable and unified culture, more nuanced political readings have begun to emerge, as illustrated in the recent chapters on these plays by Phyllis Rackin and Leah Marcus. For while these studies continue to read the plays as patriarchal histories, they break with earlier work by underscoring the disjunction between the stage and the state, focusing on the differences between the history plays and the complex realities of Elizabethan politics in the 1590s.

For both Rackin and Marcus, the patriarchal narratives of the history plays offer a counterexample to Elizabethan England, one that manages contemporary instabilities and anxieties within the closed space of the public stage. For Marcus, *1 Henry VI* performs a kind of collective therapy, "working through" public tensions by airing and displacing "suppressed cultural anxieties about the Virgin Queen" onto the scapegoat figure of Joan of Arc.[13] Rackin also emphasizes the stage's role in mediating social and political instabilities. In a chapter entitled "Patriarchal History and Female Subversion," Rackin acknowledges that women's participation in history constitutes a challenge to patriarchal authority, especially in a play like *King John*, but in the end she argues for Shakespeare's orthodoxy, aligning the politics of the history plays with their chronicle sources. In his nostalgic vision of the past, she writes, "Shakespeare, no less than his chronicle sources, participated in the construction of genealogical myths of martial valor that repressed the reality of female authority and discredited expressions of female power."[14] In the face of the rapid changes and insecurities characterizing late-sixteenth-century England, these two studies suggest, the spectacle of a rigorously patriarchal history allowed audiences a chance to escape, if only for a few hours, with a story of better days.

Like both Rackin and Marcus, I too am concerned with the differences between Shakespeare's history plays and the Elizabethan culture in which they were produced. But at the same time I want to open up the binary of "patriarchy" and "subversive women" that has underwritten most discussions of gender politics in the history plays, and the early plays especially.[15] This is not to say that patriarchal structures are not dominant in these plays. They are. Nor is it to deny a relationship between Elizabethan anxieties about powerful women and Shakespeare's staging of historical narratives. My intention, rather, is to refigure that relationship by considering the extent to which these plays contest, as well as validate, their own authorizing structures. As many have argued, these plays adopt, and even intensify, the patriarchal narratives of their chronicle sources. But little attention has been paid to the ways in which they also complicate and disrupt these narratives, denying the fulfillment of moral and political order promised at the outset. The plays may evoke patriarchal patterns in their focus on subversive women—detailing the dangers of Joan of Arc, Eleanor Cobham, and Margaret of Anjou, for example—but they also offer a critique of these patterns, especially in their staging of male triumph. More political than ideological, this critique of patriarchal history develops out of, and speaks to, specific concerns of late Elizabethan England.

This study differs from recent discussions of women in the histories, then, in privileging the challenges these plays make to a sixteenth-century discourse of patriarchal power. It also differs in its assumptions about Shakespeare's use of his chronicle sources. Rather than simply reasserting the patriarchal stories of his sources, this book argues, Shakespeare reworked them for his Elizabethan audience in part by registering the political concerns of the 1590s on the narratives of a fifteenth-century past. As the following chapters demonstrate, the Elizabethan contexts for these plays often have the effect of altering the historical record, not only in turning attention to powerful women but also in charting their effect on moral and political order and, in the process, undermining the authority of the nation's cultural narratives. If the plays thus record the pressures of the present on the past, then we may begin to trace the shaping Elizabethan contexts—and Shakespeare's politics—by setting the playtexts against their sources.[16]

If, as Rackin has argued, the Elizabethan fascination with history can be explained in part by "a desire to recuperate an older, better world" and to take "refuge in nostalgic historical myths of a stable, Edenic past,"[17] then Shakespeare's staging of history frustrates as well as encourages that desire. The plays may tease their audiences with the promise of an escape from present concerns, yet their staging of chronicle history often works in the opposite direction. For by writing the present onto the past, they close off history both as a place of refuge and as a locus of authority for representations of state power and national identity. The effects of this practice of inscribing present concerns on history's texts are complex. One effect is to heighten, and to critique, the instabilities and anxieties of the times. But in rewriting Tudor history in Elizabethan terms, Shakespeare also "makes strange" the gendered discourse of chronicle history and, as a result, points out the limitations of the past as a model for the present. In this sense, Shakespeare's histories call into question, even as they draw upon, humanist notions of the past as a mirror for the present.

To argue that the present rewrites the past is to go against the grain of the humanist model informing the study of Shakespeare's history plays inaugurated by E. M. W. Tillyard and Lily B. Campbell earlier in the century.[18] According to this model, the past provides a mirror for the present, from which readers of history, including the monarch, might draw valuable lessons. Contemporary references to Shakespeare's history plays confirm this cultural practice. As Thomas Nashe claimed in defense of the stage in 1592, the history play, by celebrating "our forefathers valiant acts," offers a "reproofe to these degenerate effeminate dayes of ours."[19] Nearly a decade later, the queen herself assumed a similar correspondence between past and present in her alleged response to Essex's commission of *Richard II* on the eve of his rebellion: "I am Richard II. know ye not that?"[20] In spite of their radically different attitudes to the politics of the history play, both the queen and Nashe assume that the past can speak to the present, and the stage to the state. My own reading of Shakespeare's history plays also depends on this assumption. But while aligning myself with Queen Elizabeth and Nashe, I also want to reverse the direction of their thinking in order to consider the ways in which these plays, situated in the Elizabethan present, also invite a critique of the past. This is not to argue, with Graham Holderness, that Shakespeare is himself writing historiography and is concerned in the history plays with chronicling the fifteenth-century past.[21] It is to understand the playwright as a skeptical reader of both the chronicle accounts and contemporary politics.

Given the centrality of the past and present to the politics of these plays, my method in the chapters that follow is necessarily two-fold and involves situating Shakespeare's histories in relation to two fields of reference that are themselves unstable and contradictory. The fifteenth-century past, as recorded in the plays' chronicle sources, constitutes one field, while the Elizabethan present, defined in part by its own contested representations of power, makes up the other. In both of these areas, gender figures centrally in signifying relations of power, but, as we might expect, often in radically different ways. While seeking to avoid fixing either of these areas as a stable point of reference, this book examines the ways in which Shakespeare's representations of women interpret the tensions and intersections between these two fields. In calling attention to the complexities, and the difficulties, involved in representing a gendered discourse of state power and national identity in the 1590s, the history plays also begin to give voice to a multivocal drama of nation that differs radically from their chronicle sources.

The Tudor chronicles provided Shakespeare, as they provide scholars today, with a vast repository of social and political history. Epitomized by the great volumes of Edward Hall, Richard Grafton, Raphael Holinshed, and John Stow, the sixteenth-century chronicle was, in Richard Helgerson's words, "the Ur-genre of national self-representation,"[22] popularizing the nation's past for an expanding and ever more interested reading public. But what images of the nation did these texts present? As Rackin has argued, women received little attention in "the ideologically motivated discourse" of the Tudor chronicles: "Renaissance historiography constituted a masculine tradition, written by men, devoted to the deeds of men, glorifying the masculine virtues of courage, honor, and patriotism, and dedicated to preserving the names of past heroes and recording their patriarchal genealogies."[23] John Stow, for instance, makes no mention of women when he justifies his project to his "gentle Reader." Arguing for the value of chronicles above all other books, Stow praises history for presenting "examples of men deserving immortalitie" that might encourage the aristocracy to "noble feates" and, at the same time, discourage "unnaturall subjects" from treason, rebellion, and "damnable doctrines."[24] To be sure, the picture of women that emerges from the Tudor chronicles is by no means monolithic, as evidenced by the differences between an Elizabethan chronicle, like the 1587 edition of Holinshed's *Chronicles of England, Scotland, and Ireland*, for example, and a Henrician chronicle, like Hall's *The Union of the Two Noble and Illustre Famelies of Lancastre and York* (1548), upon which Shakespeare drew for the *Henry VI* plays. But in spite of these differences, Rackin's observations still hold. Like the "unnaturall subjects" given to treason and rebellion, women most often warrant a place in these texts not for performing heroic acts but for disrupting order and threatening the nation's welfare.

The Tudor chronicles nonetheless offered Shakespeare more than a patriarchal "ground" against which to measure his own times. As Annabel Patterson's recent work on Holinshed's *Chronicles* reminds us, we should not assume that these sources are themselves univocal, ideological texts or that they are purely political, concerned only with propagandizing the reigns of the monarchs who commissioned them. Instead, we may read the Tudor chronicles as Shakespeare may have read them, as multilayered and multivocal "documentary histories" shaped by a variety of sources and motives.[25] Bringing together multiple and often conflicting accounts of the same event, the chronicles recorded the discrepancies in historical materials and thereby gave the attentive reader access to history's political and ideological faultlines. Shakespeare's chronicle sources thus provided him not only with a vast supply of "raw" historical material but with a method as well, inviting him to explore the conflicts and instabilities of their own multivocal texts. Like a palimpsest whose text has been written over by successive generations, the Tudor chronicles, together with other Elizabethan "sources," offered Shakespeare a model for his own inscriptions of history.

Elizabethan representations of women in power, beginning with images of the queen herself, constitute a second field of reference for understanding the politics of gender in the history plays. In many ways, Elizabethan iconography precisely inverts the Tudor chronicles' figuring of women and dynastic power. The presence of a woman on the throne necessitated revisions in England's gendered discourse of state and nation, revisions that in some form or other had to reconcile her position as monarch, to whom all were subject, with her status as a woman who "by nature" was considered subordinate, "subject" to men. Much has been written in recent years about the strategies by which the queen and her court addressed the contradictions of female rule and attempted to turn cultural expectations about gender to advantage.[26] Representing Elizabeth in her various incarnations as Virgin Queen, the court celebrated the monarch's gender even as it worked to accommodate it to the beliefs and expectations of the patriarchal culture. By controlling production of the queen's image, the court was able to confer a mythical and even divine aura on her reign, and it is perhaps a sign of her success that these "official" portraits have for so long provided us with a single, idealized image of Elizabethan England.[27]

But the queen and her court did not retain exclusive control over production of the queen's image. Instead, as Susan Frye has argued, various parties competed for control in representing the monarch throughout her reign. This competition became especially intense in the last decade of the sixteenth century as the queen entered her sixties and the nation's peace and prosperity appeared threatened on a number of fronts: continued conflict with Spain, deepening economic problems, factionalism within the court, together with the queen's refusal to name an heir—all contributed to the nation's uneasiness during these years.

Elizabeth, for her part, responded by retreating from the public eye while at the same time engaging in what Roy Strong has called a "policy of deliberate rejuvenation" designed to recapture in royal portraits and pageantry the power of a youthful Virgin Queen and to efface the visible signs of her own mortality.[28] But while the queen worked to idealize her image, and even to deny her inevitable death, her subjects sometimes represented her in less flattering terms. As the French ambassador reported in 1597, the queen's government was "little pleasing to the great men and the nobles; and if by chance she should die, it is certain that the English would never again submit to the rule of a woman."[29] But if the 1590s ushered in a decade of instability and uncertainty, as the increased competition for the queen's image suggests, it paradoxically offered Elizabethans a radical freedom to dream about the future, to imagine both the state and the nation in their own terms.

That Shakespeare sought to take advantage of this freedom at the start of his career by turning to the English history play might seem unlikely, the choice of fifteenth-century history hardly suggestive of a young playwright's iconoclasm. At the start of the 1590s, however, both the public theater and the new genre of the national history play offered opportunities and freedoms of their own. Elizabethan playhouses, as Steven Mullaney has argued, were located in the liberties just outside London's city walls, in a marginal space that served as an "ambivalent staging ground, as a place where the contradictions of the community— its incontinent hopes, fears, and desires—were prominently and dramatically set on stage."[30] And Shakespeare's history plays, themselves an ambivalent genre mixing fact and fiction, history and poetry, past and present, stood to take full advantage of the license afforded by this location. Scholars have, of course, long approached these plays as political writings and, beginning with Tillyard's ground-breaking study earlier in the century, have sought to establish connections between the public stage and the Elizabethan state.[31] But consensus on Shakespeare's politics has still not emerged, and if we set the Essex conspirators against Tillyard, as Stephen Greenblatt does in his now-classic introduction to new historicism, it becomes clear that plays which some find subversive of Tudor authority others read as supportive.[32] That we may see both the rabbits and the ducks in these plays, to borrow from Norman Rabkin's discussion of *Henry V*, may be in part a product of our own theoretical assumptions, but it also argues that the plays are themselves complex and contradictory, interested less in inculcating the lessons of moral history than in interrogating the politics informing that history.[33] And it is in this sense that the plays may be viewed as radical.

This study begins with the *Henry VI* plays and then turns to

Richard III and *King John*, following the order in which Shakespeare wrote them. Although scholars continue to debate the dates of the early plays, and *1 Henry VI* in particular, most agree that they were written more or less in order during the first half of the 1590s.[34] My analysis does not depend on establishing a more precise dating, but approaching the plays chronologically, beginning with *1 Henry VI* and ending with *King John*, does allow some general patterns to emerge. This is not to suggest that the histories offer a teleological narrative, one that moves toward suppressing female "misrule,"[35] as Leah Marcus has argued, by setting right the gendered conflicts of the early plays with the celebration of Henry's marriage to Katherine of France at the close of *Henry V*. The patterns that do emerge from these plays, though irregular and not without contradiction, argue against such conclusions. We may notice, for example, that women become less "strange" over the course of these plays and, as a result, pose less of a threat to England's national identity. Indeed, as the scene shifts from France to England, and French maids give way onstage to English queens and mothers, the structuring binaries of gender become more unstable and more subject to critique. At the same time, the stage gradually makes a place for women in history.

This book begins by examining the gendered structures of the *Henry VI* plays, the first three chapters focusing on the figures of Joan of Arc, Eleanor Cobham, and Margaret of Anjou, respectively. Epitomized by Talbot's struggle against Joan in *1 Henry VI*, discourses of gender figure importantly in all three plays as a means of legitimating power and authorizing aggression. But while the gendered discourse in some ways grows more insistent over the course of the *Henry VI* plays, especially as dynastic conquest gives way to civil conflict in the absence of a strong male monarch, its moral authority becomes dangerously compromised by political interest. For in all three plays, negative stereotypes of women are framed, and qualified, by political contexts—both on- and offstage— as ambitious women come into conflict with conspiring noblemen. The dynastic struggle of the War of the Roses furnishes the most pervasive political context, one that consistently works to critique the stereotypes of domineering women found in the chronicles. The Elizabethan present, as Shakespeare writes it into the historical record, provides another.

Attending to these contexts, the first three chapters situate the representations of women in the *Henry VI* plays in relation to the contradictions between the chronicle sources, on the one hand, and the political concerns and needs of the Elizabethan present, on the other. Chapter 1 considers Joan of Arc's confrontations with England's heroic warriors in *1 Henry VI* in relation to both Hall's chronicle and to the chivalric fictions of the Elizabethan court, and the Accession Day ceremonies in particular, to argue that the play points out the limitations of a national identity grounded in gendered oppositions. Turning to the case of Eleanor Cobham in *2 Henry VI*, chapter 2 examines the stereotype of the witch-traitor within a number of political and historical frameworks that extend from the Yorkist conspiracy onstage to John Foxe's *Acts and Monuments*, which serves as both source and context. Exposing the witchcraft-treason trial as a persuasive but also dangerous means of legitimating aristocratic ambition, the play opens up a wider critique of representations of power. Chapter 3 considers Queen Margaret in *2* and *3 Henry VI* in relation to sixteenth-century debates over female rule and a chronicle tradition in which Margaret epitomizes the dangers of ruling women. In contrast to his chronicle sources, Shakespeare's presentation of the Lancastrian queen raises questions about gendered attacks on women rulers and calls instead for a political ethos based on the nation's welfare.

Turning to *Richard III* and *King John*, the remaining chapters concentrate less on individual female characters and more on the roles of women in general in matters of succession and dynastic conflict. Women in these plays are clearly less subversive of English interests than their counterparts in the *Henry VI* plays: as English queens they now fight *for* rather than against the nation's welfare, and as mothers they are concerned primarily with protecting their sons' rights to the succession. Thus transforming the independent women of the *Henry VI* plays into protective queen-mothers, Shakespeare rewrites chronicle history in both *Richard III* and *King John* in order to acknowledge the importance of women in ensuring patrilineal succession. At the same time, however, the presence of women on history's stage also generates a critique of patrilineal inheritance and legitimacy that speaks to the concerns raised by the unsettled Elizabethan succession.

Chapter 4 takes up *Richard III* to argue that Richard's dependence on women, figured in a double bind of misogyny and marriage, registers a central paradox of patriarchy and, more specifically, the dilemma of dynastic succession in Tudor England. Turning to *King John*, chapter 5 reconsiders the Elizabethan succession question in relation to the struggle between John and Arthur, examining the play alongside some of the more radical succession tracts circulating in the 1590s. In spite of acknowledging women's importance in succession matters, both plays close with a restoration of patriarchy, with the accession of Henry VII in *Richard III* and Henry III in *King John*. As these chapters argue, however, the closing celebrations of male monarchs do not go uncontested. Taken together, *Richard III* and *King John* register a range of contemporary responses to the unsettled Elizabethan succession, marked at one end by misogyny and a kind of reactionary politics and at the other by a more radical revision of traditional patriarchal structures, as figured in the image of the powerful male monarch.

In its attention to the early history plays, this study reverses the conventional emphasis on Shakespeare's second cycle of English history plays that closes, at the end of the decade, with *Henry V*. This is not to suggest that under strong Lancastrian rule the "woman's part" is so fully suppressed that there is little to discuss in these later plays. Rather, my design in pushing the *Henriad* to the margins was to show that the early histories afford rich material for political criticism. But as I have come to realize in the process of writing this book, it is also to give shape to a "story" of nation within Shakespeare's canon that moves, however fitfully and anxiously, toward including women on history's stage. In many ways more experimental, and more skeptical, than the later histories, these early plays demonstrate the freedoms to be found in the new genre of the national history play.

1

The Politics of Chivalry in *1 Henry VI*

In the second act of *1 Henry VI*, Lord Talbot leads the English in recapturing Orleans from the French. Shouting "'Saint George!' 'A Talbot!'" (2.1.38), his men scale the city walls while the dauphin and Joan of Arc sleep "secure" within. If the "subtile-witted French" (1.1.25) and their "magic verses" (27) can be blamed at the start of the play for the death of Henry V—and for the loss of French lands and English manhood—Talbot's offensive promises to restore those losses by exacting England's revenge on all "conjurers and sorcerers" (26), now conveniently embodied in the figure of the French Joan. The rhetoric resounds with a jingoism reminiscent of the Armada pamphlets, as Talbot imagines the attack as visiting a kind of divine justice on the "baleful" enemy:

> Well, let them practice and converse with spirits.
> God is our fortress, in whose conquering name
> Let us resolve to scale their flinty bulwarks.
>
> (2.1.25–27)

In this scene, as in others, England's identity depends on a discourse of alterity that associates the English with God, country, and aristocratic male warriors, and the French with "witches and the help of hell" (2.1.18). Within this allegory of nation, the noble Talbot represents the best of the English—he is valiant, courageous, and heir to a string of titles—whereas the demonic and cross-dressed Joan, a "shepherd's daughter," exemplifies the French, at their worst.

Not surprisingly, critics have long argued that the Joan-Talbot opposition is key to the play's politics, with the result that divergent approaches have often converged in assuming that the play endorses orthodox notions of the nation-state as represented in the aristocratic male warrior. The play has been understood, for instance, as a moral history, in which Talbot "represents the forces of England and righteousness" and Joan "the forces of demonic malice."[1] The opposition also supports David Riggs's reading of the play as a political-heroic history, in which Talbot "represents English chivalry" and Joan "the forces that threaten the aristocratic ideal of military service and gentle blood."[2] Most recently, the gendered oppositions have come into play in feminist-political readings in which, as Barbara Hodgdon observes, Joan represents "a subversive challenge to gender as well as to the closed chivalric code owned by males."[3] Leah Marcus also draws on this opposition in her provocative "local" reading of the play, in which Joan stands in for Elizabeth I, airing "cultural anxieties about the Virgin Queen, her identity, and her capacity to provide continuing stability for the nation."[4] The parallels between Joan and the English queen may revise earlier assessments of the play's patriotism, transforming a post-Armada play into a potentially seditious celebration of aristocratic warriors triumphing over unnatural female dominance, but Elizabeth aside, the message is much the same. "It is as though, in *1 Henry VI*," Marcus writes, "despising female dominance is a necessary part of being male, English, and 'Protestant.'"[5]

Seen through the frame of the Joan-Talbot opposition, the play's politics are orthodox, and even reactionary, reiterating a gendered discourse of nation that celebrates the triumph of the aristocratic male warrior over an unruly foreign female. But this is not the only story the play tells. England's aristocratic warriors may cast the nation in their own image, but their discourse is not without contradiction and danger on Shakespeare's stage. One source of contradiction lies in Joan's Elizabethan face, which has the effect of confusing national borders as well as oppositions based on rank and gender. Another source is to be found within the warriors themselves, whose factionalism undermines England's position abroad as well as its unity at home. Though criticism of the play has tended to focus on Joan and Talbot, aristocratic rivalry figures prominently in *1 Henry VI*, setting the stage for the civil conflict that drives the action of the *Henry VI* plays as a whole.[6] In the end, the most serious threat to Talbot—and to England—comes not from the outside, not from low-born French women like Joan, but from within the ranks of the English aristocracy itself, from men like York and Somerset, born to power and privilege. As Sir William Lucy tersely sums up the situation on the battlefield before Talbot's death: "The fraud of England, not the force of France, / Hath now entrapp'd the noble-minded Talbot" (4.4.36–37). The play may privilege the interests of the so-called chivalric warrior, but, as

Lucy's words argue, it also subjects these interests to scrutiny, challeng-
ing both the authority and the motive of the aristocratic code.[7]

The task of this chapter is to reconsider Shakespeare's representation
of the nation-state in *1 Henry VI* by examining issues of gender and
power in conjunction with aristocratic rivalry. In its staging of
aristocratic ambition, the play not only revises a discourse of nation
founded principally on oppositions between heroic warriors and alien
women but does so in a way that speaks to the complex business of
mediating relations within the Elizabethan court. Much has been said
over the years about *1 Henry VI*'s topicality and the ways in which
Shakespeare's version of the fifteenth century reflects the political
realities of the early 1590s. The English campaigns in France in 1590–91
offer one point of comparison, which has been especially useful in dating
the play.[8] The parallels between Joan and Elizabeth offer others, opening
up a range of local contexts that extend from the queen's self-
presentations to the seditious rumors circulating among her subjects.
While drawing on this tradition of reading the history play as a mirror of
the present, my own analysis narrows the contextual field to focus on
relations between the queen and her aristocratic courtiers as played out in
the annual Accession Day tournaments. This is not to privilege this
particular context as one that "unlocks" the play's political meaning, nor
to argue that the play directly comments on the processes of court
pageantry. Like other parallels between the play and its Elizabethan
contexts, the Accession Day tilts simply provide one more point of
reference, but one that serves well to elucidate the political resonance of
the conflicts between the unruly woman and the contentious English
aristocrats on history's stage.

Shakespeare's play, like the Accession Day ceremonies, rewrites
medieval myths of chivalry for the Elizabethan present. But while both
the stage and the state illustrate ways in which the present might rewrite
the past, even as the past serves as a mirror for the present, the results of
these revisions are radically different. The court, for its part, tended to
refurbish the past in the hopes of mediating contemporary political
tensions. Conversely, Shakespeare's revisions heighten those tensions.
As we will see, the play achieves this effect in large part by
interrupting—and at times even inverting—the anticipated patterns of
patriarchal history in which virtuous English warriors triumph over
demonic French women. Thus denying the pleasures that come from
stories of England's heroic past, *1 Henry VI* invites a reconsideration of
fictions of power, past as well as present. In the process, Shakespeare
begins to give shape to a complex political drama that moves beyond the
familiar binaries of a gendered national discourse.

Elizabethan Chivalry

The romance between the queen and her court constituted one of the central fictions of Elizabeth's reign and appeared in a variety of forms, from the verse of courtiers seeking favor and patronage to the queen's own forays into Petrarchism in her speeches and verse. But it was the Accession Day tournament, in which noblemen came together each year "in open presence" to tilt in honor of their queen, that enacted this romance in one of its most visible—and most political—forms. Under the direction of Sir Henry Lee in the 1580s, the annual tilts developed into elaborately choreographed and well-attended spectacles that celebrated Elizabeth's reign by calling up a romanticized chivalric past. According to William Segar, writing in 1602, the tilts were prompted by Lee's "earnest desire to eternize the glory of her Majestie's Court" and to fulfill his promise to "performe, in honor of her sacred Majestie."[9] But in spite of these claims, the Accession Day ceremonies were probably shaped more by the specific political and economic needs of the participants than by the chivalric ideals they continually evoked.

As Richard McCoy has persuasively argued, the annual tilts provided a formal ritual by which the queen and the nobility came together to negotiate longstanding conflicts of power and privilege. "Its ceremonial forms," McCoy writes, "constitute a kind of cultural resolution of one of the central contradictions of Elizabethan politics, the conflict between honor and obedience, the 'customary rights' of knighthood and the duty to 'right royal majesty.'"[10] In allowing courtiers to parade their martial abilities and ambitions before the court even as they paid tribute to their monarch, the Accession Day ceremonies ideally offered a means of balancing the aristocracy's belief in its right to autonomous power and privilege with the queen's demand for honor and obedience. The chivalric displays were also well-suited to mediating the unique situation of the Elizabethan court, where the presence of a woman ruler had the potential to aggravate tensions by turning aristocratic obedience into unnatural, and unmanly, submission. Celebrating a chivalric ideal based on service to the chaste monarch, the court worked to translate obedience into heroic virtue.

The Accession Day rituals were not always successful, however, at resolving conflicts between the queen and her courtiers. This was especially the case in the last decade of the reign when, after the retirement of Lee in 1590, the decorous rituals of chivalric devotion began to give way to the more militaristic displays of aristocratic power associated with the earl of Essex, whose aggressive style of tilting came to dominate the annual events. As the decade wore on, the chivalric fiction became more and more difficult to sustain. Court factionalism had escalated to dangerous levels, and rival parties now attempted to use the ceremonies as a staging ground for their own power and influence. At the same time, the pretense of romancing the royal mistress was itself becoming less convincing, with Elizabeth, now in her sixties, beginning to show clear signs of aging. Even so, the difficulty of sustaining Elizabethan fictions of power also had its advantages, for the courtiers if not for the queen. As Eric Mallin has argued, late Tudor chivalry was "a forum for the visibility of masculine courtier power,"[11] in which women, the queen included, participated only as observers.

If the Accession Day tilt of 1600, from which Essex was excluded, saw "the collapse of the chivalric compromise,"[12] the 1590 tilt furnishes a starting point for charting the decline. The ceremonies of 1590 marked Lee's retirement as director of the annual tilts and, as such, were especially elaborate and well-attended. They were also well-documented. "An infinite number of people"[13] turned out for the occasion, Segar writes in "Honor Military and Civill" (1602), and those unable to witness the spectacle could read about it in George Peele's *Polyhymnia* (1590), which went to press within the month. In allowing us access to both the forms and the conflicts shaping Elizabethan fictions of power, these two accounts provide a fitting introduction to the contemporaneous staging of chivalry in *1 Henry VI*, a play written, we may assume, between 1590 and 1592.[14] Both Peele and Segar emphasize the centrality of the queen's place in the ceremony and suggest the importance of the tilts for staging royal power. But they also offer evidence of the tensions the ceremonies worked to allay, raising concerns about ruling women and aristocratic privilege in accounts clearly dedicated to praising the "peerelesse Soveraigne: / High Maistresse of their service."[15]

Segar's account of the ceremonies details the harmonious rituals of Lee's resignation and begins with a description of how Lee and his successor, the earl of Cumberland, "first performed their service in armes." At the conclusion of the tilts, the spectacle shifted from the knights to the queen herself when music suddenly sounded and the ground opened to reveal a white taffeta pavilion "like unto the sacred Temple of the Virgin's Vestall." After an interlude of song and the presentation of gifts, the official ceremony began as Lee "disarmed, offered up his armour at the foot of her Majestie's crowned pillar: and kneeling upon his knees, presented the Earle of Cumberland, humbly beseeching she would be pleased to accept him for her Knight, to continue the yeerely exercises aforesaid." In place of his armor Lee then donned a "side coat of blacke velvet" and "covered his head (in lieu of an helmet) with a buttoned cap of the countrey fashion."[16] The transformation from knight to beadsman was complete.

The ceremony of Lee's resignation presents an image that in another context might undermine traditional notions of aristocratic strength and independence—that of a knight disarmed and suppliant before a ruling female. Yet, as it draws on familiar and idealized representations of the queen and her court—Elizabeth as Vestal Virgin and her courtiers as chivalric suitors—the ceremony ritualizes and so controls the potentially disturbing image, but maybe not completely. For, as the words of the song remind the audience—"A Man at Armes must now sit on his knees, / And feed on prayers, that are old ages almes"—the transition to the contemplative, religious life is not without a loss of manly stature and strength. Segar himself further disturbs the ceremony's balance when, in a curious elucidation, he compares Lee's laying down of arms at Elizabeth's feet to "the auncient Romane[s], who . . . offered his armes unto Mars."[17] Behind the image of Elizabeth as Vestal Virgin, Segar places the god of war in a comparison that strangely pairs opposing images of virgin and warrior, female and male, in the context of a ceremony that celebrates Elizabeth as virginal female and her courtiers as male warriors.

If Segar's comparison discloses Elizabethan anxieties about submitting to a female monarch, Peele's description of Essex's participation in the tilts offers the counterexample by reminding us of the aggressive independence of powerful courtiers that these ceremonies worked to control. Focusing on the tilts themselves, Peele details the entrances of each of the thirteen pairs of contenders, beginning with the stately appearance of Lee "mounted on puissant horse" and Cumberland bearing "plumes and pendants al as white as Swanne," in keeping with the theme of the Vestal Virgin. By contrast, Essex's appearance "proudly shocks," his dark presentation equivocating between mourning and militarism. With his company outfitted "in funerall blacke," the earl himself bore "mightie Armes of mourners hue" to pay tribute to "Sweete Sidney . . . whose successor he / In love and Armes had ever vowed to be."[18] But even as the device honors Sidney's memory, it also speaks to the queen's decision not to name Essex as Lee's successor. As one of the most enthusiastic participants in the Accession Day tilts of the previous decade, Essex had expected to step into Lee's place when he retired, but having displeased the queen, he was now passed over in favor of Cumberland. Rather than playing the penitent, however, Essex boldly asserted his strength and, in linking himself to the Sidneys, as McCoy suggests, "sought to upstage the new champion by establishing a line of chivalric succession worthier and more heroic than that bequeathed by

Lee and formally declaring himself its heir."[19] Royal authority might be challenged, as Essex was to demonstrate more than once in the last decade of Elizabeth's reign, even within the rituals of court ceremony and celebration.

It is within this political context that Shakespeare brings his version of English chivalry to the stage in the early 1590s. With its battle scenes, its static tableaus, and its patterned speeches evocative of a heroic past, *1 Henry VI* invites comparison with Elizabethan pageantry.[20] But in place of the accommodating chivalric fictions, the play presents a story of loss and division that brings forward the very tensions the court sought to control. For those in the audience involved in the not-so-successful French campaigns of the early 1590s, for example, the play's foreign landscape and abortive sieges may have been all too familiar. Similarly, for those struggling to maintain the estates and privileges enjoyed by their forefathers, the successive deaths of Salisbury, Bedford, and Talbot would have provided an equally poignant reminder of loss. In contrast to the ceremony of Lee's retirement, where the mantle passes to his successor, there is no one worthy enough to take up the armor of these chivalric lords in *1 Henry VI*. Those who do triumph in this play, men like York and Suffolk, bear little resemblance to these fallen heroes. Talbot may have served as a reminder of a heroic past, but the "factious emulations" (4.1.113) of York and Suffolk surely invited comparison with the realities of the late Elizabethan court, whose policy, as Robert Naunton later described it, depended on "faction and parties."[21]

Most provocative, however, are the associations between Joan of Arc and England's queen. As Marcus and others have argued, the figure of Joan bears a remarkable resemblance to Elizabeth, particularly at the beginning of the play where the French maid makes much of her chastity and, in words that echo Elizabeth's habitual refrain, claims to "exceed [her] sex" (1.2.90).[22] By bringing this Elizabethan figure into confrontation with England's heroic warriors, *1 Henry VI* works an unsettling variation on court romance, one that again exposes the tensions that the Elizabethan chivalric fiction sought to mediate and control. Like the 1590 ceremony of Lee's retirement, the image of a knight disarmed at a maid's feet also appears in *1 Henry VI*, but as a disturbing parody that lays bare the danger of the courtly image for the aristocratic male. For, in place of the Roman Vestal Virgin, the play substitutes a demonic, Amazonian figure, who in her confrontations with aristocratic warriors provides a menacing image of female dominance, as witnessed first in the scene of the dauphin Charles "prostrate" at the feet of the sword-wielding Joan and again in the scene of Talbot's death, when the French maid looks down on the slain hero to mock his mortality.

1 Henry VI thus presents a striking contrast to Elizabethan court pageantry, prominently displaying the tensions and conflicts that, as we have seen with the accounts of Peele and Segar, were already beginning to show through the bright surfaces of court ritual. In its presentation of a demonic Joan, the play registers aristocratic male anxieties about ruling women and thereby disallows the accommodating fictions of power played out in court romance. But in simultaneously registering concerns about a self-interested aristocracy, the play does not simply revert to a patriarchal fantasy of masculine power. Qualifying the authority of both aristocratic males and the ruling female, *1 Henry VI* endorses no alternative to the double bind of contemporary gender politics. Rather than unifying conflicting interests in a celebration of the monarch's glory, or in a nostalgic evocation of a mythical chivalric past, the play instead refuses to converge on a single, authorized locus of power. In the absence of a positive, and clearly defined, model of authority, we must locate the play's politics in its double critique of ruling women and self-interested aristocratic warriors. The remainder of this chapter examines these critiques both singly and in relation to each other, as they are raised first by the Amazonian figure of Joan and then by the intersection of gender with aristocratic ambition as played out in the scenes of Talbot's death and York's capture of Joan at the play's close.

"Thou art an Amazon"

1 Henry VI begins with the funeral of Henry V in 1422 and ends with the truce between England and France in 1444, compressing twenty-two years of the Hundred Years War into the space of one play. In the process, Shakespeare significantly revises the loosely structured narratives of his sources, bringing coherence to chronicle accounts that are more episodic than usual. Neither Edward Hall's *The Union of the Two Noble and Illustre Famelies of Lancastre and Yorke* (1548) nor the 1587 edition of Holinshed's *Chronicles of England, Scotland and Ireland* reveals an organizing structure for these years, and neither presents one character as central to the events.[23] Instead, they record what seems to be an endless cycle of conflict, telling a story, in Hall's words, of "the marciall feactes, the mortal strokes, and daily skirmishes, practised betwene the English and Frenche nacion in the Region of Fraunce."[24] What structure there is in these accounts is provided by a refrain of national stereotypes—the French are always deceitful, fraudulent, and cowardly; the English are brave, honest, and courageous—but even this opposition weakens as the war persists and England fails to emerge victorious. The gendered confrontations central to *1 Henry VI* are absent from the sources, and the scenes of civil discord are limited to the conflict between Gloucester and Winchester. Neither Joan nor Talbot figures prominently in the chronicle accounts of these years.[25]

To turn from the chronicles to *1 Henry VI* is to be struck, then, by the extent to which Shakespeare reorganized the historical record around a binary opposition of gender. The opening moments of the play establish this opposition, as the funeral procession of Henry V moves across the shrouded stage. One of the points of this scene is to show that with the death of Henry V—"that most phallic of English kings,"[26] Leslie Fielder remarks—all order collapses. Eulogized by Gloucester, Henry represents the heroic ideal, a warrior-king whose strength, and that of the nation, is figured in the powerful image of the raised hand holding a sword:

> England ne'er had a king until his time:
> Virtue he had, deserving to command;
> His brandish'd sword did blind men with his beams;
> His arms spread wider than a dragon's wings;
> His sparkling eyes, replete with wrathful fire,
> More dazzled and drove back his enemies
> Than midday sun fierce bent against their faces.
> What should I say? his deeds exceed all speech:
> He ne'er lift up his hand but conquered.
>
> (1.1.8–16)

But in the fallen world of *1 Henry VI*, the manly king is succeeded by an "effeminate prince" (1.1.35), the strong father by the weak son. Before Henry V's funeral is over, England has lost ground in France, and the mourning nobles, not unlike many of Shakespeare's contemporaries, express their concerns about the present by nostalgically evoking a virtuous and virile past. As the play progresses, the gendered oppositions become more pronounced, staged in a series of confrontations between Englishmen and each of the play's women—Joan of Arc, the countess of Auvergne, and Margaret of Anjou.[27] But it is the sword-wielding Joan, who directly turns her power against England's chivalric exemplars, who most embodies the danger of the French woman. As the dauphin himself declares when first confronted by Joan's martial prowess: "Thou art an Amazon, / And fightest with the sword of Deborah" (1.2.104–5).

In its overarching structure of gender confrontation, played out in Joan's face-to-face encounters with chivalric warriors, *1 Henry VI* alludes to a mythology of patriarchal power that extends from ancient stories of Amazons to the large body of sixteenth-century misogynistic literature. But in borrowing from this tradition, Shakespeare gives it an unusual Elizabethan form by allowing Joan to triumph over her male opponents. The classical narratives, by contrast, centered on the triumph of the male warrior over the alien Amazons, linking the hero's victory to the defense of the patriarchal city-state. In the exemplary Athenian legend, in fact, the very founders and protectors of the state were men like Theseus who had warred with the Amazons and won.[28] Shakespeare's version of the story thus rewrites the reassuring conclusion of male triumph. But what were the politics of Shakespeare's choice to throw the garland to Joan? As with the other *Henry VI* plays, the spectacle of a powerful woman offers a resonant point of comparison between past and present, and between patriarchal fictions of power and the complexities of present-day politics. In staging Joan's confrontations with chivalric warriors, the play revises a patriarchal mythology for an Elizabethan present and, at the same time, replays Elizabethan concerns within the framework of chronicle history. This conjunction of gendered fictions and contemporary realities is in many ways key to the play's politics.

Joan's initial entrance onto the stage immediately leads to armed conflict, but because her opponent here is the French dauphin, the sexual politics are ambiguous, a source of both pleasure and fear for an English audience. Announcing herself as a maid divinely chosen to "free my country from calamity" (1.2.81), this shepherd's daughter invites the dauphin to try her courage by combat, "if thou dar'st" (1.2.89). The prince takes up the challenge, and Joan makes short work of her opponent, besting him with her wit and her "keen-edg'd sword" (1.2.98). Within minutes, the dauphin lies at Joan's feet, her "prostrate thrall" (1.2.117). The echoes of Elizabeth are especially striking in this scene, as Shakespeare alludes to many of the queen's roles: as Deborah, as pastoral queen of the shepherds, and as Petrarchan mistress. Seen one way, these echoes give a nationalistic cast to the comic motif of virago versus braggardly coward and may have prompted many in the audience to applaud the virgin warrior who triumphs over the French prince.[29] But for those dependent on the queen for power and patronage, the figure of the dauphin "prostrate" at Joan's feet may have been more disturbing than comic. Serving up a pastiche of Elizabethan court "romance," Shakespeare here transforms the noble Petrarchan mistress into a base-born, cross-dressed woman who cannot be mastered by courtly discourse. From this perspective, Joan's triumph lays bare the threat that female rule posed to relations of rank and gender within the patriarchal nation-state.[30]

When Joan turns her strength against the English—and the echoes of Elizabeth give way to a catalogue of misogynistic stereotypes—the political effects of her dominance are less equivocal, and certainly less comic. On the English stage, the sight of a French woman in armor, with brandished sword *"driving Englishmen before her"* (1.5.s.d.), offers a frightening image linking female strength with male impotence. Like the dauphin, Talbot attributes Joan's unsettling power to her Amazonian appearance:

> Where is my strength, my valor, and my force?
> Our English troops retire, I cannot stay them;
> A woman clad in armor chaseth them.
>
> (1.5.1–3)

And like the dauphin, Talbot too is disoriented and disarmed by her "unnatural" powers: "My thoughts are whirled like a potter's wheel, / I know not where I am, nor what I do" (1.5.19–20). The heroic English warrior has promised to "chastise this high-minded strumpet" (1.5.12), but faced with Joan, his oaths come to nothing. Not only is Talbot unable to vanquish the armed woman in single combat, but she "scorn[s] [his] strength" (1.5.15) and leaves him for other conquests. Unmanned by her power, Talbot cries out: "The shame hereof will make me hide my head" (1.5.40). In the battle of Orleans, it is Joan who has "play'd the m[a]n" (1.6.16). By contrast, Talbot and his men "crying run away" (1.5.26).

There was nothing new, to be sure, in the association between domineering women and male fears of emasculation; the motif is commonplace in centuries of misogynistic literature.[31] What was new was the way in which this association had become politically volatile in sixteenth-century England with the accession of women to the throne. John Knox's *The First Blast of the Trumpet against the Monstruous Regiment of Women* (1559), one of the century's most vociferous attacks on female rule, powerfully illustrates how a familiar antifeminist discourse might be put to political use. Imagining how "the ancients" would react to the sight of a woman ruler, Knox warns of the dire effects of such a monstrosity:

> I am assuredlie persuaded, I say, that suche a sight shulde so astonishe them, that they shuld judge the hole worlde to be transformed in to Amazones, and that suche a metamorphosis and change was made of all the men of that countrie, as poetes do feyn was made of the companyons of Ulisses, or at least, that albeit the outwarde form of men remained, yet shuld they judge that their hartes were changed frome the wisdome, understanding, and courage of men, to the foolishe fondnes and cowardise of women.[32]

The real danger of female rule, Knox's hysterical prose suggests, is that these Amazons will remake "the hole worlde" in their image. For Knox, the woman ruler is a frightening and unnatural hybrid of Amazon, witch, and temptress—a Circe who debases men by transforming them not into beasts but, worse yet, into women.

It is out of this same unholy trinity that Shakespeare forms his portrait of an emasculating Joan, linking martial and sexual aggression with witchcraft and, in the process, deepening the misogyny of his chronicle sources.[33] Hall, for example, condemns Joan at length for her "unwomanly behavior" but makes no mention of any sexual offense; instead, he jokingly asks whether her chastity "wer because of her foule face, that no man would desire it."[34] On a more skeptical note, the Holinshed chronicler writes that Joan displayed "great *semblance* of chastitie"[35] but refrains from elaborating. In Shakespeare's version, by contrast, both the French and the English discredit Joan's chastity through repeated bawdy punning that equivocates between the opposing images of "Pucelle or puzzel" (1.4.107), maid or whore.[36] As Bedford puts it, joking about her military prowess: "A maid? and be so martial?" (2.1.21). Burgundy's comeback—"Pray God she prove not masculine ere long, / If underneath the standard of the French / She carry armor as she hath begun" (2.1.22–24)—picks up the sexual innuendo, allaying fears about Joan's martial strength (her "armor") by transforming it into a promiscuous sexuality (amour). In *1 Henry VI*, as in the Elizabethan court, to depict the ruling woman as less than a virgin is to take away the identity that authorizes her power. In this context, the attacks on Joan within the play recall contemporaneous French jokes about "whether Queen Elizabeth was a maid or no."[37] To recast the virgin as whore is to turn the fiction of chivalric romance on its head and thereby denigrate the power and authority of the chaste mistress.

It is the association between Joan and the Amazons, however, that generates the most provocative variation on traditional relations of gender and power. A popular figure in the sixteenth century, Amazons appeared not only in attacks on female rule but also in traveller's narratives to the new world, court pageantry, and Elizabethan literature.[38] Sixteenth-century writers like William Painter, in *The Palace of Pleasure*, passed on the fascinating stories of women-warriors who refused to submit to marriage, who raised only female children (maiming or murdering the males), and who waged battles against men with skill and valor.[39] As evidenced by Knox's polemic, sixteenth-century references to Amazons, like their classical counterparts, also mobilized patriotism in the service of patriarchy, celebrating male dominance over women as vital to the strength and welfare of the nation-state. Given the traditional opposition between heroic warriors and subversive Amazons, it is not surprising that the figure of the Amazon was seldom directly associated with Queen Elizabeth.[40] Nor is it surprising that when Elizabethan writers did place Elizabeth in proximity to the Amazons, they often revised the classical narrative in order to mediate the potentially seditious celebration of male dominance.

As Louis Montrose has argued, both Sir Walter Ralegh's account of the Amazons in *The Discoverie of Guiana* (1596) and Edmund Spenser's tale of the Amazon Radigund in book 5 of *The Faerie Queene* illustrate how those seeking favor with the queen might refashion the classical narrative for the Elizabethan court: both writers diplomatically substitute a brave and noble woman in the role of the heroic male warrior. Ralegh, for instance, after detailing the habits of the Amazons of Guiana, closes his text by inviting Elizabeth to play the conquering hero and turn her strength against these alien women. The "Empire of the *Amazones*," he writes, "shall heereby heare the name of a virgin, which is not onely able to defend her owne territories and her neighbors, but also to invade and conquere so great Empyres and so farre remoued."[41] Spenser similarly alters the classical amazonomachy by casting the martial Britomart in the role of the male warrior. A mirror for Elizabeth, Britomart defeats Radigund and rights the inverted order of Amazon rule. In both texts, the substitution of a woman for the heroic male in the war against the Amazon works to associate Elizabeth with the protection of the state. But, at the same time, by placing the queen in opposition to the Amazons, both Ralegh and Spenser continue to insist on the unnatural condition of female rule in general even as they set their own ruling woman apart as a singular exception.[42]

Shakespeare's version of the war against the Amazon in *1 Henry VI* likewise insists on the unnatural state of a ruling woman. But in marked contrast to the strategy that Spenser and Ralegh would employ, Shakespeare's staging of the classical confrontation makes no effort to mediate the contradictions of Elizabeth's rule. Instead, it brings the Knoxian nightmare to life, altering legend at its most crucial moment in order to allow the armed woman to conquer, and feminize, the male hero. The play thus refuses to stage either the insistently patriarchal story of male triumph or the more diplomatic Elizabethan version in which a heroic woman warrior stands in for the triumphant male. Instead, Shakespeare looses his Amazon to wreak destruction on the guardians of England's patriarchal ideals in a succession of scenes that has no basis in chronicle history. Shakespeare's first violation of chronicle "fact" in this context involves Salisbury's death, an event that the chronicles see as a turning point in England's fortunes. Historically, the death of Salisbury occurs *before* Joan's involvement with the dauphin and the French forces, but Shakespeare reverses the sequence so that his death comes as a result of Joan's gathering power and thus provides proof of that power.[43]

In his presentation of Joan tormenting the duke of Bedford in act 3, scene 2, Shakespeare again contradicts the historical record. The chronicles portray the duke as a strong military leader. As regent of France, Bedford had built a powerful sphere of influence and is, accordingly, eulogized in the chronicles as a "noble prince, and valeaunt capitain, the bright sunne, that commonly shone in Fraunce faire and beautifully upon the Englishmen."[44] In his appearance with Joan in *1 Henry VI*, however, Bedford has degenerated into "a man half dead" (3.2.55). Carried onto the stage in a litter, Bedford provides an easy mark for the "railing Hecate" (3.2.64), who irreverently taunts him for his loss of heroic stature: "What will you do, good greybeard? Break a lance, / And run a-tilt at Death within a chair?" (3.2.50–51). This display of female domination—with Joan standing over the dying Bedford, mocking his impotence—is achieved only through Shakespeare's ironic rewriting of his sources. For not only did Bedford die four years *after* Joan, and at the age of forty-five, but, more significantly, it was he along with Cauchon and others who presided over her trial and execution. As Hall succinctly puts it, "Ione was sent to the duke of Bedford to Roan, wher (after long examinacion) she was brent to ashes."[45]

In writing Joan into the scene of Talbot's death in act 4, scene 7, Shakespeare effects an even more startling revision of history since, according to the chronicles, Talbot died in battle some twenty-two years *after* Joan's execution. As Shakespeare presents it, Joan enters the stage, backed by the French forces, immediately following the poignant scene of Talbot and his son dying on the field of battle. The son now "inhearsed" (4.7.45) in his father's arms, the two bodies remain onstage, vulnerable to the enemy's power. And Joan does not disappoint. Irreverently undercutting Lucy's recitation of Talbot's many titles and heroic deeds, Joan mocks the great warrior with this levelling epitaph: "Him that thou magnifi'st with all these titles / Stinking and fly-blown lies here at our feet" (4.7.75–76). Radically altering the chronology of his sources, Shakespeare cuts Talbot's life short by nearly a quarter century in order to allow Joan to triumph over his death. That Shakespeare might just as well have allowed Talbot to triumph over Joan at her death, with far less offense to the historical record, raises questions about the political and cultural forces at work in this highly charged scene.

Remarkably, the one extant contemporary account of the scene, by Thomas Nashe, omits mention of Joan altogether and rewrites the play to celebrate Talbot's "triumphe." Nashe's reference to Talbot comes as part of his defense of the stage in *Pierce Penilesse, His Supplication to the*

Divell (1592), and has been important in setting an upper limit on the
play's date. The reference is also important, however, in testifying to the
play's contemporary reception and its enormous popularity. According to
Nashe, the Talbot play shows theater at its best: like other history plays,
it performs a "rare exercise of vertue" by raising the nation's valiant
forefathers from "the Grave of Oblivion" and bringing them "to pleade
their aged Honours in open presence."[46] As Nashe remembers it, the play
allows Talbot to "triumphe againe on the Stage, and have his bones newe
embalmed with the teares of ten thousand spectators at least, (at severall
times) who in the Tragedian that represents his person, imagine they
behold him fresh bleeding." Concerned with the play's effect on the
weeping spectators, Nashe's account writes Joan out of the scene
altogether and in her place substitutes an idealized image of heroic valor
that serves to illustrate the larger argument of his defense—that the
history play offers a "reproofe to these degenerate effeminate dayes of
ours."[47]

If the history play invited comparisons between past and present, as
Nashe's defense of playing contends, then what conclusions would
Shakespeare's London audience have drawn from the scene of Talbot's
death? While Nashe insists on the differences between past and present,
implying that the sight of Talbot's "triumphe" would have made the
audience ashamed of its own "degenerate effeminate dayes," Shakespeare's staging of Talbot's death suggests that the reproof may have
depended on the audience's perceiving similarities as well as differences
between history and the present time. At the very least, it seems,
Shakespeare's provocative rewriting of Talbot's death argues that
relations between the past and the present in the Elizabethan history play
were not unidirectional. The past may indeed serve to reform the present,
as Nashe claims, but as Shakespeare's revisions of the chronicles
demonstrate, the present may also rewrite the past. Shakespeare's
audience might have understood the failure of the aristocratic hero not
only as an expression of its own anxieties but as evidence of the extent to
which the reign of women in sixteenth-century England had revised
longstanding patriarchal fictions of power, and perhaps even history
itself. Gauging the political effects of these revisions, however, is
difficult. Nashe's account suggests one possibility, that Shakespeare's
Elizabethan remake of English history provoked some members of the
audience to rewrite the scene according to their own desires and thus
collectively imagine a heroic past that could serve as a reproof not only
to the present times but also to the stage before them.[48] But if the
spectacle of female dominance in the scene of Talbot's death ignited
audiences' desires for the aristocratic male hero, as Nashe's reference to

"brave *Talbot*" suggests, the play's simultaneous critique of aristocratic ambition tempers and even checks those desires.

"Factious emulations"

The dangers of aristocratic ambition are visible even at the start of the play, when the smoldering quarrel between Winchester and Gloucester erupts in the midst of Henry's funeral. This bickering between Englishmen of comparable rank stands in counterpoint to the gendered presentation of foreign conflict, complicating the familiar binaries of national identity with internal conflicts and dissension. Aristocratic contentions proliferate at an alarming rate in *1 Henry VI* and extend from the long-standing animosities among the older peers to the new and more dangerous rivalries of the younger generation, of York, Somerset, Suffolk, and their followers. At one point the conflict even spreads to the city streets, with London's citizens organizing into armed gangs. "Civil dissension is a viperous worm / That gnaws the bowels of the commonwealth" (3.1.72–73), the king notes, and though he underestimates the complexity of civil discord, there is a certain truth to his moral platitude. Not only is the factionalism of Henry's court obvious; its consequences are obvious as well, as Exeter sadly observes:

> . . . no simple man that sees
> This jarring discord of nobility,
> This shouldering of each other in the court,
> This factious bandying of their favorites,
> But that it doth presage some ill event.
> (4.1.187–91)

Warnings are sounded at the start of the play when Bedford bluntly predicts that there will be "none but women left to wail the dead" (1.1.51). Civil discord threatens to destroy the noble patrilineage that forms the basis of the nation's strength and identity, yet, paradoxically, it is the struggle over patrilineal inheritance among the nobility that gives rise to the civil discord in the first place.

The magnification of "factious emulations" (4.1.113) in *1 Henry VI* constitutes the play's most extensive departure from its chronicle sources. That Shakespeare takes more liberty with the historical record here than he does with his portrait of Joan argues that the feuding nobles are even more central to the play's politics than is the Amazonian French woman. The attention to aristocratic rivalry in *1 Henry VI* indeed gives shape to the complex political drama that ultimately refuses the simple binaries of moral history associated with the Talbot-Joan conflict. The war with France may generate a series of predictable oppositions—between English noblemen and base French women, between the forces of good and evil—but the civil conflicts cut across these clear divisions, complicating and at times even contradicting traditional moral and political categories. One important effect of the conjunction of civil dissension and foreign war in *1 Henry VI* is to expose the potentially dangerous conflict between aristocratic self-interest and the interests of the nation-state.

The play's most direct critique of aristocratic self-interest comes with the events surrounding Talbot's death. In this instance, Shakespeare freely invents his history, not only in bringing Joan back from the dead, but also in dramatizing the feud between York and Somerset and in linking it to the death of Talbot and his son.[49] In many ways, this scene simply replays the pattern we have seen from the start, where English losses actually stem not from French "treachery" but from "want of men and money" (1.1.69) and division among the generals. But the pattern has become complicated by the emergence of York, whose desire—"Either to be restored to my blood, / Or make mine ill th' advantage of my good" (2.5.128–29)[50]—directly conflicts with the interests of the Lancastrian Crown. For York, to reclaim his "blood" is to lay claim to the throne itself. That the York-Somerset rivalry finally spills onto the battlefield is also the fault of the king, who unwisely commands the nobles to resolve their differences by joining forces against the French. Predictably, the squabbling continues, and Talbot is "bought and sold" (4.4.13) by their "worthless emulation" (4.4.21). As Lucy chorically laments: "Whiles they each other cross, / Lives, honors, lands, and all, hurry to loss" (4.3.52–53). Joan may stand over Talbot's body to mock his lineage, but it is York's quarrel with Somerset—rooted in a conflict over the "rights" of patrilineal inheritance—that most undermines England's strength abroad.

If the scene of Talbot's death in act 4 displays dynastic interests in conflict with the interests of the nation-state, the scene of Joan's capture and trial in act 5 would seem to bring these interests back into alignment as the play stages the long anticipated moment of male triumph that enacts justice with all the tidiness of a morality play. The English, it seems, have come together in the war against the Amazon; they have discovered their common identity—and fraternity—by battling the outsider. The armed woman, the image of disorder and anarchy, is led onto the stage in chains, her containment made visible to the audience before she is taken away to be burned. Order has been restored, and

England is victorious. Once again, however, Shakespeare's revision of patriarchal fictions complicates the play's politics. Casting the machiavellian York as Talbot's successor in the war against the Amazon, the play brings together the two strands of aristocratic dissension at home and gendered conflict abroad—and with unsettling results. York may be victorious over the unruly French woman, but he is hardly representative of England itself. Rather than resolving civil discord with a unified attack on the French woman, the scene only intensifies the play's double critique of female domination and aristocratic self-interest.

Part of what makes York's triumph so unsettling is the presentation of Joan, and for many, the sight of the maid's brutal end has remained the play's most disturbing feature. *1 Henry VI* "ends in mere scurrility," George Bernard Shaw remarked.[51] Others have argued that the problems lie more with modern sensibilities than with the play itself and may be attributed to differences between our own "modern taste" and that of a "Renaissance Englishman," while still others contend that Shakespeare shared our own sensibility but "blackened [Joan] to satisfy the prejudices of his audience."[52] Sixteenth-century presentations of Joan were by no means monovocal, however, and ranged from positive accounts like that of Polydore Vergil—who writes that Joan's sentence "was thought the hardest that ever had beene remembred, which could neyther be mollified nor mittigated by tract of time"—to the negative accounts of Holinshed.[53] Although it may be fair to say that Shakespeare did indeed "blacken" Joan, my concern here is with understanding these revisions within the play's political framework and in relation to the critique of aristocratic factionalism in particular. And so, before turning to Shakespeare's handling of Joan's capture and death, it may be helpful to look briefly at his sources.

According to Keith Thomas, there were not more than a half dozen executions for witchcraft in England between the time of the Norman Invasion and the Reformation, and although witchcraft trials significantly increased during the Tudor and Stuart reigns, the actual number of executions in England remained low, particularly in comparison with Scotland and the Continent.[54] Given the English reluctance to prosecute for witchcraft, it may not be surprising that chronicles from the fifteenth and sixteenth centuries display a certain uneasiness in detailing Joan's fiery end.[55] Hall, for example, deflects legal and moral questions by reproducing the letter Henry VI sent to Burgundy following Joan's death. Justifying England's position, the letter emphasizes the depth of Joan's crimes against the English and at the same time makes much of England's willingness to temper justice with mercy.[56] The account in Holinshed also seeks to exonerate the English, but less by emphasizing their merciful behavior than by making Joan even more deserving of death.[57] The Holinshed chronicler also displays a sophisticated awareness of the propaganda produced by Joan's rehabilitation and the questions it raises. Accordingly, he details the contradictory accounts of Joan's death as a way of unmasking the "gentle Ione" produced by "hir good oratours." He then shrewdly elicits his reader's own good judgment in deciding the truth of Joan's actions: "So sith the ending of all such miraclemongers dooth (for the most part) plainelie decipher the vertue and power that they worke, by hir shall ye be advertised what at last became of hir; cast your opinions as ye have cause."[58]

Like the Holinshed account, *1 Henry VI* also offers to resolve the moral dilemma of Joan's execution by removing all questions about the source of her power with a Faustian scene of conjuring. Compared with the presentation of Joan earlier in the play, this scene is remarkably unequivocal, prompting one critic to observe that "Shakespeare himself seems unable to tolerate any uncertainty about the source of Joan's potency."[59] The scene of Joan's rejection of her father, which has no basis in the chronicles, likewise seems calculated to brand her even in her moment of death as wholly unnatural and without redemption. The scene between father and daughter is also important in playing out the final variation on the Joan-Talbot opposition: Joan here repudiates all familial bonds, refusing to "stoop" (5.4.26) for her father's blessing, in stark contrast to the heroic community of Talbot and his son, who "side by side, together live and die" (4.5.54). But if we read these scenes against the equivocating discourse of the chronicles, the very efficiency with which they seem to resolve the problem of Joan's aggression argues against their authority. Moreover, when political concerns begin to intersect with moral ones in the subsequent confrontation between Joan and York, the easy conclusions invited by these scenes become even less tenable.

As Talbot's successor, York's pronouncement on Joan's denial of her parentage—"This argues what her kind of life hath been, / Wicked and vile, and so her death concludes" (5.4.15–16)—would seem to establish him as the voice of moral authority. But, as this scene transforms itself into a theater of cruelty, York's voice, like Joan's, seems more demonic than sanctioned. Refusing to show either mercy or a concern for law, York and Warwick mock Joan as she attempts to stay her execution first by claiming to be "chaste, and immaculate" (5.4.51) and then, when that fails, to be "with child" (5.4.62). Although omitted by Hall, the reference to Joan's plea of pregnancy was a standard feature in the English chronicles, which used the detail both to incriminate "the maid" and to display the leniency and humanity of her judges (who "gave her nine moneths staie," Holinshed reports).[60] Shakespeare, by contrast, uses the detail to denigrate both Joan and her English captors. For the English, Joan's claim to be with child only gives them more cause to spin cruel jokes, and the scene quickly descends into a grotesque drama as Joan grows more and more desperate, naming a string of possible fathers, and York and Warwick continue to torment her.[61]

In striking contrast to the chronicles whose discourse negotiates the moral and legal questions raised by Joan's execution, Shakespeare revises his sources in order to make the event at first more straightforward but in the end even more complicated and troubling. Much of what makes this scene so unsettling has to do, finally, with the disturbing choice it offers the audience. We cannot support the damnable Joan, who is, after all, England's enemy, but if we root for the English, we not only become complicitous in their cruelty, we also give legitimacy and power to aspiring noblemen whose interests are clearly against those of the nation at large. The scene is further unsettling in the variation it plays on earlier scenes of Amazonian confrontation. Once again, the play calls attention to the difficult problem of gaining control over the unruly woman, but in this instance, the grotesque trial scene helps to clarify the previous confrontations by reminding the audience that the very ideals of civilization which the Amazon is thought to subvert paradoxically argue against her destruction. Only York, who lives by policy rather than a code of chivalry, is able to capture and destroy the alien female. Though York's political aspirations are not yet apparent to all onstage—he "suppress[es] [his] voice" (4.1.182), Exeter remarks—the audience knows that he stands not only outside the community but against it as well. Unlike the noble Talbot, who is disarmed by the "woman clad in armor," York is immune to Joan's power to transform her opponents, for as Joan bluntly tells him: "Chang'd to a worser shape thou canst not be" (5.3.36).

What may have made this scene most unsettling to Elizabethan audiences is its relationship to the political world outside the play. For if *1 Henry VI* speaks to the tensions between Elizabeth and the aristocracy in the 1590s, rather than celebrating a "chivalric compromise," this confrontation between Machiavel and Amazon instead pushes tensions to dangerous extremes and so perhaps issues a warning to both sides. The figure of the chivalric hero immobile before the "ruling" female may well have its counterpart in the Elizabethan mythology of chivalry that required the male warrior to obey—and submit to—the woman ruler. That it is the self-interested York and not the heroic Talbot who succeeds in triumphing over the unruly female raises even more troubling questions. Those who succeed in capturing the French woman in this play come from the new breed of English noblemen whose loyalties are to themselves and not their monarch. Significantly, Suffolk's winning of Margaret replays York's capture of Joan, and though this scene takes its cue from a courtly discourse more in tune with the fictions of the Elizabethan court, the power this triumph furnishes the victor is no less menacing than that displayed by York in his cruel capture of Joan. In contrast to the older peers, this new version of English hero is able to exploit and manipulate available fictions of power and authority in ways that predict the rise of a courtier like Essex, whose image as an armed and triumphant male warrior was to become by the end of the century a "dangerous image" indeed.[62]

If the play thus demonstrates both the limitations and the dangers of the aristocratic warrior, in the figures of Talbot and York respectively, then what figure of the nation-state, if any, does the play finally offer? J. P. Brockbank, writing of the *Henry VI* plays as a whole, makes this general assessment: "Shakespeare's early histories are addressed primarily to the audience's heroic sense of community, to its readiness to belong to an England represented by its court and its army, to its eagerness to enjoy a public show celebrating the continuing history of its prestige and power."[63] But while Shakespeare clearly appeals to this sense of a heroic community, he does so most often to mark its failure within the play's politically complex world. *1 Henry VI* may offer glimpses of a heroic community based on aristocratic identification, witnessed in Talbot's vow to avenge Salisbury's death or in the haunting image of Talbot and his son together in death. But the most sustaining narrative this play offers is shaped by the failure of aristocratic ideals. From the opening report from France of Sir John Falstaff's cowardly retreat, to Suffolk's closing promise to "rule both her, the King, and realm" (5.5.108), the play shows the aristocratic code of heroic virtue to be a fiction, one that may be exploited when it is politically convenient but which has no power in itself, not even to bring a "band of brothers" together against the female enemy.

2

Dangerous Practices:
Making History in *2 Henry VI*

When Buckingham in *2 Henry VI* interrupts the royal party at St. Albans with news of the arrest of Eleanor, duchess of Gloucester, his report concisely articulates a familiar narrative, one that links female aggression with witchcraft and treason.[1] This is the tale that his "heart doth tremble to unfold" (2.1.162):

> A sort of naughty persons, lewdly bent,
> Under the countenance and confederacy
> Of Lady Eleanor, the Protector's wife,
> The ringleader and head of all this rout,
> Have practic'd dangerously against your state,
> Dealing with witches and with conjurers,
> Whom we have apprehended in the fact,
> Raising up wicked spirits from under ground,
> Demanding of King Henry's life and death,
> And other of your Highness' Privy Council,
> As more at large your Grace shall understand.
>
> (2.1.163–73)

As it inscribes the duchess's treason within an age-old stereotype of virago-witch-traitor, Buckingham's report gains a certain authority for the characters onstage and perhaps for some members of Shakespeare's London audience. On the stage, the report's effectiveness is demonstrated at once by the response of the duke of Gloucester, who promises that if his wife is at fault, he will "banish her my bed and company, / And give her as a prey to law and shame, / That hath dishonored Gloucester's honest name" (2.1.193–95). Eleanor is promptly tried and sentenced and, at the close of act 2, is led away to a life of exile on the Isle of Man. With predictable speed, the duchess's treason brings down her husband. Forced to resign his office as England's lord protector, Gloucester is himself accused of treason and, before he can be brought to trial, is found "dead in his bed" (3.2.29).

Like the armed figure of Joan of Arc in *1 Henry VI*, Eleanor Cobham would seem to offer yet another warning about the dangers of ambitious women: her desire for power leads not only to her own fall but to her husband's as well, and without the "good Duke of Gloucester" (1.1.159) to protect the nation's interests, the country descends into civil strife. But like *1 Henry VI*, this play places the familiar narrative of patriarchal power within a wider political context that alters its meaning and authority. Once again, to reduce the play to a cautionary tale that sets subversive women in opposition to the patriarchal state is to tell only part of the story. In Shakespeare's version of the crime, in contrast to Buckingham's, the duchess may think treasonous thoughts, and even consort with necromancers, but she is also the victim of what we might call political entrapment. Hoping that "her attainture will be Humphrey's fall" (1.2.106), the "rich Cardinal" (1.2.94) and the "new-made Duke of Suffolk" (1.2.95) hire a double-agent to set up the duchess, to "buzz these conjurations in her brain" (1.2.99). Her ambitions are thus exploited and even manipulated by her husband's enemies to further their own ambitions for power over the Lancastrian state.

Although Eleanor's case has received only cursory attention in most discussions of the play's politics, which usually focus on Jack Cade's rebellion, those who do take up the matter tend to accept the validity of Buckingham's report and, like the "good Duke of Gloucester," neglect to attend to the complex politics underwriting the duchess's crime and punishment.[2] Even those who acknowledge the framing conspiracy resolve the question of Eleanor's guilt by pointing to the play's conjuring scene, which they see as a kind of "ocular proof" that stands on its own, quite apart from the plot to bring down her husband.[3] The conjuring scene does offer impressive stagecraft, to be sure, but because the theatrics are managed by the conspirators, the scene loses much of its probative value. The paper of scribbled prophecies that would seem to offer material proof of her guilt—"the devil's writ" (1.4.57), as York refers to it—becomes suspect when understood within the context of the conspiring Lancastrian court.

In this play, as in the other *Henry VI* plays, the figure of the ambitious woman again provides a source of instability that calls into question a familiar discourse of power that would reduce political struggles to simple binaries and so suppress their historical and political contexts.

Buckingham's report may invite the audience to find Eleanor guilty simply because his story sounds so familiar, but Shakespeare's double-voiced presentation of the duchess as both victim and aggressor warns of the dangers of this practice. Rather than simply reinforcing the witchcraft-treason stereotype, 2 Henry VI instead opens up, and interrogates, the political faultlines in this gendered story, inviting consideration of the conflicts and contradictions at work in representations of power, both past and present. As the play demonstrates in its complex presentation of Eleanor's crime and punishment, representations of power, whether in the chronicles or in Elizabethan society, are not simply reproductions or repetitions of some original event, but interpretations shaped by specific contexts and motives.[4] Undermining the authority of these representations, the play invites a skepticism about evidence and, with this, a reconsideration of the legal and historical record that extends beyond the issue of women's participation in politics.

This chapter thus continues the practice of examining Shakespeare's presentation of women in the history plays in relation to a past and present, delimited by the chronicle sources, at one end, and Elizabethan contexts, at the other. Generally considered the play's principal source, Edward Hall's chronicle provides one obvious starting point and a kind of baseline for charting Shakespeare's variations on Tudor history's patriarchal themes. I want to begin elsewhere, however, with a text that could be considered both a source and a context. Although not usually put forth as either a source or a context for Shakespeare's duchess, John Foxe's defense of Eleanor Cobham in Acts and Monuments yields an especially resonant point of entry into the politics of representation in 2 Henry VI. As a source, Foxe's text is important in supplying methods as well as materials for interrogating orthodox representations of power. Writing against the chronicle record in order to expose the religious and political interests at work in the case against Eleanor, Foxe's polemical discourse raises questions about the authority of the very texts that served as Shakespeare's sources. As a result, Acts and Monuments may well have furnished the young dramatist with interpretive methods with which to translate chronicle history to the Elizabethan stage. At the same time, by instructing Elizabethans in the contradictory "facts" of the duchess's story, Foxe's widely read text may also have formed part of the play's contemporary context, one that would have shaped the audience's response to the story of treason and witchcraft before them.

Given the importance of sources and contexts in shaping Eleanor's crime in 2 Henry VI, this chapter begins by setting Foxe's interpretation of the case alongside those of the chronicle accounts, reviewing the development of Eleanor's story from the fifteenth to the sixteenth centuries in order to bring into relief the political and religious motives at work in the historical record. From there, the discussion turns first to a close reading of Shakespeare's presentation of the case and then concludes, in the final section, with a more general consideration of the play's politics. While giving us access to history's faultlines, Foxe's defense of Eleanor Cobham is also useful in complicating the ongoing debate about the play's politics, which has been recently rekindled by Richard Helgerson's insistence that Shakespeare is in the business of "staging exclusion," of discrediting commoners—and women, one could add—who attempt to participate in the political nation.[5] When read alongside its sources and contexts, Shakespeare's double-voiced presentation of Eleanor argues against this conclusion and provides a model for reading, and interrogating, other cases of treason and rebellion within the play, within the historical record, and within the Elizabethan state.

"A Matter Made"

In the 1570 edition of *Acts and Monuments*—the edition that, beginning in 1571, appeared by law in every cathedral in England alongside the Bishop's Bible—Foxe interrupted his apocalyptic history of the English church in order to answer the charges levied against the first edition by the recusant Nicholas Harpsfield.[6] As part of his *Dialogi Sex* (1566), published in Antwerp under the name of Alan Cope, Harpsfield had denounced Foxe's calendars of Protestant martyrs, calling them "false martyrs," and, more generally, had accused the martyrologist of misrepresentation and falsehood. Harpsfield especially objected to Foxe's inclusion of men like Lord Cobham, Thomas Cranmer, and Sir Thomas Wyatt among the ranks of Protestant martyrs, men whom Harpsfield and other Catholics deemed traitors and rebels. Also at issue was Foxe's brief mention of another Cobham, Eleanor, duchess of Gloucester. In this instance, Harpsfield again objected to Foxe's choice to include this so-called traitor in the Book of Martyrs, claiming that he had misrepresented Eleanor's crime as heresy. Foxe's response to these charges was direct and effective: he lay the dispute before his readers in a point-by-point response to Harpsfield's "cavillations."[7]

One of the results of Foxe's choice to wage the debate with Harpsfield within the pages of *Acts and Monuments* was that many Elizabethans would have been well-acquainted with the details of Eleanor Cobham's story long before Shakespeare brought it to the stage in the early 1590s.

But what is even more important about Foxe's defense in relation to *2 Henry VI* is that it marked Eleanor's story as a site of controversy. For Foxe, the controversy turned on two points—the truth of the crime itself, and the authority of the chronicles that propagated the story of her treasonous necromancy. Arguing that chroniclers like Hall and Robert Fabyan were unreliable, Foxe's defense worked to make visible the religious and political forces that had been obfuscated and even effaced by the historical record. Influenced by Foxe's arguments, many Elizabethans, including Shakespeare, were likely to have associated Eleanor Cobham's story less with warnings about the dangers of overreaching women than with fears of ambitious churchmen. At Foxe's prompting, they may also have been attuned to the faultlines in the historical record. In order to understand the particulars of Foxe's defense of Eleanor, and the importance of his methods for Shakespeare's own staging of history, we need to look first at the historical ground on which, and against which, both Foxe and Shakespeare wrote. For an Elizabethan trained by Foxe to read between the lines of historical materials, earlier accounts of Eleanor's story offered rich material indeed. Before turning to these materials, however, it may be useful to rehearse what modern historians know of the facts of Eleanor's case.

If fifteenth-century accounts are any indication, Eleanor Cobham's crime was a national sensation: her story appears in every extant fifteenth-century English chronicle and in popular ballads as well.[8] Eleanor was, as one ballad puts it, "amonge alle women magnyfyed,"[9] and her rank and position alone may explain the attention given her case. A former lady-in-waiting, Eleanor Cobham had boldly taken her mistress's place as wife to Humphrey, duke of Gloucester, who held the position of protector during the minority of Henry VI. In the absence of a queen, Eleanor occupied the highest position among women in England, and after the death of John, duke of Bedford, in 1435, she and her husband stood to inherit the throne in the event of the king's death. Six years later, in 1441, Eleanor was accused of conspiring with necromancers, of plotting against the king's life so that she, along with her husband, might assume the royal seat. Two of her three accomplices were executed, while the duchess herself was sentenced to a life of exile on the Isle of Man, where she died eighteen years later.[10]

According to J. G. Bellamy, treason based on necromancy was a relatively new offense in the fifteenth century. Previously, those charged with conjuring against the king had been sentenced as felons rather than traitors. During the first half of the century, however, two high-profile cases, both involving aristocratic women with connections to the Crown, confirm that the scope of treason had expanded to include necromancy.

The first concerned Henry IV's widow, Queen Joan of Navarre, who was accused in 1419 of using sorcery and necromancy in an attempt to destroy the life of her stepson Henry V. Never officially charged or brought to trial, Queen Joan was kept under house arrest for three years.[11] In 1441, Eleanor Cobham, by contrast, was subjected to both civil and ecclesiastical examinations, forced to undergo public penance and humiliation, and sentenced to a life of exile. Historians do not know the exact terms of the charges against Eleanor and her accomplices, but, as Bellamy conjectures, treason in this case was probably construed as "imagining or compassing the death of the king," in accordance with the great treason statute of 1352.[12] Chronicle accounts indicate that Eleanor underwent a series of examinations and that, after the clergy found her guilty of heresy, a civil inquest was commissioned to look into the treason charge. In the end, the state did not actually put Eleanor on trial for treason, probably because there was no precedent for prosecuting a peeress. Within months of her sentencing by the ecclesiastical courts, however, Parliament enacted legislation that clarified the legal status of peeresses accused of treason or felony: they now would be judged by the same judges and peers of the realm as their male counterparts.[13] The result was to increase the penalties for ranking women, for while ecclesiastical courts typically imposed sentences of public penance, the civil court alone could request a death sentence.

That Eleanor's story was first recorded by her husband's enemies, by Yorkist chroniclers writing during the reign of Edward IV, clearly shapes the facts of the narrative that found its way into Shakespeare's Tudor sources. It is not surprising, then, that these early accounts give little attention to the troublesome legal issues of the trial or that they fail to draw a connection between her fall and her husband's. As we might expect, the Yorkist accounts make much of Eleanor's involvement in sorcery and necromancy—she is said to have admitted to several of the charges against her—and locate the motive for her treason in her unnatural ambition and pride. By suppressing political motives altogether, in a move that would seem to be at odds with the charge of treason, these accounts authorize their censure by translating Eleanor's crime against the state into a moral framework, one that is in some cases reinforced by a misogynistic discourse. One of the most detailed fifteenth-century accounts, for example, found in a manuscript that had belonged to John Stow, concluded that the duchess's "pride, fals covetise and lecherie were cause of her confusioun."[14] For popular audiences, the duchess's fate furnished a cautionary tale directed at women in general. In one fifteenth-century ballad written by a London citizen and still being sung in Shakespeare's day, the lamenting duchess confesses her "gret offence" and reiterates the moral in the poem's echoing refrain: "Alle women may be ware by me."[15]

Another strategy for representing Eleanor's crime in the fifteenth-century chronicles was to place her alongside other traitors and heretics who were brought to justice during Henry VI's reign. In one London chronicle, a brief account of the duchess's crime and punishment is followed by a reference to the fighting in Smithfield between an armorer and his servant and the rise and fall of Jack Cade.[16] One of the longest extant accounts from the period, found in *An English Chronicle*, makes an even more provocative connection by placing Eleanor's story immediately after that of Richard Wyche, an Essex vicar, who had been burned for heresy earlier that year. Wyche's execution had stirred up trouble among the populace: "Some said he was a good man and an holy, and put to deth be malice," the chronicle reports.[17] Wyche quickly achieved the status of martyr as crowds flocked to the site of his burning at Tower Hill until the authorities put an end to this "fals ydolatrie."[18] This account thus attests to the link between heresy and Lollard martyrs that Foxe would exploit in his church history a century later when he too would set Eleanor's case alongside Wyche's martyrdom.

In contrast to their Yorkist predecessors, Tudor chroniclers writing in the first half of the sixteenth century began to hint at the possibility of political maneuvering, as their focus shifted from Eleanor's crime to the injustices done to her husband. Fabyan's account, for example, first published in 1516, retains the familiar story of Eleanor's crime and punishment but prefaces it with a telling paragraph on the duke of Gloucester's enemies who, he writes, "left nat tyll they hadde brought hym unto his confucion."[19] Hall, in *The Union of the Two Noble and Illustre Famelies of Lancastre and Yorke* (1548), follows a similar strategy of rehearsing the facts of the duchess's treason within the context of Lancastrian politics. Although Hall carefully avoids linking the animosity against Gloucester directly with his wife's fall, he insinuates a connection by placing the brief tale of Eleanor as a conclusion to the lengthy presentation of the duke of Gloucester's complaints against Cardinal Winchester, complaints that bring to a head the long-standing political struggle between the duke and the cardinal. After documenting Gloucester's accusations, Hall asserts that "secret attemptes were advaunced forward this season, against the noble duke Humfrey of Glocester, a farre of, whiche in conclusion came so nere, that they bereft hym both of lyfe and lande, as you shall hereafter more manifestly perceyve."[20] Hall here begins the story of the duchess's crime and punishment.

But while Hall thus links the cardinal's "injury" with the subsequent falls of the duchess and her husband, when he turns to the story of the crime itself, he continues to record the incriminating details of her necromancy and public disgrace. The effect is to produce a contradictory narrative that, on the one hand, foregrounds the political context suppressed in earlier accounts but, on the other, reiterates, and even elaborates on, earlier condemnations of Eleanor. Hall's account, not unlike Buckingham's in *2 Henry VI*, compresses the crime and punishment into one sentence that neatly contains the treasonous event. A concise *exemplum*, it seems, of the dangers of aspiring women, this is the account that Abraham Fleming would later reproduce in the pages of Holinshed's *Chronicles*:

> For first this yere, dame Elyanour Cobham, wyfe to the sayd duke, was accused of treason, for that she, by sorcery and enchauntment, entended to destroy the kyng, to thentent to advaunce and to promote her husbande to the croune: upon thys she was examined in sainct Stephens chappel, before the Bisshop of Canterbury, and there by examinacion convict and judged, to do open penaunce, in. iii. open places, within the citie of London, and after that adjudged to perpetuall prisone in the Isle of Man, under the kepyng of sir Jhon Stanley, knyght.[21]

To readers today—and to Elizabethan readers like Foxe—what is perhaps most startling about Hall's account is its failure to adjudicate the contradictions of its own narrative.

We may understand these contradictions in part as a product of Tudor historiography. As F. J. Levy has argued, chroniclers like Hall, Grafton, and even Holinshed were essentially compilers, who drew on an ever-increasing array of materials. Rather than selectively editing the multiple and sometimes conflicting accounts of their sources, these writers instead followed the principle of inclusion, which led to massive compilations that omitted nothing. In its most extreme form, this practice resulted in disjointed accounts and contradictory "facts," about which the politic chroniclers usually remained silent. Choosing to record rather than arbitrate the conflicts that arose among their sources, these writers left it up to the reader to rule on the authority of earlier accounts.[22] As Annabel Patterson has argued of the Holinshed chroniclers, the practice of allowing the reader to adjudicate conflicting accounts also furnished important protection in what could be a dangerous business. "The reader was left to be his own historian," she writes, "not because the historian had abrogated his interpretative task, but because he wished to register how extraordinarily complicated, even dangerous, life had become in post-Reformation England, when every change of regime initiated a change in the official religion, and hence in the meaning and value of acts and allegiances."[23] Holinshed gives ample support for this assertion in the opening words of his "Preface to the Reader": "It is dangerous (gentle Reader) to range in so large a field as I have here undertaken, while so manie sundrie men in divers things may be able to controll me."[24] Even a chronicler like Hall, who rarely acknowledged the contradictions he set before the reader, offered a disclaimer in presenting the controversial matter of Lord Cobham's death. Whether the charges against Oldcastle were fabricated or genuine, he writes, "the judgement whereof I leave to men indifferent."[25]

For Elizabethans habituated to a rhetoric of deference and diffidence, the edition of Foxe's *Acts and Monuments* placed before them in their churches constituted a radical departure from the methods of the Tudor chroniclers. Concerned with setting forth the apocalyptic history of the "true" church, Foxe made no claim to being a disinterested compiler of historical records. Instead, as he wrote in the dedicatory letter to Elizabeth I in the 1570 edition, he intended that his book would serve to instruct a nation "long led in ignorance, and wrapped in blindness" (1:viii). In contrast to the unbiased reporting claimed by the chroniclers, Foxe's text revealed its Protestant agenda at every turn, recounting story after story of evil churchmen and suffering believers. To Foxe's critics, his apocalyptic project was clearly at odds with historical practices grounded in accuracy and objectivity, and it is on this basis that his work has been attacked, first by sixteenth-century Catholics like Harpsfield and Robert Parsons, who accused him of writing "wholly to deceive,"[26] and later by historians in the nineteenth and twentieth centuries. Recent scholarship on Foxe, however, urges a more balanced assessment, one that distinguishes between the obvious biases built into the book's overarching argument and Foxe's historical practices.[27] As some have argued, Foxe's methods, characterized by careful attention to primary sources and a respect for documentation, may have proved as influential as his Protestant message, providing a model of historiography for those who came after, including the Holinshed chroniclers.[28] Influencing the way Elizabethans wrote and read chronicle history, Foxe's widely read text may also have helped to shape the new genre of the English history play that emerged in the early 1590s.

Foxe articulates his concern for historical methods at length in his polemical additions to the second edition, as illustrated in the debate about Lord Cobham's treason and again in his defense of Eleanor. Arguing against Harpsfield's use of English chroniclers like Hall and Fabyan to disprove his accounts of Lord Cobham and Eleanor, Foxe begins by questioning the authority of these writers: "What authority do they avouch? what acts, what registers, what records, or out of what court do they show, or what demonstration do they make?"(3:373). Since the chroniclers did not actually witness the events they recorded, Foxe contends, they depended on rumor and hearsay, which could be especially unreliable in controversial cases involving treason and heresy. Rather than blindly relying on the chronicles, Foxe calls instead for a careful scrutiny of the historical record:

> Diligence is required, and great searching out of books and authors, not only of our time, but of all ages. And especially where matters of religion are touched pertaining to the church, it is not sufficient to see what "Fabian" or what "Hall" saith; but the records must be sought, the registers must be turned over, letters also and ancient instruments ought to be perused, and authors with the same compared: finally, the writers amongst themselves one to be conferred with another; and so with judgment matters are to be weighed; with diligence to be laboured; and with simplicity, pure from all addition and partiality, to be uttered. (3:376–77)

Foxe's desire to weigh the evidence is not exactly disinterested, to be sure, and he can be accused of replacing the biases of earlier histories with his own. But, at the same time, Foxe's scrutiny of historical documents provides a model for a far more radical project. Dedicated to recovering the voices of the oppressed within the oppressors' records, Foxe's text demonstrates a way to generate alternative narratives out of the orthodox accounts of church histories and English chronicles.

Foxe's defense of Eleanor Cobham brings up similar questions of methodology, again in response to Harpsfield's objections. Recapitulating the quarrel for readers of the second edition, Foxe explains that he had included "a short note" about Eleanor Cobham in the first edition of *Acts and Monuments* in order to document the persecutions that continued in the years after Lord Cobham's death. Eleanor's case represented a widening of persecution, Foxe had claimed, as the papists "began now to execute their cruelty upon women" (3:704). In this instance, Harpsfield had accused Foxe of mixing up the facts of the case. Again, Foxe responds by contesting the authority and accuracy of Harpsfield's facts as derived from English chronicles. "Why is it not as free for me to credit John Bale and Leland," Foxe asks, "as for him to credit Robert Fabian and Edward Hall?" (3:705). Foxe continues this line of argumentation by representing his defense of Eleanor as a disinterested critique of historical methods:

> *I do but only move a question by way of history,* not as defending, nor commending, nor commemorating the thing, if it be true, but only moving the question, whether it is to be judged true, or suspected rather to be false and

forged; and so, having briefly propounded certain conjectural suspicions or supposals concerning that matter, I will pass it over, neither meddling on the one side nor on the other. (3:707) (emphasis added)

Although Foxe's protestations here may be largely rhetorical—he is, after all, defending his earlier note on Eleanor—his call for a reexamination of historical records reiterates his method of recovering church history.

Exemplifying this method in Eleanor Cobham's defense, Foxe sets his own account of the crime alongside that of Harpsfield and the chroniclers, leaving "the determination and judgment hereof to [the] indifferent and free arbitrement" of his "gentle reader" (3:708–9). Foxe begins by conjecturing that the duchess was framed and that her treason was, therefore, "a matter made, and of evil-will compacted, rather than true indeed" (3:707). Both Eleanor and her so-called accomplice were followers of Wycliff, Foxe explains, and thus "hated" by the clergy. The link between Eleanor's persecution and the "grudge kindled" between the duke of Gloucester and Cardinal Winchester, noted by Fabyan and Hall, leads Foxe to conjecture that "all this matter rose of that cardinal, who was then a mortal enemy to the house of Gloucester & c" (3:708). Foxe then closes his argument against Harpsfield by proposing an alternative story to the one informing the chronicle accounts, delineating a tradition in which charges of witchcraft are exploited for political gain. "The frequent practices and examples of other times may make this also more doubtful," he writes of Eleanor's treason, "considering how many subtle pretences, after the like sort, have been sought, and wrongful accusations brought, against many innocent persons" (3:708). Foxe then validates his argument with specific historical cases, citing, for instance, the false charge laid to "the queen and Shore's wife, by the protector, for enchanting and bewitching his withered arm" (3:708). Situated within the wider framework of Foxe's book of martyrs, this alternative tradition widens even further to connect Eleanor with a chain of martyrs that includes Elizabeth I, who at the start of her sister's reign was herself suspected of treason, by another Winchester, Bishop Stephen Gardiner. Foxe may leave the decision about Eleanor's case up to the judgment of his "gentle reader," but the choice for Elizabethan Protestants is clear.

Foxe's argument that the charges against Eleanor were "a matter made" may leave its mark on 2 Henry VI's emphasis on conspiracies, but what is more important in terms of Shakespeare's staging of history in this play is Foxe's larger project of reexamining, and rewriting, the historical record. Granted, Foxe's apocalyptic history may on the face of it bear little resemblance to Shakespeare's complex and pervasively

skeptical staging of English history. But Foxe's text nonetheless provides
an important model for interrogating the documents of the past,
particularly as they are codified, and authorized, by popular chroniclers
like Hall and Fabyan. Foxe's defense of Eleanor, together with his
expressed concern for historical procedures, illustrates a method by
which a dramatist interested in staging English history might open up the
faultlines of his chronicle sources and, in the process, generate a drama
of nation that reexamines, and revises, orthodox narratives of patriarchal
power and national identity. In this regard, Eleanor's story confirms a
link between Shakespeare and Foxe that supports recent work by Robert
Weimann and Donna Hamilton on representation, Protestantism, and
early modern drama. For if Shakespeare incorporated "the idioms of
protestant polemical discourse" into his plays, as Hamilton has
persuasively argued, 2 Henry VI may have served as an early testing
ground for these practices.[29]

"A pretty plot, well chosen to build upon"

Setting Foxe's text alongside Shakespeare's urges us, as it may have
urged audiences in the 1590s, to see the play's double-voiced narrative of
Eleanor as both criminal and victim less as a strategy of deference or
indirection than as a means of interrogating instabilities in the historical
record and, in the process, of raising far-reaching questions about
evidence and authority. To be sure, Shakespeare's presentation of the
duchess in 2 Henry VI is in many ways more indebted to Hall than to
Foxe. Shakespeare's Eleanor is certainly no proto-Protestant, and even
the resonant name of Cobham is seldom heard during the course of the
play. Nor is Eleanor's crime solely "a matter made" in 2 Henry VI.
Instead, Shakespeare, like Hall, replays the incriminating scene of
necromancy and, in reiterating the old warnings about aggressive
women, appears to restore the gendered narrative of the earlier accounts
that Foxe had all but effaced. The play also recalls the Tudor chronicles
by placing the conspiracy to bring down the duke of Gloucester
alongside Eleanor's crime and then refusing to offer a clear resolution to
the resulting contradictions. But while Hall may have provided a source
for the play's contradictory narratives of crime and conspiracy, Foxe
offered a model for situating these contradictions within a wider context.
Like Foxe's polemical defense of Eleanor, which sets earlier accounts
alongside his own, Shakespeare's double narrative requires its audience
to become involved in sifting the evidence and evaluating the authority

of the representations before them onstage and, by extension, in the world outside. In contrast to Foxe, however, the answers in Shakespeare are not so clear, nor are they resolved by an explanatory, and totalizing, narrative of history.

If the play offers a theatrical version of Foxe's interrogation of the chronicle accounts, it stages its skepticism by exploiting what Weimann has referred to as the "bifold authority" of the Elizabethan stage. According to Weimann, the theatrical conventions of an upstage *locus* and a downstage *platea* allowed authority to be represented both as an object and as a process of authorization. The *locus*, Weimann writes, "tended to privilege the authority of what and who was *represented* in the dramatic world," whereas the *platea* "tended to privilege the authority of what and who was *representing* that world."[30] Generating a dissonance between "authorities represented" and "authorities representing,"[31] in this case between the representation of Eleanor's crime and the conspirators acting as agents in that representation, Shakespeare calls attention to the ways in which authority might be constructed, in the performance of justice as well as in the historical record. Locating the conjuring on the upstage *locus*, the play may appear to privilege the chronicle accounts of Eleanor's crime by confirming her guilt. But in simultaneously staging the crime's political context on the downstage *platea*, in the asides and soliloquies of the conspirators, the play offers a challenge to the *locus*-centered authority of the conjuring scene. Understood in terms of the bifold authority of the Elizabethan stage, Shakespeare's double presentation of Eleanor as both traitor and victim enacts a debate about the authority of evidence not unlike that set forth in Foxe's polemical defense.

The play institutes this bifold authority with Eleanor's entrance in act 1, scene 2, as Shakespeare adopts, and even intensifies, the familiar stereotypes of his chronicle sources. Almost a caricature of a domineering female, Eleanor begins by imperiously urging her husband to take the throne. "Put forth thy hand, reach at the glorious gold," she commands, only to mock her husband's manhood: "What, is't too short? I'll lengthen it with mine" (1.2.12). Gloucester provides the moral gloss, advising his wife to "banish the canker of ambitious thoughts" (1.2.18), yet his "troublous" (1.2.22) dream of his staff "broke in twain" (1.2.26) gives form to his fears. Gloucester's civic impotence, the play suggests, has its origins in his marital impotence, in his failure to command his wife. True to the stereotype, the duchess chafes at the limitations imposed on her sex in terms that anticipate those of Lady Macbeth:

> Were I a man, a duke, and next of blood,
> I would remove these tedious stumbling-blocks,

And smooth my way upon their headless necks;
And, being a woman, I will not be slack
To play my part in Fortune's pageant.

(1.2.63–67)

Denied the means of power available to her husband, the duchess turns to necromancy.

On the basis of this scene alone, one could argue that the play simply reproduces the patriarchal discourse of chronicle history. Eleanor's ambitions, it seems, are just another symptom of the social and political instabilities stemming from Henry VI's weak rule and his "fatal" marriage to Margaret of Anjou. With Eleanor's desires replicated in Margaret's, the play not only "mobilizes specific ideologies of gender to voice its political anxieties,"[32] as Jean Howard has argued, it also appears to validate, if not exacerbate, those anxieties by insisting on the dangers of female misrule. But if the play seems to endorse a gendered discourse that casts the ambitious woman as a danger to the nation's welfare, the bifold authority of the stage soon calls that discourse into question by placing Eleanor's ambitions within a political context that extends from the contentions between Winchester and Gloucester to the political machinations of York and Suffolk.

Shakespeare may dramatize the familiar paradigm of virago-witch-traitor in the play's opening scenes, but he significantly alters our understanding of it by qualifying the duchess's aspirations with the framing soliloquies of York and Hume, soliloquies that show the duchess to be an unwitting pawn in a larger and far more dangerous conspiracy to take the Crown. The duchess makes her entrance, in fact, immediately after York's lengthy speech in which he voices his grievance against the king and vows that with "force perforce I'll make him yield the crown" (1.1.258). Her expressed desire for "King Henry's diadem" (1.2.7) thus parodies (or "boys," to be more precise) York's own treasonous desire to possess "fertile England's soil" (1.1.238). It is York, after all, who actually acts out the duchess's desire to "smooth my way upon their headless necks" (1.2.65). The duchess will indeed "play" her part in "Fortune's pageant," but on Shakespeare's stage it is a part set down for her by her husband's enemies, as the ambidextrous Hume confides to the audience at the close of this scene. Delivered from the downstage *platea*, the framing soliloquies of York and Hume serve to circumscribe the duchess's ambition, containing it within the larger, and more dangerous, plots to undermine the monarchy. Rather than validating the familiar story of virago-witch-traitor as a universal truth, Shakespeare's presentation, like Foxe's, makes visible the ways in which this story is exploited, and even fabricated, by the Crown's "true" enemies.

Shakespeare's staging of the conjuring scene similarly complicates the supposedly transparent facts of the case by raising questions about Eleanor's involvement and the nature of her crime. Enacting the conjuring onstage should offer proof of Eleanor's guilt, and to some extent it does. But Shakespeare, like Foxe, undermines that proof by asking the audience to see the crime in part as "a matter made" by Gloucester's enemies. In contrast to Hall's account, which shows Eleanor to be the initiator of the plan to "destroy the kynges person"—her accomplices undertook their sorcery "at the request of the duchesse,"[33] Hall writes—2 *Henry VI* presents her as a passive observer. On Shakespeare's stage, the conjuring has become a "performance" (1.4.2), as Hume puts it, paid for by the duchess, who takes her place "aloft" (1.4.8), as audience to Bolingbrook's "exorcisms" (1.4.4). Again, Shakespeare exploits the bifold capacity of his stage, this time placing Bolingbrook and his associates in the *locus* of authority and setting Eleanor apart, as witness to the spectacular events, in a move that aligns her more with the play's own audience than with the conspirators onstage. By distancing Eleanor from the events staged before her, and thus transforming the crime itself into a kind of play-within-a-play, Shakespeare shifts the location of authority away from Eleanor and onto her enemies.

The conjuring scene indeed exposes itself as theater as Bolingbrook, prompted by the double-dealing Hume, acts as stage manager, directing his players: "Mother Jordan, be you prostrate and grovel on the earth. . . . John Southwell, read you; and let us to our work" (1.4.10–12). Bolingbrook's fears about the duchess's courage, absent from the chronicle accounts, further diminish the extent of her involvement. "I have heard her reported to be a woman of an invincible spirit," Bolingbrook confesses to Hume, "but it shall be convenient, Master Hume, that you be by her aloft, while we be busy below" (1.4.6–9). Hume, after all, must ensure that the scene is set for the duchess's arrest. Before the spirit rises, Bolingbrook advises her to "fear not" for "whom we raise, / We will make fast within a hallow'd verge" (1.4.21–22), words that might apply just as well to the "raising" of Eleanor. Never a real threat to the monarchy, it seems, the duchess too is made "fast," securely contained within the circle of conspiracy drawn by Gloucester's enemies. By foregrounding the master plot of the cardinal, Shakespeare thus radically alters the facts of the duchess's conjuring as they will later be reported by Buckingham. Eleanor does, to be sure, consort with spirits to learn of the king's death, though she is conspicuously silent during the ceremony itself. When framed by the machinations of the cardinal and York, however, the conjuring scene itself appears as a trick or, as York himself describes it, "a pretty plot, well chosen to build upon" (1.4.56).

Another alteration Shakespeare makes in his chronicle sources that alters the audience's understanding of Eleanor's crime is the substitution of a prophesying spirit for the wax image commonly cited in the Tudor accounts. Hall, for instance, had described how the duchess's accomplices, following her instructions, "devised an image of waxe, representyng the kynge, whiche by their sorcery, a litle and litle consumed, entendyng therby in conclusion to waist, and destroy the kynges person, and so to bryng hym death."[34] In suppressing the wax image, *2 Henry VI* recalls the story of Eleanor's tragedy found in the 1578 edition of *The Mirror for Magistrates*, in which the duchess confesses that she intended no harm to her prince but only "to cast and calke, the kinges constellation / And then to judge by depe dyvination."[35] The raising of a spirit is, as some have argued, far more spectacular onstage than is a diminutive wax figure—witness the success of Marlowe's *Doctor Faustus*—but neither theatrical reasons nor the play's sources fully explain the effect the substitution may have had on the audience's perception of Eleanor's crime.[36]

Once again, Shakespeare's revision of chronicle history complicates interpretations of the scene. Paola Pugliatti, for instance, has argued that the substitution makes the scene more subversive, in part because it displays Margery Jourdain's "conjuring competence."[37] The presence of a spirit onstage does indeed prove the efficacy of conjuring in a way that a wax image would not—the prophecies come true, after all, but the king lives. Yet the substitution of a spirit for the wax image also alters the legal status of Eleanor's crime, reducing its magnitude and, at the same time, raising questions about intention and proof that go to the heart of Elizabethan treason legislation. Again, it may be useful to begin with Hall's account, which clearly establishes the intention (she "entended to destroy the kyng"), the evidence ("an image of waxe, representyng the kynge"), and the nature of the crime ("treason"). Because the crime of treason rests with intention—with "compassing" or "imagining"—the scope of treason legislation may be measured in part by what is accepted as proof of intention. During Elizabeth's reign, treason was broadly defined, and accusations could be based on evidence as questionable as spoken words, which frequently came down to one man's word against another's.[38] Even so, Shakespeare's version of Eleanor's crime— "Raising up wicked spirits from under ground, / Demanding of King Henry's life and death" (2.1.170–71), as Buckingham reports it—places it outside the scope of Elizabethan treason law.

For an Elizabethan audience, the substitution of a talking head for a wax image would have reduced the seriousness of Eleanor's crime considerably, changing it from high treason to a felony offense. Still, the change would not have been without political resonance since, by Elizabethan standards, Eleanor's crime would now fall under the repressive antisedition statute of 1581 (23 Eliz. c. 2), which made prophesying the king's future a crime punishable by death. Between the years of 1549 and 1581, penalties for prophesying had been minimal, and even those convicted of prophesying the king's death were subject only to a fine and a year in prison.[39] But in 1581, in an effort to clamp down on recusants and sympathizers of Mary Stuart, Parliament had enacted strict antisedition legislation, refurbishing a 1554–55 statute originally designed to suppress vocal Protestants. That Shakespeare's substitution of prophesying for treason might have prompted some members of his audience to see a connection between Foxe's proto-Protestant heroine and the recusants of the 1580s is not without its ironies. We cannot know Shakespeare's intentions, but if there is a message to be found here, it points to the dangers of repressive legislation that, in a century characterized by radical shifts in religious and political authority, could be turned against the legislators.[40]

When submitted to the scrutiny of Elizabethan statute law, the "ocular proof" of the conjuring scene becomes less and less definitive. The scene supports a charge of prophesying, not treason, and shows Eleanor to be a pawn in a larger conspiracy. Still, it does not exonerate Eleanor of the crime altogether. On Shakespeare's stage, as in Hall, it is a deed arranged and paid for by the duchess herself. Shakespeare's skepticism of sources and facts may be indebted to Foxe, but in the end his presentation of Eleanor differs from the martyrologist's in refusing to offer an alternative story of the crime, one that simply replaces ambition and treason with heresy and persecution. Indeed, what distinguishes Shakespeare's rewriting of chronicle history is his refusal to resolve political complexity with yet another binary narrative of good and evil. Without the kind of assured truths that shape *Acts and Monuments*, Shakespeare's skepticism of authority in this play is more extensive than Foxe's, and far more radical.

Local Politics

To argue that *2 Henry VI* provokes skepticism about the authority of familiar representations of power is to challenge, or at least qualify, longstanding assumptions about the play's conservative politics. Largely on the basis of Jack Cade's rebellion, critics have pointed to the play as evidence of Shakespeare's orthodox support for the ruling elite. Through Cade, M. M. Reese writes, Shakespeare explored "what happens in the state when authority passes to the uninstructed multitude."[41] More recently, both Richard Wilson and Richard Helgerson have extended this argument by proposing a historical ground for Shakespeare's conservatism. Reading the play's supposedly law-and-order staging of artisan riot as a response to the Southwark riot in the summer of 1592, Wilson puts Shakespeare on the side of the Crown against the rioting city apprentices.[42] Helgerson likewise associates Shakespeare with the ruling elite, arguing that in its staging of popular revolt, the play moves to "efface, alienate, even demonize all signs of commoner participation in the political nation."[43] Helgerson's argument rightly acknowledges the complexity of staging history during this period, created in part by the tensions between the theater's artisan identity and its dependence on aristocratic patronage and protection from the Crown. But while Helgerson sees the national history play of the 1590s as "a scene of contention" that is not fully resolved, he argues that Shakespeare's histories are concerned "above all with the consolidation and maintenance of royal power."[44]

Shakespeare's handling of Eleanor's case, however, argues against the opposing choices these readings offer. As in *1 Henry VI*, the conjunction of aspiring women and conspiring noblemen complicates, and even invalidates, the binary categories of a patriarchal and aristocratic narrative of power. Once again, the play refuses to resolve the competition for power, in part by failing to converge on a single, authorized locus, as identified in the figure of the king, for instance, or the unified state. The scenes of Eleanor's arrest and trial, not unlike Joan's in *1 Henry VI*, may promise to restore order, but here Shakespeare evokes the patriarchal resolution only to register its dangers. Captured and led onto the stage under guard, Eleanor recalls the tragic figures from *The Mirror for Magistrates*, humbly accepting responsibility for her fate—"Welcome is my banishment, welcome were my death" (2.3.14)—in words that echo the repentant scaffold speeches of the period. But even as the play stages Eleanor's trial within a familiar, if not formulaic, moral pattern, it continues to undermine the efficacy of that pattern.

In *2 Henry VI*, Shakespeare again raises questions about familiar patriarchal fictions of power and national identity in which control of women is deemed essential to the well-being of the nation-state. As Shakespeare stages it, the capture of the unruly female leads not to the restoration of order in the state but to its collapse. Radically compressing the chronology of the chronicles, the play links Eleanor's arrest and sentencing directly to her husband's removal from office (2.3.23), and without the lord protector, civil strife soon breaks out. The play further disrupts traditional models of power by identifying the enemies of the witch-traitor as the enemies of the Crown. As we have seen in the previous chapter, the dominant national discourse tended to glorify the hero who succeeded in gaining control over the female enemy and bringing order to the state. That Shakespeare should again cast the conspiring York as the "hero" who triumphs over the subversive female, a choice that like York's capture of Joan in *1 Henry VI* involved rewriting chronicle history, calls into question the model of power that derives its authority from a myth of patriarchal domination. In Shakespeare's version of English history, the unruly female is brought under control not by a divinely sanctioned hero or by a civilized code of law but by the forces of anarchy, by York and Winchester who operate outside the law. For, despite York's mouthing concern for "King and commonweal" (1.4.43) as he makes the arrest, the capture of the witch-traitor is anything but a patriotic act.

2 Henry VI's presentation of Eleanor Cobham thus contests the authority of the patriarchal narrative by dramatizing a specific, historic case in which "containment" ironically not only fails to preserve the state but in fact contributes to its ruin. In the process, the play warns of the ease with which outsiders may exploit familiar narratives of power as a means of subverting the nation-state. This is not to recirculate a new historicist argument that power is simply theatrical or that it depends on "the constant production of its own radical subversion and the powerful containment of that subversion," as Stephen Greenblatt argued in his essay on the *Henriad*.[45] In interrogating relations between power and the production of subversion, *2 Henry VI* could be said to anticipate the "invisible bullets" of Lancastrian authority in the *Henriad*, but with an important difference. For in *2 Henry VI*, both subversion and containment—in the cases of Eleanor's conjuring scene and Cade's rebellion—are produced as a means to power, but in this play, those controlling this production are not princes but aspiring aristocrats who conspire against the Crown. "Invisible bullets" may have offered the early modern nation-state an important means of power, but, as *2 Henry VI* warns, it is a form of power that is difficult to keep within the control of the ruling elite. Indeed, as the play amply documents, this is a form of power that proliferates rapidly, appropriated by aristocratic conspirators like York and by upstart artisans like Cade.

The case against Eleanor is, in fact, only the first of a series of treason trials within the play. And, as treason accusations come to provide a central means of establishing power and authority within the contentious Lancastrian state, the play's critique of the gendered stereotype of witch-

traitor widens to include other discourses of state power. The case against
the armorer Thomas Horner, presented in scenes interwoven with
Eleanor's crime and punishment, offers the most immediate parallel. The
evidence in this case is far more tenuous than Eleanor's, based not on
material proof but spoken words, for "saying that the Duke of York was
rightful heir to the crown" (1.3.26–27). That the accusation is made by a
servant against his master raises even more questions about evidence: as
master Horner points out, his apprentice may simply be seeking revenge,
for "when I did correct him for his fault the other day, he did vow upon
his knees he would be even with me" (1.3.198–200). But if the
accusation is prompted by the apprentice's desire to get back at his
master—and we can never be sure that it is—what brings the case to
court is the fact that the apprentice's charges serve the interests of the
queen and Suffolk, who want to block York's appointment as regent to
France. Again, as in Eleanor's case, the politics shaping this case
complicate, and perhaps prevent, the working out of justice. Once again,
the play refuses to resolve the truth of the matter with a just verdict.
Horner may confess his crime before he dies, and the apprentice may
proclaim his innocence, but, aside from the king, few are convinced by
this staging of justice.[46]

If treason's discourse serves those who struggle for power within the
Lancastrian court, it also works for those like Jack Cade, who practice
their power within the London streets. Like his social betters, Cade also
launches his rise to power with accusations of treason, stringing up the
clerk Emmanuel because "he can write and read and cast accompt"
(4.2.85–86). With the clerk's summary trial, the play fully exposes both
the politics of treason and the dangers of interpreting evidence in
accordance with familiar narratives, in this case the rebels'
counternarrative equating illiteracy with morality. Like Eleanor, the clerk
is condemned on the basis of material proof when the rebels discover "a
book in his pocket with red letters in't" (4.2.90–91). As this scene
demonstrates, proof is not transparent but depends on the interpretation
of the "judges," who in this case regard writing as dangerously
subversive. "Nay, then he is a conjurer" (4.2.92), Cade declares at the
sight of the book, his words echoing York's performance with Eleanor
earlier in the play. The final piece of evidence against the clerk is the fact
that he can write his own name. "He hath confess'd!" the rebels shout,
and Cade pronounces the sentence: "Hang him with his pen and inkhorn
about his neck" (4.4.107, 109–10). This grotesque display of injustice
clearly underscores the horrors of Cade's rebellion and thus offers
support for a conservative Shakespeare. But the fact that the scene, in
part a parody of the trials of Eleanor and Horner, finds its source in the

manipulation of authorizing narratives of power by those struggling for control within the Lancastrian court counters this conclusion.

If Eleanor's case opens up a wider critique of representations of power within the play as well as the historical record, as this chapter has argued, it also offers a way of reading the intersection of politics and familiar displays of power within the early modern nation-state. For the play's London audience in the early 1590s, Eleanor's case may have invited comparison with the recent wave of witchcraft-treason trials in Scotland, in which more than three hundred witches were said to have conspired against James VI by raising storms at sea as the king returned from Denmark with his bride.[47] Not unlike the characters within the play, James had tried to control the events, frequently breaking with tradition to preside over the trials himself. In 1591, the king attempted to influence public opinion in England with the publication of *Newes from Scotland*, a pamphlet in which Shakespeare's audience could have read for themselves about the trials of the North Berwick witches. Carefully tailored for its English readers, *Newes from Scotland* offered a sensational account, both titillating and gruesome, designed to enhance the king's standing in England by presenting him as "the Lords annointed" and the enemy of the devil.[48] Using the trials not only to hunt down his political enemies but also to advertize his own authority, England's future king worked to fashion his own brand of patriarchal power.

But if the play invited comparison with contemporary events—and Elizabethan representations of power no doubt provided other resonant points of reference for Shakespeare's audience—it did not offer easy solutions to the complexities of early modern politics. Shakespeare's histories may be concerned with the "consolidation" of royal power, as Helgerson argues, but in this play, as in *1 Henry VI*, that power exists only as a myth, nostalgically evoked by the ghost of Henry V that haunts all three *Henry VI* plays. Rather than converging on the figure of a powerful king, *2 Henry VI* instead launches a sweeping critique of representations of power that crosses boundaries of rank and gender. In place of a powerful king, or a single and authorized locus of power, the play offers its audience fractured authorities and contradictory images of power—with the staging of Eleanor's crime, as we have seen, with Horner's trial, and again with Cade's rebellion. Inviting skepticism rather than acceptance of authority, the play asks its audience to sift historical evidence and to scrutinize the validity of the representations before them. With these demands, the play gestures toward a more inclusive drama of nation, one in which the audience, even more than the king and contending aristocrats onstage, is asked to participate.

3

Ruling Women and the Politics of Gender
in *2* and *3 Henry VI*

If York's characterization of Margaret of Anjou as a "tiger's heart wrapped in a woman's hide" became an instant sound bite when the play was first performed in the early 1590s, as Robert Greene's infamous parody suggests, it has also come to dominate discussions of Margaret in the years since. Not unlike York in his claim that "women are soft, mild, pitiful, and flexible," many critics have held the Lancastrian queen up to normative categories of gender, describing her as an unnatural mother, "a vicious woman," and "an archvillainess" that Shakespeare "used to epitomize the worst qualities of her sex."[1] The *Henry VI* plays offer ample support for such assertions, to be sure, vividly detailing Margaret's adultery, her participation in Gloucester's murder, and her torment of York on the battlefield at Wakefield. But just because the plays support censure of Margaret's rule, they do not necessarily endorse the gendered terms of York's attack. That York speaks out of self-interest, specifically out of his desire to possess the Lancastrian Crown, once again invites consideration of the complex processes that give shape to the politics of gender in Shakespeare's history plays.

Taking York's attack at face value has the effect not only of minimizing questions about politics and gender raised within the plays themselves. It also limits our understanding of Margaret's political resonance on the Elizabethan stage. For if we accept the Lancastrian queen unconditionally as a figure of misrule, as York would have us do, we are likely to understand her relation to Shakespeare's own queen as one of opposition only. In a recent study of fifteenth- and sixteenth-century representations of Margaret, Patricia-Ann Lee concludes, for example, that Shakespeare's portrait of the Lancastrian queen "posed no practical threat" to Elizabeth, in large part because the Tudor queen had been so successful in forging "her own royal icon of triumphant and compelling brilliance" against the "dark and powerful images of illegitimate queen-ship" we see in Margaret.[2] It is indeed unlikely that Shakespeare's London audience would have directly identified Margaret with their own reigning monarch; as Leah Marcus and others have observed, "the echoes of Elizabeth are faint."[3] Margaret had, after all, already been popularized as a figure of misrule by Tudor chroniclers, with the result that the two queens were rarely, if ever, linked during Elizabeth's reign. John Aylmer, for example, includes Joan of Arc but not Margaret of Anjou in a cata-logue of exemplary women put forth in his defense of female rule, written in response to John Knox's polemical attack.[4] Queen consort and mother, the foreign-born Margaret was hardly a suitable model for England's singular queen regnant.

But if Shakespeare's Margaret did not provoke specific associations with Elizabeth, she almost certainly raised questions about ruling women in general. Her prominence in these plays alone calls attention to many of the concerns voiced in both formal and informal debates about women rulers in the sixteenth century. Margaret is, in fact, the only character to appear in all of the plays of the first tetralogy and, aside from brief appearances by the two Yorkist queens in *Richard III*, she is the only English queen to appear within the span of the two tetralogies. Returning the Lancastrian queen to the London stage again and again in these early plays, Shakespeare offered his audience a sustained presentation of a ruling woman who was more than his own queen's "dark" opposite. For while Shakespeare's Margaret may not have shared specific attributes with Elizabeth, she nonetheless recalled the Tudor queen in more general ways. Both queens hold power within a patriarchal state and both "play the Amazon," leading their troops into battle in defense of the nation. And in both cases, opposition to their reigns frequently devolves into an attack on gender.

Given the general nature of the associations between the two queens, this chapter approaches the gender politics of *2* and *3 Henry VI* by looking less to precise topical parallels than to the broader contexts marked out by the century's discourse on female rule, contexts whose shape may be read in the Tudor chronicles and, more directly, in the debate over female rule waged by Knox and Aylmer in the late 1550s. As in previous chapters, the multileveled accounts of the Tudor chronicles furnish a useful starting point, allowing us to map the ways in which political circumstances write and rewrite the historical record over time. The sixteenth-century debate over female rule offers a second point of entry into the plays' politics, one that, like the chronicle sources, is important in historicizing the relationships between gender and politics that are central to this chapter. More specifically, the arguments of Knox and Aylmer also demonstrate the ways in which controversy ostensibly grounded in female rule had the potential to open up more sweeping political debates during the sixteenth century. For while the controversy over female rule centered on questions of gender, in situating those questions within the context of contemporary politics, it also offered an occasion to redefine traditional structures of power and authority.

Shakespeare's presentation of Margaret in 2 and 3 Henry VI likewise documents the interplay of politics and history while, at the same time, registering the radical potential of the century's debate over female rule. On Shakespeare's stage, as in the chronicle sources, Margaret's assumption of power continues to come under censure. What does change in the translation to stage, however, are the terms of that censure. The plays may criticize Margaret's misrule, but in doing so on the basis of policy rather than biology, they effect a subtle but provocative shift that allows for an alternative discourse of power, one based not on expectations about gender but on an appeal to the nation's welfare. Thereby refiguring the terms of the patriarchal critique of female rule, these plays allow women a place on history's stage and, in the process, alter orthodox assumptions about state power and national identity.

Margaret of Anjou and the English Chronicles

To trace the story of Margaret's misrule from fifteenth-century Yorkist accounts to the Tudor chronicles that served as Shakespeare's sources is to understand the extent to which cultural assumptions about gender worked in tandem with political interests in the years before the accession of the Tudor queen regnants. Remarkably consistent in their condemnation of the Lancastrian queen, the chronicles reiterate a persuasive narrative of female misrule in which censure was almost always framed in misogynistic terms. Yet even as these accounts document the pervasiveness of misogyny in fifteenth- and sixteenth-century political discourse, they also reveal the potential problems this discourse raised for Elizabethans. Differences between the Elizabethan chronicles of Raphael Holinshed and the Henrician chronicles of Edward Hall and Polydore Vergil, for instance, suggest that the presence of a woman on England's throne altered the historical record, affecting the way Elizabethans represented historical queens as well as their own queen regnant. These differences also suggest that Elizabethans would have been attentive to similarities as well as differences between Margaret and Elizabeth. Before turning to the Elizabethan versions of the Lancastrian queen—in Holinshed's *Chronicles* and in *2* and *3 Henry VI*—it may be helpful, then, to look first at the earlier versions of Margaret's misrule that supplied the sources for both Holinshed and Shakespeare.

As far as the English chroniclers were concerned, Margaret's story began in 1445 when, at the age of sixteen, she became the wife of Henry VI. The daughter of a landless king, Margaret brought no dowry or land to England, a condition that set many against her from the start. Historically, her involvement in politics began in 1453, when Henry was no longer able to rule because of mental infirmity, and ended nearly twenty years later, in 1471, when the king and the crown prince were killed and the Yorkists came to power. As might be expected, it was during the years that Margaret led the Lancastrians in their struggle to maintain the Crown against Yorkist aggression that the propaganda against Margaret first emerged.[5] Establishing the version of misrule that was to dominate the Tudor chronicles, the London chronicles, with their obvious Yorkist sympathies, typically censured Henry for his failure to rule and Margaret for her corrupt and immoral actions. *An English Chronicle*, compiled in the decade between Edward IV's accession in 1461 and Henry VI's death in 1471, asserts that "the reame of Englonde was oute of alle good governaunce" under Henry VI's reign because "the kyng was simple" and the queen "rewled the reame as her lyked."[6]

Although Margaret's position as consort would seem to raise a very different set of problems from those posed by the Tudor queen regnants, opposition to her rule followed similar lines of attack. Because she was a woman, the argument went, Margaret's rule was unnatural and therefore destructive to the realm. As an anonymous poem, written shortly after Edward IV's coronation in 1461, put it:

> . . . it ys right a gret abusion,
>   A womman of a land to be a regent,
>   Qwene Margrete I meme, that ever hathe ment
> To governe alle Engeland with hyght and poure,
>   And to destroye the ryght lyne was here entent,
> Wherfore sche hathe a fal, to here great langoure.[7]

Margaret's rule was deemed illegitimate, this verse suggests, not because she was a consort who stepped out of her place to act as a regnant, but simply because she was a woman. These early attacks on Margaret's rule characteristically authorized their opposition by combining moral objections to ruling women with a familiar misogynistic discourse.

With the accession of the Tudors in 1485, it became politic to improve upon Yorkist condemnations of the Lancastrians. But while the Tudor chroniclers showed sympathy toward Henry, recasting his weakness as a sign of his saintliness—"there was not in this world a more pure, more honest, and more holye creeture,"[8] Polydore Vergil declares—they deepened the attack on Margaret, transforming the queen into a scapegoat for Lancastrian losses. With Robert Fabyan's chronicle, published in 1516, Henry's "unprofitable" marriage to Margaret emerged as a central theme in the story of the Lancastrian decline, one that was to be repeated by chroniclers for the rest of the century.[9] Extending this line of argument, Polydore Vergil offered a detailed critique of Margaret's misrule. More direct in his moralizing than the earlier chroniclers, Vergil's censure is also clearly misogynistic. "By meane of a woman, sprange up a newe mischiefe that sett all out of order,"[10] he announces before describing how Margaret helped to stir up "envie" against the duke of Gloucester. Vergil offers a number of explanations for the Lancastrian decline, but it is his emphasis on Margaret's unnatural involvement in politics, together with the duke of York's unlawful aggression, that predominates.[11]

Edward Hall's *The Union of the Two Noble and Illustre Famelies of Lancastre and Yorke* (1548), the principal source for *2* and *3 Henry VI*, intensifies Vergil's moralizing, and his misogyny. Hall's narrative obsessively details Margaret's masculine characteristics in ways that underscore the unnaturalness of her ambition. The queen was "of stomack and corage, more like to a man, then a woman,"[12] he writes. The first to depict Margaret's direct involvement in Gloucester's death, Hall explains that "this manly woman, this coragious quene . . . practised daily"[13] to take the rule away from the protector and to rule herself. Hall also includes the Yorkist rumor of the prince's bastardy, a detail omitted in Vergil's account. Hall's moralistic approach to historiography may offer a partial explanation for this attack on ruling women. According to F. J. Levy, "Hall's principal purpose, the justification of the Tudors and the encouragement of order, depended less on inculcating a sense of political realism than it did on convincing men that certain forms of political activity were sinful and that political quietism was much the safest course open to them."[14] But the insistent misogyny invites speculation about other factors as well. Did the aggressively masculine Henrician court foster criticism of women in power, especially aspiring queen consorts?

If misogyny could be said to be normative during the first half of the sixteenth century, it began to acquire a seditious resonance in the century's second half with the reigns of the Tudor queens. Accordingly,

Holinshed's *Chronicles*, published in two separate editions during Elizabeth I's reign, invite consideration of the ways in which the presence of a woman on England's throne may have influenced representations of the Lancastrian queen. As we might expect, the *Chronicles*, while repeating many of the standard features of earlier accounts of Henry VI's reign, diminish the criticism of Margaret. The Elizabethan chronicles continue to emphasize the role of the royal marriage and Gloucester's death in "the decaie of the house of Lancaster,"[15] for instance, but they place these events within a wider political context that looks not only to the Crown's misrule and aristocratic ambition but also to the growing discontent among the populace, who suffered "through misgovernment."[16] The emphasis on the realm as a complex sociopolitical entity no doubt registers broad changes in political thought in Elizabethan England. So too may the altered portrait of Margaret, which goes to considerable lengths to reduce the misogyny of the earlier accounts. The *Chronicles* also reduce Margaret's role in Gloucester's fall; she may be an instigator, but it is the conspiring nobles who actually bring about his death.

The chroniclers' care in revising Margaret's portrait would seem to offer evidence of the need for diplomacy in representing queens, even historical ones, in Elizabethan England. Consider, for example, these successive versions of the initial description of Margaret. The first is from Hall's chronicle, printed in 1548, the second from the 1577 edition of Holinshed's *Chronicles*, and the third from the 1587 edition, which together with Hall served as a source for Shakespeare's representation of Margaret. Hall begins, interestingly enough, by praising the queen, but soon transforms compliment into censure by showing Margaret's virtues to be manly. Conversely, her one womanly trait is negative:

> The Quene his wife, was a woman of a greate witte, and yet of no greater witte, then of haute stomacke, desirous of glory, and covetous of honor, and of reason, pollicye counsaill, and other giftes and talentes of nature, belong-yng to a man, full and flowyng: of witte and wilinesse she lacked nothyng, nor of diligence, studie, and businesse, she was not unexperte: but yet she had one poynt of a very woman: for often tyme, when she was vehement and fully bente in a matter, she was sodainly like a wethercocke, mutable, and turnyng.[17]

In revising this passage, the 1577 edition of the *Chronicles* restores the compliment simply by eliminating many of the negative terms of the original:

> The Queene contrarywyse, was a woman of a greate witte, and no lesse courage, desyrous of honour, and furnyshed wyth the gyftes of reason,

policye and wysedome, but yet to shew hir selfe not altogether a man, but in some one poynte a verie woman, oftentymes when she was vehemente and fully bente on a matter, she was sodeynly lyke a Weathercocke, mutable and tournyng.[18]

The 1587 edition, however, eliminates all references to Margaret's manliness, with the result that her gifts no longer appear as masculine and therefore unnatural:

The queene contrariwise, a ladie of great wit, and no lesse courage, desirous of honour, and furnished with the gifts of reason, policie, and wisdome; but yet sometime (according to hir kind) when she had beene fullie bent on a matter, suddenlie like a weather cocke, mutable and turning.[19]

Although the 1587 edition continues to present women—now more ambiguously referred to as "hir kind"—as changeable, it significantly alters previous accounts by treating reason, policy, and wisdom as queenly virtues rather than as "gifts" belonging only to men.

We know that the 1587 edition of the *Chronicles* was subject to censorship, as evidenced by a number of excised pages, but there is no evidence that the passages on Margaret were among them.[20] Yet the fact that the editors of the second edition should take the trouble to rework previously published sections of the chronicle, not simply adding new material but painstakingly editing the old, would seem to confirm Annabel Patterson's argument that writers during this period, including the Holinshed chroniclers, practiced a form of self-censorship.[21] In both editions, the chroniclers' care in reducing Hall's misogyny suggests that while Elizabeth might not have objected to criticism directed against Margaret's actions, she may have been displeased when that criticism went further to raise questions about women rulers in general. Differences between the 1577 and 1587 editions may also reflect specific changes in policies on sedition in the 1580s, as instituted by the repressive 1581 statute (23 Eliz. I. c. 2) that made it a felony punishable by death to print, write, or speak seditious words.[22] In general, the *Chronicles'* representation of Margaret—and the 1587 edition especially—tactfully avoids drawing conclusions about women rulers as a whole. In marked contrast to Hall, who most often refers to Margaret as "this woman," the focus in Holinshed is on the specific actions of a particular queen.

The variations in chronicle accounts of Margaret's rule thus provide evidence of a shift in representations of historical queens with the accession of the Tudor queens. As this brief survey documents, the misogynistic censure of Margaret's rule, authorized by nearly a century of chronicle accounts, gives way in the latter half of the sixteenth century to a more nuanced, and more diplomatic, presentation. The subtle revisions of the *Chronicles* also suggest that Elizabethans, including the queen herself, would not automatically have dismissed an association between Elizabeth and Margaret, nor would they would have seen the Lancastrian queen simply as a dark inversion of their own. Accommodating the historical record to the realities of contemporary politics, the chroniclers engaged in a rewriting of history that reduced the offensive misogyny of the earlier accounts and, in the process, criticized Margaret's reign on the basis of policy, not gender.

Debating Female Rule

If the chronicles provide one field of reference for understanding the politics of Shakespeare's representation of the Lancastrian queen, the sixteenth-century debate over female rule provides another that is both more polemical and more radical. With the accession of Mary Tudor in 1553, the debate about female rule was no longer theoretical, and for many in England, political necessity quickly overruled longstanding objections to women as rulers. But the accession of a Catholic queen prompted opposition, especially among radical Protestant exiles like Christopher Goodman and John Knox, who circulated their objections to the ruling woman in tracts published on the Continent in the late 1550s. These men objected to female rule on the grounds that it was a violation of natural law that deemed women subordinate to men within the family and state. A woman is "a tendre creature, flexible, soft and pitifull,"[23] Knox affirms in *The First Blast of the Trumpet Against the Monstruous Regiment of Women* (1558), in words echoed by York in *3 Henry VI*. Arguing that these assumptions are authorized both by scripture and Aristotle, Knox concludes that a ruling woman "is repugnant to nature, contumelie to God, a thing most contrarious to his reveled will and approved ordinance, and finallie it is the subversion of good order, of all equitie and justice."[24] On the other side, writing in defense of female rule, and Elizabeth's rule in particular, John Aylmer set forth a point-by-point response to Knox's polemic in a tract titled *An Harborowe for Faithful and Trewe Subjectes* (1559). Countering Knox's privileging of natural law, Aylmer grounded his argument in the authority of positive law and the custom of nations and, at the same time, bolstered his defense of female rule with a historical catalogue of successful ruling women.

Much has been written about the midcentury debate, particularly in recent years as feminist scholars have reconsidered the controversy over female rule within historical contexts that extend from humanist defenses of women to discourses on political theory.[25] What these studies emphasize is that, contrary to what we might expect, the defenses of female rule may have influenced discussions of women in general, but they had little long-term effect on political thought. As Constance Jordan concludes: "Neither the presence of a woman on the throne for the better part of the century nor the arguments for the legality of her rule seem to have encouraged an acceptance of the idea that women could assume magistracies or participate in political life in other capacities."[26] But if the debate about women's rule did not measurably alter attitudes toward women's participation in politics, it may have influenced political theory in other ways. When understood in relation to sixteenth-century theories of resistance, for example, the Protestant opposition to Mary Tudor's rule generates far-reaching political implications, furnishing a test case for active disobedience that may be extended to male monarchs as well.[27] Exemplifying a condition under which rebellion against the magistrate could be sanctioned, the presence of a woman ruler, who was also a Catholic, focused and even intensified the century's ongoing debate about resistance and rebellion. The subject of female rule thus authorized broader discussions of political theory—among defenders as well as opponents—and, in some cases, prompted a reconsideration of the state as figured in the monarch.

For Knox, the debate over female rule led to an attack on English law and the custom of hereditary monarchy. As a result, even though Knox had directed his diatribe against Mary Tudor, his arguments deeply disturbed the Elizabethan government as well. As William Cecil reported: "Of all others, Knoxees name, if it be not Goodmans, is most odiouse here; and therefore I wish no mention of hym hither."[28] One explanation for the queen's anger is that Knox's arguments undermined the institution of female rule in general and therefore constituted an attack on her own authority as well as her sister's. But what may have appeared even more dangerous to the English was Knox's insistence that natural law should supersede positive law and the customs of nations. When obedience to the monarch and nation comes into conflict with divine or natural law, the choice for Knox is clear: "I have determined to obey God, not withstanding that the world shall rage therat."[29] Placing his own conscience above man's law, Knox moves toward a radical Protestant theory of government that would supplant the power of the Crown with the truth of divine authority—an authority revealed by Knox's own inspired speech. Claiming the special status of prophet,

Knox effectively situates himself above English law.

Equating female rule with idolatry, Knox calls for rebellion against the monarch and urges the nobility "to remove from authority all such persones, as by usurpation, violence, or tyrannie, do possesse the same."[30] Knox's attack thus extends far beyond either Protestant objections to a Catholic monarch or orthodox arguments against female rule in order to make the case for rising up against a specific ruler. At the same time, Knox's call for rebellion would overrule, and even eliminate, England's custom of hereditary monarchy. From the perspective of the Elizabethan government, the offense in Knox's tract was clearly more than a matter of its antifeminist position or its bad timing (the attack on Mary Tudor had been published only a few months before Elizabeth's accession). Supplanting national loyalties with religious ones, Knox mounts a treasonous offensive against England itself, authorizing his attack on the nation's laws and customs by drawing on familiar objections to women in government. Although Knox subsequently wrote to Elizabeth in 1559, assuring her that his book was not "prejudicial to anie libertie of the realme" or to "your Grace's just regiment," he continued to assert his objections to the authority of English law and custom: "Neither the consent of the people, process of time, nor multitude of men can establish a law which God shall approve," he warned the queen.[31]

Not surprisingly, Aylmer's response to Knox's *First Blast* goes beyond a simple defense of Elizabeth's right to rule in order to confront the dangerous politics embedded in his polemic. Characterizing Knox's arguments as "pikaxes to under mynde the state," Aylmer refers to the tract as treasonous. It is written by "a stranger," he charges, with the intention of making war on the monarch and the nation by altering England's ancient laws:

> This is the cannon shot to batter the walles of themperial seate, and to beate the crowne of the true heires head. It is *a sore enterprise to alter so auncient an order, and to chaunge lawes of suche antiquite*, specially at suche tyme as the realme is full of trouble, mens myndes otherwise disquieted, and the forren enemies gaping for occasion to invade and overrenne us. (sig. C2v) (emphasis added)

Although Aylmer devotes most of his tract to the question of the monarch's gender, as with Knox, the concern with matters of law and national interest points to the wider political context of this debate.

Aylmer mounts a direct challenge to Knox's emphasis on natural law, for instance, by insisting instead on the authority of positive law and custom. Even Aylmer's often-cited defense of Elizabeth as a divinely sanctioned exception—how else could "a woman weake in nature, feable in bodie, softe in courage, unskilfull in practise" (sig. B2v) rule the nation, he asks—turns, finally, on questions of law. For while Aylmer invokes divine authority for Elizabeth's rule, he then locates that authority in the nation's custom of lineal succession: "But when God chuseth him selfe by sending to a king, whose succession is ruled by enheritaunce and lyneall discent, no heires male: It is a plain argument, that for some secret purpose he myndeth the female should reigne and governe" (sig. B3). At the same time, Aylmer shrewdly identifies English law with Parliament, a forum in which Knox has no place. A stranger's voice is to be heard in the pulpit "so long as he speaketh Gods worde," Aylmer declares: "But a straungers voyce is not alowed . . . in the parliament about pollycie, bycause he is not a citezen" (sig. F2). Where Knox insists on the authority of divine or natural law, as interpreted by his own status as prophet, Aylmer insists on the authority of positive law, as set forth by England's Parliament.

For Aylmer, the preservation of the commonwealth provides a crucial test of the monarch's authority. "What so ever preserveth common wealthes, and destroyeth them not: is not againste nature, but the rule of women hath preserved common wealthes, ergo, it is not against nature" (sig. D2), he exclaims in a brazen appeal to national interests. In his emphasis on commonwealth, Aylmer shrewdly appropriates a principal argument of the radical Protestants, who would make obedience conditional on the magistrate's "preservation of the comon welthe,"[32] as Christopher Goodman puts it in *How Superior Powers Oght To Be Obeyed* (1558). But when Aylmer extends this argument to link the commonwealth with Parliament and positive law, he himself begins to exert pressure on royal prerogative that, like the arguments of the radical Protestants, sets conditions on the monarch. What better place than England to have a woman ruler, Aylmer declares in one of his more radical digressions, for in England, the Crown's powers are dependent upon Parliament:

> The regiment of Englande is not a mere Monarchie, as some for lacke of consideracion thinke, nor a meere Oligarchie, nor Democratie, but a rule mixte of all these, wherein ech one of these have or shoulde have like authoritie. . . . *[I]f the parliament use their privileges: the King can ordein nothing without them.* If he do, it is his fault in usurping it, and their follye in permitting it. (sig. H2v–H3) (emphasis added)

Boldly insisting on the limited powers of the English Crown, Aylmer explains that for this reason alone, "it is lesse daunger to be governed in

England by a woman then any where els" (sig. H2v). The power Aylmer ascribes to Parliament may have been wishful thinking rather than an accurate description of political realities in the 1550s. Nevertheless, his argument remained influential, for though Aylmer would later renounce this position when he became bishop of London in 1577, arguments for a mixed government continued to be voiced, by radical Puritans like Thomas Cartwright and by the authors of the Martin Marprelate tracts later in the century.[33]

The examples of both Aylmer and Knox argue for the need to understand the sixteenth-century debate over female rule within a political context that includes but also goes beyond issues of gender. The inherently political nature of the occasion furnished by women rulers during this period cautions us, just as it probably cautioned Elizabethans themselves, against taking any argument about gender and power, negative as well as positive, at face value. This is not to say that the discourse on female rule should simply be dismissed as opportunistic and self-serving. As the number of recent studies on Elizabethan attitudes toward women in power amply illustrate, the presence of a woman on England's throne was inevitably unsettling, in large part because it conflicted with longstanding notions that female rule was unnatural and dangerous. But while the reigns of Mary and Elizabeth may have contradicted deeply entrenched beliefs about female subservience, they also furnished their loyal subjects and enemies alike with an opportunity to engage in political debates that touched on even more dangerous questions of government and sovereignty.

2 Henry VI

The presentation of the Lancastrian queen in 2 Henry VI might seem to offer a clear exception to arguments that the presence of a woman on the throne invited Elizabethans to rethink traditional assumptions about state power and national identity. Relying more on Hall than Holinshed, Shakespeare chooses, in what may have been his first play, not to minimize the potentially offensive features of earlier accounts of Margaret's misrule. If anything, the play intensifies the negative pattern of queenship set forth in the early Tudor chronicles. The royal marriage and Gloucester's death continue to be central themes in the story, but Shakespeare takes the liberty of fabricating the incriminating details of Margaret's role in Gloucester's murder and her adulterous liaison with Suffolk. Moreover, he freely extends the play's critique of the queen to censure aggressive women in general. "These are no women's matters" (1.3.117), the duke of Gloucester curtly declares of Margaret's first intrusion into court politics. Spoken with the fatherly authority that comes with his office as protector of the realm, Gloucester's words apply just as well to the other women in the play, to his own wife, Eleanor, and to Simpcox's wife.[34]

In translating chronicle history to the stage in *2 Henry VI*, Shakespeare could be said to reinforce, and even heighten, the patriarchal narratives he found ready-made in writers like Hall. As Phyllis Rackin has argued, there are few roles for women within the chronicles, and when women do appear, they are typically seen as subversive of patriarchal history and authority.[35] With its attention to the confrontation between Gloucester and Margaret, the first half of *2 Henry VI* neatly illustrates Rackin's point. As in *1 Henry VI*, Shakespeare again appears to represent national interests in explicitly gendered terms, replaying the Joan-Talbot conflict on the homefront. The scene has shifted from France to England and from the battlefield to the court, but the confrontation is much the same. Gloucester's civic heroism echoes Talbot's chivalric virtue, and, like his predecessor, Gloucester too struggles to defend his nation against a usurping female outsider. "England's bloody scourge" (5.1.118) is once again cast as a French woman, whereas Gloucester, by contrast, is "an insulated stand of manly virtue," as A. P. Rossiter puts it, representative of England itself.[36]

Reinforcing an opposition between the patriarchal state and subversive women, the play draws on the correspondence between domestic and national relations informing political discourse. Just as the royal marriage renders the king fond and foolish—ravished by his wife's beauty, her speech makes him "from wond'ring fall to weeping joys" (1.1.34)—it is equally disastrous for the realm, as Gloucester somberly warns the nobles at the start of the play:

> Fatal this marriage, cancelling your fame,
> Blotting your names from books of memory,
> Rasing the characters of your renown,
> Defacing monuments of conquer'd France,
> Undoing all, as all had never been!
>
> (1.1.99–103)

The marriage will not simply "undo" England's past victories over France, Gloucester predicts. It will wipe out history itself, defacing even the memory of past victories as they are recorded in monuments, books, and in the "deep scars" (1.1.87) of the nation's heroic warriors. As Jack

Cade later puts it, in terms that even the unschooled artisans will understand, the marriage, purchased with Anjou and Maine, "hath gelded the commonwealth, and made it an eunuch" (4.2.165–66).

But just because *2 Henry VI* does not offer an Elizabethan remake along the lines of Holinshed does not mean that it simply returns to, and so endorses, the pattern of female misrule found in the Henrician chronicles and popularized by antifeminist tracts circulated in the years before either Mary or Elizabeth took the throne.[37] The spectacle of Margaret's misrule may invoke anxieties about ruling women, but it also urges a reconsideration of the place of gender within a critique of power. Once again, Shakespeare effects this reconsideration in part by setting questions of gender within a wider political context. The play establishes this pattern, for example, in the first scene when "the brave peers of England" (1.1.75) fall to their "ancient bickerings" (1.1.144), their quarrels soon eclipsing the concerns about Margaret and the royal marriage voiced at the play's opening. What is significant here, in contrast to the Henrician chronicles, is that Margaret is no longer the primary cause of civil unrest.[38] Her presence in the court exacerbates the antagonisms, to be sure, and for some, like York, it serves as a spur to treasonous desires. But it does not confirm the sweeping claim of chroniclers like Hall, who declared that "a sodain mischief, and a long discorde, sprang out sodainly, by the meanes of a woman."[39] Self-interest and old antagonisms, not a "manly woman," determine the shifting political alliances of Shakespeare's Lancastrian court. As in *1 Henry VI*, the play's proliferating contentions qualify longstanding objections to women in power by examining the problem of gender in relation to other, more dangerous, threats to the nation's strength and stability.

With Margaret, however, Shakespeare deepens the reconsideration of gendered stereotypes by inviting a critique of rule in which questions about gender are not only subordinate to, but even independent of, larger questions about the nation's welfare. In a move reminiscent of both Aylmer's defense of Elizabeth's rule and the presentation of Margaret in Holinshed's *Chronicles*, Shakespeare defines the queen principally in terms of her policies and their effects on the nation-state. Thus, while the play, like its sources, continues to condemn Margaret, and while misogynistic complaints echo throughout the play, the concern for commonwealth supersedes gender as the principal criterion for assessing her rule. And with gender no longer a stable referent in the critique of power, the familiar opposition between patriarchy and subversive women begins to collapse. On the basis of these revised standards, Margaret may still be a figure of misrule, but the shift in thinking does at least allow for the possibility of effective female rule. As a result, when Margaret finally

begins to fight for England's interests, as she does at the close of
2 Henry VI and throughout much of 3 Henry VI, her rule gains a certain
authority and sanction. At the same time, these revised standards also
open the door to other, more radical, ways of configuring authority and
power within the nation-state.

The opposing categories of state and nation informing Richard
Helgerson's recent discussion of the play provide a useful model for
understanding the place of gender within traditional structures of power.
Identifying the state, or Crown, with "the governing order," and the
nation with "the governed," Helgerson observes that during this period
"discursive forms that emphasize state over nation, power over custom
and individual conscience, are also more upper-class and male. Those
that emphasize nation over state include—and even identify with—
women and commoners."[40] Although Helgerson sees 2 Henry VI as
exclusive rather than inclusive—arguing that the play "eliminates the
inclusionist position with which it seemed to begin"[41] with the staging of
Jack Cade's revolt—his categories provide a ground against which to
chart shifting notions of gender and power in the histories. Hardly a
stable marker of either state or nation, exclusion or inclusion, the
aristocratic women in this play cross the lines between opposing
categories and thus complicate orthodox notions of power. One could
argue, of course, that the play's treatment of women simply reinforces
Helgerson's position on the play's exclusionist politics: like the
rebellious Cade, who makes his bid for power against the ruling
aristocracy, both Margaret and Eleanor desire to wrest power from the
noblemen and in the process endanger the stability of the state. But the
fact that the play defines Margaret's misrule primarily by placing her in
opposition to the nation as a whole disrupts this binary.

One of the difficulties in arguing that the play stages exclusion, and
thus endorses state over nation, lies in its refusal to offer a model of state
power that is both effective and legitimate. Neither Gloucester nor the
king is successful in maintaining the Crown's power, and York, whose
interests are exclusively with the Crown, shows himself to be morally
and politically corrupt. Instead, as even Helgerson acknowledges, "the
people" are fundamental to England's identity and to the legitimacy of its
governing order as evidenced when the play, at its start, places
Gloucester's "solidarity with the commons in opposition to aristocratic
ambition."[42] Like "the good duke" of the London chronicles and John
Foxe's Acts and Monuments, Shakespeare's Gloucester lines up on the
side of the nation. He identifies his own grief with "the common grief of
all the land" (1.1.77) and speaks for the public good and the shared
interest of the community. He is, the cardinal complains, favored by "the

common people" (1.1.158). Thus while Gloucester's insistence that women should stay out of court politics evokes orthodox images of a patriarchal state, his concern for the commonwealth, especially as it is figured in the nation's laws, takes him closer to the more radical positions voiced in sixteenth-century political debates.[43]

If we associate the lord protector with the commonwealth, however, where does this leave the play's women? In contrast to *1 Henry VI*, where the armed peasant maid figures the interests of the populace even as she aligns herself with the dauphin, in *2 Henry VI* both Margaret and Eleanor identify themselves exclusively with the institution of the Crown. What makes these women dangerous is not the fact that they are different from "the brave peers" they would control, but that they are all too similar. Like the conspiring nobles, Margaret and Eleanor are driven by self-interest and an elitist desire to assert dominion over others, and as these aristocratic women come to resemble their male counterparts— aspiring, corrupt, and unconcerned with the nation's welfare—sex no longer functions as the main category of difference. Thus minimizing the otherness of gender, the play opens up other criteria by which we may evaluate Margaret's rule. Like the defenses of Elizabeth's rule, this shift in perspective invites a critique of ruling women that is grounded less in claims about the unnaturalness of female rule than it is in specific, political concerns. In the case of *2 Henry VI*, these concerns focus on the administration of justice that extends from the aristocrats to the populace.

Viewed from this perspective, Margaret's conflict with Gloucester may be understood more in terms of what it says about commonwealth and nation than about ruling women and the problem of gender. Gloucester, for example, speaks for a commonwealth grounded in the authority of law, whereas Margaret defines herself by her contempt for both the law and the common people, a contempt she displays repeatedly in a series of judgments culminating in Gloucester's trial. In contrast to the lord protector who strives to remain a disinterested judge, Margaret judges solely out of self-interest, to further her own power in the realm. The queen first abuses her authority in response to the petitioning commons in a scene whose importance is signaled by the fact that it does not appear in any of Shakespeare's sources. The petitioners, waiting to have their suits heard by Gloucester, are intercepted by Margaret and Suffolk, and the results are predictable. The queen dismisses two of the complaints, including one on behalf of the "whole township" (1.3.24) against "the Duke of Suffolk, for enclosing the commons of Melford" (1.3.20–21). But she retains the third, a treason charge touching on the duke of York, because it will be useful politically. Margaret's injustice is especially strong in the Folio text where she, rather than Suffolk, *"tear[s] the supplication*" (S.D. 1.2.39). Her crude dismissal—"Away, base cullions" (3.3.40)—only reinforces her elitist contempt. Although we may understand Margaret's tyranny as exemplifying Knox's warning that female rule "is the subversion of good order, of all equitie and justice," we should also recognize that Shakespeare's insistence on bringing Margaret into opposition with the common people in this scene begins to shift the terms of censure away from gender and thus to open up a wider critique of state power.

Within this context, Margaret's sudden shift into a courtly discourse after she dismisses the petitioners and is alone with Suffolk only deepens the opposition between nation and state, common law and royal prerogative, populace and ruling elite. First registering her contempt for English law and custom—"Is this the fashions in the court of England? / Is this the government of Britain's isle, / And this the royalty of Albion's king?" (1.3.43–45), she sneers—the queen takes refuge in her memories of France and the tournament in which Suffolk "ran'st a-tilt in honor of my love" (1.3.51). The Petrarchan discourse, so effectively employed by Shakespeare's own queen, is less successful for Margaret. Rather than ennobling her desire for power within the court, and allowing her to demand both submission and service from her suitors, Margaret's amatory discourse marks her adultery with Suffolk as elitist and dangerous to the commonwealth.[44] In contrast to *1 Henry VI*, where the language of chivalry is still capable of evoking nostalgia for heroic ideals, in this play it only reinforces divisions between the ruling elite and the common people.

Political conflicts involving Crown and nation again intersect with questions of gender in the brutal scene of Gloucester's trial in act 3. Following Hall, Shakespeare makes much of Margaret's participation in Gloucester's fall and so invites us to read the confrontation as yet another example of the dangers of women's participation in politics. Accordingly, we may understand Margaret's defeat of Gloucester much as we did Joan's victory over Talbot, as an inversion of traditional patriarchal myths of masculine triumph. Going beyond his chronicle sources, which are silent on the extent of Margaret's involvement in Gloucester's death, Shakespeare actually stages the so-called trial and casts the queen in the lead. The first to enunciate the charge of treason, Margaret aggressively lays out her case with the skill of a seasoned attorney. Interestingly, it is Margaret who brings up matters of gender in this scene, and not unlike her opponents earlier in the play, she too shows the success with which expectations about women may be exploited for political gain. Refashioning herself into a woman who is "by nature" weak and afraid, the queen uses her sex as an excuse for opening the inquiry against Gloucester: "If it be fond, call it a woman's fear; / Which fear, if better reasons can supplant, / I will subscribe, and say I wrong'd the Duke," (3.1.36–38) she humbly explains. Later in the scene, she again invokes this "fear" in calling for Gloucester's death. Margaret thus effectively transforms Gloucester's murder into a defensive act, "To rid us from the fear we have of him" (3.1.234). Her gendered rhetoric attempts to authorize the violence against Gloucester by urging her coconspirators to display their masculinity in protecting her.

At the same time, however, Margaret's fellowship with the conspiring noblemen extends the conflict beyond the simple opposition of subversive women and patriarchal state informing the accounts of the Henrician chronicles. Once again, tensions between state and nation—figured in the commons' love for Gloucester—end up overshadowing concerns about gender. Margaret is the first to voice suspicion about Gloucester's fabled relation with the common people, accusing him of having "won the commons' hearts" with "flattery" (3.1.28). This love, she warns, makes Gloucester all the more dangerous because treason may quickly lead to rebellion: "And when he please to make commotion,/ 'Tis to be fear'd they all will follow him" (3.1.29–30). Speaking in his own defense, Gloucester too makes much of his link with the people: he has stayed up nights "studying good for England" and spent "many a pound of mine own proper store, / Because I would not tax the needy commons" (3.1.115–16). Just as Margaret fears, Gloucester's care for the common people does cause problems for the conspirators. When the good duke is discovered "dead in his bed," the commons cry out for justice. And with the commons' demand for Suffolk's death—a request effectively delivered to the king by Salisbury—Shakespeare again brings Margaret into conflict with the populace as she pleads with the king to spare "gentle Suffolk." This time, backed by the support of Warwick and Salisbury, the commons' request for justice is met.

In bringing Margaret into opposition not only with Gloucester but with the populace as well, Shakespeare goes beyond the narrow focus of Hall's patriarchal narrative. What is perhaps most significant about Shakespeare's version, however, is that while gender continues to act as a marker, reinforcing the seeming unnaturalness of Margaret's political involvement, it does not in itself explain or justify her misrule. Instead, Shakespeare invites us to evaluate Margaret much as we do others in the play—ambitious noblemen and aspiring artisans alike—according to national interests, interests that are represented most fully in Gloucester. The play thus encourages its audience to censure Margaret not because she is a woman but because she, like both York and Cade, abuses the common people and the nation's laws. In this regard, *2 Henry VI* points toward a political theory not unlike that suggested by Aylmer earlier in the century in his argument that in "a politike weale" like England, authority rests finally not with the monarch but with law and custom.

With the confrontation between Margaret and the duke of York at the play's close—a confrontation that significantly revises the moral and political terms of the Margaret-Gloucester conflict—*2 Henry VI* offers one final qualification to the play's presentation of female misrule. Playing the machiavel to Gloucester's lord protector, York thinks not of the commonwealth but of himself. For York, the Crown is property, "goods" that he should own, and he possessively speaks of "the realms of England, France, and Ireland" (1.1.229) as "his own lands."[45] In contrast to Gloucester, York attempts to exploit the commons, seducing Cade "to make commotion" (3.1.58). And at the end of the play, when York returns from Ireland, to "pluck the crown from feeble Henry's head" (5.1.2), he gives free reign to his absolutist desires. Calling for bells and bonfires "to entertain great England's lawful king" (5.1.4), York sets himself above his subjects: "Let them obey that knows not how to rule; / This hand was made to handle nought but gold" (5.1.6–7), he boasts with Marlovian excess. Henry may not be a strong king, and York may have a claim to the throne, but York's absolutism clearly taints his right, especially given the play's concern for commonwealth. Echoing Cade's earlier promise that his "mouth shall be the parliament of England" (4.7.11), York now announces his own authority: "Here is a hand to hold a sceptre up / And with the same to act controlling laws" (5.1.102–3). The self-proclaimed heir has begun to mimic his own devilish "substitute" (3.1.371).

Diametrically opposed to Gloucester's concern for commonwealth, York's tyrannical absolutism also has the effect of shifting Margaret's politics toward the center. The queen's boldness now becomes almost heroic. No longer needing to pretend that her aggression is defensive, the queen here fights to maintain the Crown for her husband and son. Within this context, York's vitriolic attack on Margaret—"O blood-bespotted Neapolitan, / Outcast of Naples, England's bloody scourge!" (5.1.117–18)—loses much of its power and authority by betraying its own political interests. In its closing moments, the play revises the gendered oppositions with which it began. Aligned with Crown and country against the rebellious nobles, Margaret now emerges as a courageous and pragmatic leader. "We shall to London get, where you are lov'd, / And where this breach now in our fortunes made / May readily be stopp'd" (5.3.81–83), she instructs the king, taking command in the face of his cowardly retreat from authority. This is not to say that Margaret is rehabilitated by the end of the play, or that her assumption of her husband's authority is fully sanctioned. But in adopting a strategy similar to those deployed in early defenses of Elizabeth's rule, Shakespeare here allows a place for women in politics, however qualified and temporary, by suggesting that national interests—in this case peace and unity— overrule arguments that would not only dismiss female rule as unnatural but also exploit it as justification for revolt. As Aylmer declares in defense of Elizabeth, upholding the authority of the commonwealth: "What so ever preserveth common wealthes, and destroyeth them not: is not against nature, but the rule of women hath preserved common wealthes, ergo, it is not against nature" (sig. D2).

3 Henry VI

Reinforcing the notion that a ruler's authority depends on policies and principles directed toward the preservation of the commonwealth, *3 Henry VI* returns to the figure of a heroic queen fighting for Crown and country. In this play, the adulterous queen of *2 Henry VI* has been rehabilitated as a mother: Margaret appears in every scene but one with her son at her side, her aggression now sanctioned by the fact that she fights solely to preserve her son's succession. In donning armor to do battle against England's noblemen, Margaret clearly recalls the cross-dressed Joan of Arc, but with an important difference that boldly refigures the gendered conflicts structuring the previous histories. For in this play, the Amazonian woman fights for, rather than against, England, while her aristocratic male opponents stand for rebellion, disorder, and the inversion of patriarchal ideals. Yet, however much Margaret is identified with the defense of state and nation in this play, misogynistic stereotypes continue to erupt onstage.

In *3 Henry VI*, Shakespeare again invites a double perspective on Margaret's rule, reiterating the patriarchal discourse of chronicle history and, at the same time, qualifying that discourse within a framework of civil contention. In this play, as in the other *Henry VI* plays, the conjunction of aggressive aristocrats and strong women again exposes the corrupt manipulation of gendered discourse by those who, like York and his sons, seek to legitimate their power within the patriarchy. In part, Shakespeare's strategy here is to counter one fear with another, to offer his audience a choice between a woman ruler and rebellious aristocrats. Like both the midcentury debate over female rule and the political debates characterizing the last decade of Elizabeth's reign, the choice brings orthodox assumptions about a woman's place within the nation-state into conflict with political necessity. Setting forth this choice in a series of oppositions between Margaret and York and his sons—in the initial confrontation within Henry's court, and again in the battles of Wakefield and Tewkesbury—the play invites its audience to revise traditional assumptions about women, power, and the nation-state.

The play immediately calls into question the gendered opposition between subversive women and patriarchal state in its opening scene when York and his sons, heady with the blood of their victory at St. Albans, demand the Crown as their own. Attempting to appease the rebels, the "faint-hearted and degenerate king" (1.1.183) "unnaturally" (1.1.193) disinherits his own son and entails the Crown to York and his heirs. And so, when the enraged queen storms onto the stage, she is already a sympathetic figure, a fiercely protective mother rather than the aspiring queen consort of *2 Henry VI*. Shakespeare does glance at the comic potential of the confrontation—the king and Exeter shrink from her fury—but Margaret's passionate lamentation quickly transforms her into a noble heroine. With her disinherited son at her side, she stands before Henry to issue her ultimatum:

> But thou prefer'st thy life before thine honor;
> And seeing thou dost, I here divorce myself
> Both from thy table, Henry, and thy bed,
> Until that act of parliament be repeal'd
> Whereby my son is disinherited.

$$(1.1.246–50)$$

Placing her duty to her son and the Crown above her duty to her husband, Margaret divorces the king *a mensa et thoro* for betraying his own successor in much the same way that Gloucester in *2 Henry VI* banished his wife from his "bed and company" for her treason against the Crown.

Neither Henry's willing abdication nor Margaret's call for divorce is to be found in the chronicles.[46] Many have argued that these revisions, in increasing Margaret's "manliness and initiative," have a negative effect on our response to the queen. Margaret's "unnatural assumption of a masculine role," one critic writes, "in effect usurp[s] her husband's kingship." "If Henry is unnatural in disinheriting his son," another asks, "what is one to say of a wife who overturns at will the political acts of her husband and king?"[47] But does the play encourage us to see Margaret's disobedience to her husband as worse, either morally or politically, than Henry's act of cutting off his own lineage? In many ways, Margaret's spirited independence from her husband recalls

Zenobia in Thomas Elyot's *Defense of Good Women*, who not only ruled in the name of her young sons but argued that a wife might disobey her husband if his wishes threatened to "tourne them bothe to losse or dyshonesty."[48]

Shakespeare's revisions, moreover, do not present Margaret's actions in this scene as the cause of, or even as a contributing factor in, the play's civil conflict. Marking a clear shift in the representation of women in the *Henry VI* plays, Margaret's assumption of power is notable in this instance in its attempt to restore rather than subvert order within the family and state. Fighting to maintain patrilineal succession, the queen offers a highly orthodox solution to the political chaos and bloodshed initiated by the dynastic struggles between men—in this case, by the parallel acts of York's assumption of the throne and Henry's "unmanly deed" (1.1.186) of giving away his kingdom. Supported by Henry's lords and by the prince himself, who nobly promises to "follow her" (1.1.262) to victory, Margaret heroically takes up arms to restore the patriarchal authority that the king has so willingly relinquished. Railing at her husband for his cowardly act of disinheriting her son, she declares:

> Had I been there, which am a silly woman,
> The soldiers should have toss'd me on their pikes,
> Before I would have granted to that act.

> (1.1.243–45)

In this instance, Margaret's courage recalls not that of the legendary Amazons but of Shakespeare's own queen, who was also in the habit of calling attention to her exceptional courage by contrasting it with the weaknesses natural to women.[49] Moreover, Margaret's taking up of arms at the start of *3 Henry VI*, like Elizabeth's legendary leadership before the victory over the Armada, offers a means of preserving both Crown and nation.

Given the sophisticated handling of gender and power at the beginning of *3 Henry VI*, Margaret's savage performance at Wakefield a few scenes later comes as something of a shock. The queen's triumph over York in this scene indeed presents one of the most horrifying representations of women and violence in Shakespeare's canon. As with Joan in *1 Henry VI*, critics again look for explanations in the chronicle sources. J. P. Brockbank writes, for example, that "in making a ritual of the atrocity Shakespeare imitates the history."[50] Yet Shakespeare does not imitate history in the part he writes for Margaret. Neither Hall nor Holinshed describes Margaret as having a direct role in York's death. As Hall tells it, York is slain on the battlefield, where his body remains until discovered by Clifford, who then "caused his head to be stryken of, and set on it a croune of paper, and so fixed it on a pole, and presented it to the Quene."[51] Holinshed adds the story of the mock coronation on the molehill but casts Margaret as audience rather than player.[52] Clearly, Shakespeare depends on Holinshed for the scene of York's torture, but he goes far beyond the scope of history to make Margaret York's chief tormentor and executioner.

The scene at Wakefield may be, as Emrys Jones has remarked, "one of the most violent in all Shakespeare's plays,"[53] but why should the death of York, who has brought on his own fate in attempting to seize the Crown, seem more violent than Clifford's brutal stabbing of the innocent schoolboy Rutland in the previous scene? The effect depends in part, surely, on the contradiction between Margaret's actions and cultural expectations about women.[54] When crimes against humanity are carried out by a woman, a mother, and a queen, the violation of civilized order is especially disturbing since, as York's own commentary on the scene instructs us, "women are soft, mild, pitiful, and flexible" (1.4.141). We must remember, however, that it is York who directs the audience, both onstage and in Shakespeare's theater, to focus on Margaret's violation of gender roles. As a result, he shifts attention away from his own violation of "his solemn oath" to permit Henry to reign "quietly" (1.2.15) until his death.

In privileging York's perspective, the play draws on Hall's report of York's address to his men on the eve of battle. In this speech, York worries about the dishonor of being beaten by "a scolding woman, whose weapon is onely her tounge, and her nayles." Since no man has yet proved me a coward, York explains, a report that "a woman hath made me a dastard" would bring "shame and infamy."[55] Hall's York thus legitimates his battle against the Crown with a passionate appeal to masculine honor. Shakespeare's York likewise resorts to misogyny in the face of his female opponent. "How ill-beseeming is it in thy sex / To triumph like an Amazonian trull" (1.4.113–14), he lectures, elevating himself by admonishing Margaret on her failure as a woman. The play itself appears to endorse York's criticism, suggesting that when crimes against humanity are carried out by a woman, a mother, and a queen, the violation of civilized order is especially disturbing. Margaret's role as queen-mother indeed lends an ambivalence to her actions, on the one hand authorizing her aggression against York, but on the other intensifying the horror of her taunts, especially when she torments York with the handkerchief stained with his son's blood. Once again, York retaliates by pointing up her failure of womanhood:

> O tiger's heart wrapp'd in a woman's hide!
> How couldst thou drain the life-blood of the child,
> To bid the father wipe his eyes withal,
> And yet be seen to wear a woman's face?
>
> (1.4.137–40)

The presence of the young prince standing silently beside the queen throughout this scene further underscores the fact that the woman who takes pleasure from destroying another's family is herself a mother.

But even as the play appears to reinstate the gendered confrontation of patriarchal history, it simultaneously offers the possibility for an alternative version of the events at Wakefield. As in the previous play, Shakespeare's strategy is to qualify negative stereotypes of women in power by situating them within a broad political context—in this case, one furnished by York's violation of his oath to the king. The play makes much of this oath in the opening scene when Henry promises to entail the Crown to York and his heirs so long as they uphold their part of the bargain:

> To cease this civil war and, whilst I live
> To honor me as thy king and sovereign,
> And neither by treason nor hostility
> To seek to put me down and reign thyself.
>
> (1.1.197–200)

In Shakespeare's version of the events, York perjures himself in the very next scene by deciding to take the Crown by force *before* he learns of Margaret's military offensive. The chronology thus supports the kind of *Mirror for Magistrates'* moralizing reported in Holinshed, that "Manie deemed that this miserable end chanced to the duke of Yorke, as a due punishment for breaking his oth of allegiance unto his sovereigne lord king Henrie."[56] Shakespeare returns attention to the oath in the scene at Wakefield; and though few critics have noticed the connection, it is Margaret's mockery of York's failure to keep his "holy oath" (1.4.99–106)—and not her display of the blood-stained napkin—that actually provokes the vituperative attack on the "she-wolf of France" (1.4.111) a few lines later.[57]

There is, of course, a certain justice in York's meeting his death at the hands of an aggressive woman. In both *1* and *2 Henry VI*, it is York who brings under control the subversive females who supposedly threaten England, first with his capture of Joan of Arc and then with his arrest of the duchess of Gloucester. Less constrained by civilized ideals than old-

fashioned heroes like Talbot and Gloucester, York is able to prevail over
these Amazonian women and to exploit his victory for political gain. In
3 Henry VI the tables turn, however, and the "ruthless queen" (1.4.156)
now defends the Crown against the rebel warrior who would be king.
York's sons may eulogize him as a heroic figure—"The flow'r of Europe
for his chevalry" (2.1.71)—but York is no Talbot, and his sons even less
so. Their father praises their valor on the battlefield—"Three times did
Richard make a lane to me / And thrice cried, 'Courage, father, fight it
out!'" (1.2.9–10)—but once he is dead, each son quickly shows himself
to be driven by self-interest, not by heroic ideals.

With the task of conquering the unruly female falling to the "lusty
sons," the play's attitude toward the gendered attack on Margaret's rule
becomes less ambiguous, especially as York's objections to Margaret's
behavior coalesce to provide justification for their revolt. For the sons, as
for radicals like John Knox, the misogynistic discourse provides a ready
means of authorizing a call for rebellion against a woman ruler. True to
form, York's sons unashamedly blame "the wrangling woman" for their
attempt on the Crown:

> For what hath broach'd this tumult but thy pride?
> Hadst thou been meek, our title still had slept,
> And we, in pity of the gentle king,
> Had slipp'd our claim until another age.

> (2.2.159–62)

The strategy of blaming Margaret, and not York, for the Lancastrian
downfall is straight out of Hall, who sympathetically reports that York
and his allies "(after long communicacion had, of the Quenes misgover-
naunce, and how she without their assent, did all thynges at her will and
pleasure) determined to raise a greate army, and by fine force, either to
die or win their purpose."[58] But while Shakespeare echoes this theme, he
places these charges exclusively in the mouths of the Yorkists and so
clearly exposes the politics of their antifeminist criticism. York's implicit
misogyny is fully discredited, of course, when it emerges full-blown in
Richard, who forges his drive to power against a feminine world he
perceives as conspiring to exclude him from making his "heaven in a
lady's lap" (3.2.148). His deformed body, he boasts, "carries no
impression like the dam" (3.2.162).

The play's refusal to endorse the Yorkist attack on Margaret's rule is
again apparent with the final confrontation at Tewkesbury near the end of
the play. Once again, Shakespeare effects a critique of the Yorkist
position by writing against his source. Hall, for example, describes how

this "unmanly queen" becomes "like a woman" in her defeat: "She like a woman all dismaied for feare, fell to the ground, her harte was perced with sorowe, her speache was in maner passed, all her spirites were tormented with Malencholy."[59] Simplifying Margaret's reign to a pattern of crime and punishment, Hall concludes her story by imposing a moral order on the chronicle events: her defeat, even at the hands of the usurping Yorkists, has a moral rightness about it, restoring the balance lost by Henry's "fatal marriage" and the murder of Gloucester. As Hall moralizes for his readers: "This Quene Margarete might well consider and thynke that these evill adventures, chaunced to her for the moste parte, for the unworthy death of Humfrey Duke of Gloucester, uncle to her husbande."[60]

By contrast, Shakespeare increases Margaret's "valiant spirit" (5.4.39), and with it the audience's sympathies, as the queen prepares for the final battle against her enemies. Margaret begins by sending word to the newly crowned and married Edward that she is done mourning and is now "ready to put armor on" (3.3.229–30). But while the change in costume prompts the Yorkists to link her with aggressive Amazons— "Belike she minds to play the Amazon" (4.1.106), King Edward quips— it may have led many in Shakespeare's audience to recall the image of their own queen popularized by contemporary accounts of her appearance at Tilbury only a few years before.[61] The associations between the two queens become especially resonant in Margaret's powerful speech to her troops before Tewkesbury, a speech that echoes the rousing words Elizabeth reportedly delivered to the troops at Tilbury: "I know I have but the body of a weak and feeble woman; but I have the heart of a king, and of a king of England too; and think foul scorn that Parma or Spain; or any Prince of Europe, should dare to invade the borders of my realms."[62] On this crucial occasion, Elizabeth is said to have, once again, turned the weakness of her gender to advantage and won the day, inspiring her men with the example of her own courage. Leicester later wrote that the queen's visit "so enflamyd the harts of her good subjects, as I think the wekest person amongst them is able to match the proudest Spainard that dares land in England."[63]

Like Shakespeare's queen, Margaret displays her own fiery courage as an example to her men. Because the king has left the helm, she explains, and "like a fearful lad, / With tearful eyes add[s] water to the sea" (5.4.7–8), the duty to pilot the ship of state now falls to her and her son. "We will not from the helm to sit and weep, / But keep our course (though the rough wind say no)" (5.4.21–22), she promises, calling for courage among her followers. Margaret's martial aggression, like Elizabeth's, appears even more admirable because she is a woman, and in words that recall Leicester's description of Elizabeth's effect on the troops, the prince praises his mother:

> Methinks a woman of this valiant spirit
> Should, if a coward heard her speak these words,
> Infuse his breast with magnanimity,
> And make him, naked, foil a man at arms.
>
> (5.4.39–42)

Like Elizabeth's willingness "to live or die" among her soldiers, Margaret's display of manly courage at Tewkesbury is hardly "ill-beseeming" to her sex.

With Margaret's final words to her men before battle, we come full circle to celebrate, if only for a moment, the figure of the heroic woman warrior. All traces of the "obdurate" Amazon have disappeared as Margaret now speaks through tears, her references to God and country lending strength and authority to her appeal:

> . . . Henry, your sovereign,
> Is prisoner to the foe, his state usurp'd,
> His realm a slaughter-house, his subjects slain,
> His statutes cancell'd, and his treasure spent;
> And yonder is the wolf that makes this spoil.
> You fight in justice; then in God's name, lords,
> Be valiant, and give signal to the fight.
>
> (5.4.76–82)

Margaret's speech may signal the vulnerability of her position—it "seems designed to ventriloquize the absent King's 'fatherly' voice,"[64] Barbara Hodgdon comments—but it also recalls the powerful discourse of nation spoken by Gloucester at the start of *2 Henry VI*. Here, at the close of the *Henry VI* plays, the very woman Gloucester spoke of as "Rasing the characters of your renown, / Defacing monuments of conquer'd France, / Undoing all, as all had never been" (1.2.101–3) now stands before the English lords, as Gloucester had before her, passionately appealing to law and justice in the nation's defense.

But even as Shakespeare allows Margaret to "speak" the nation, and thereby invokes not only Gloucester but his own monarch, the emphasis on mother and son in this scene constitutes a significant departure from Elizabethan representations of their singular queen. With this final portrait of the Lancastrian queen and crown prince, Shakespeare offers, for the first time in the *Henry VI* plays, a model for women's participation in politics that effectively counters objections to ruling women with an appeal to national interests grounded in law and the custom of patrilineal succession. Margaret now speaks modestly of a command shared with her son: "And though unskillful, why not Ned and I / For once allow'd the skillful pilot's charge?" (5.4.19–20). The prince, for his part, valiantly takes up his mother's charge and, as a result, restores heroism to its "true" place—in the male warrior. As Oxford remarks, praising his valor: "O brave young prince! thy famous grandfather / Doth live again in thee" (5.4.52–53). The prince has now assumed his place in the Lancastrian genealogy as heir to Henry V. But the glory is tragically brief, and the prince is soon taken captive by the Yorkists, who rewrite his lineage, denigrating young Henry as heir to women: "Take that, thou likeness of this railer here" (5.5.38), King Edward jeers as he stabs the prince in front of his mother.

The revised patriarchy figured in mother and son is remarkably short-lived on Shakespeare's stage, but its memory lingers as a wished-for alternative to the rule that emerges with the Yorkist victory at the play's conclusion. Viewed from a distance, the closing portrait of the Yorkist royal family would seem to offer a perfectly scripted conclusion not only to this play but to the *Henry VI* plays as a whole, promising to restore all that was lost with the death of Henry V that was mourned at the start of *1 Henry VI*. The closing scene indeed opens with the unmistakable signs of patriarchy restored. A strong male monarch now sits in "England's royal throne," flanked by his queen, his new-born male heir, and his brothers. From the Yorkist perspective, the battle has been won, the Crown "repurchased," and the "wrangling woman" captured, to be sold back to her father for "the Sicils and Jerusalem," so restoring the loss of Anjou and Maine brought by her marriage to Henry. From the audience's perspective, however, the closing portrait only mocks the ideals of family and state it appears to institute.[65] The new queen, whom Leah Marcus calls a model of "devoted female domesticity"[66] as she stands beside her husband and infant son, may seem to resolve anxieties about female misrule, but earlier complaints about this unprofitable marriage voiced by the king's brothers predict that the cycle of gendered warfare will begin all over again—and indeed it does with Richard's attack on Elizabeth at the start of *Richard III*. What most disturbs the patriarchal portrait, of course, is the menacing presence of Richard of Gloucester. "I'll blast his harvest," he promises in a vice-like aside, planting his Judas kiss on his nephew and thus boldly uncovering for the audience the full horror that lurks within the bonds of family and brotherhood.

Patriarchy has been restored, but only as a grotesque parody of the ideals that have been invoked as a battle cry throughout these plays. Richard's kiss indeed threatens to destroy the very foundation of the patriarchal state. No longer represented by a usurping female "other," the greatest threat to the nation's welfare now resides within the royal family itself, in the "brother" who would destroy the patrilineal inheritance on which stability depends. As Richard himself confesses, affirming the frightening individualism that acknowledges no bonds:

> I have no brother, I am like no brother;
> And this word "love," which greybeards call divine,
> Be resident in men like one another,
> And not in me: I am myself alone.

(5.6.80–83)

Richard's vow to "blast" the Yorkist succession at the play's close constitutes a kind of demonic inversion to Margaret's heroic fight for the Lancastrian succession throughout the play. With the final image of brother against brother and uncle against nephew thus set against the figure of the heroic mother, the play anticipates the anxieties about the succession that will figure prominently in *Richard III* and *King John*, and also the role that women will play in these plays as defenders of the nation-state.

In the end, Shakespeare's presentation of queenship may not radically revise assumptions about government and authority, along the lines of either Knox or Aylmer, say, but the closing opposition between mother and son and the Yorkist patriarchy nonetheless provokes questions about orthodox structures of power. Reconfirming a governing principle of both *2* and *3 Henry VI*, the opposition sanctions women's participation in politics when it is in the interests of the nation's welfare. As those interests come to be defined in relation to the succession, one could argue that the play transforms a potentially radical reconfiguration of authority into a fairly conservative image of dynastic power. But in defining the maintenance of lineal succession largely in terms of national interests, Shakespeare, not unlike Aylmer earlier in the century, links royal authority with preservation of the commonwealth as well as with lineage and custom. Thereby altering the categories underwriting monarchical authority, Shakespeare allows for a wider critique of patriarchal power that may be extended to Yorkist rule. If obedience is contingent in part on the magistrate's concern for the commonwealth, as this shift suggests, then the case can be made for disobedience and rebellion. What makes this argument radical is not the fact that it sanctions female rule but that it does so in part by appealing to national interests. As a result, sovereignty rests not with the monarch alone but with her subjects as well.

4

Misogyny, Marriage, and the Succession
in *Richard III*

"Why, this it is, when men are rul'd by women" (1.1.62), Richard declares in the opening scene of *Richard III*, publicly blaming the queen for Clarence's imprisonment. Refusing to accept a submissive posture as "the Queen's abjects" (1.1.106), Richard sanctions his aggression against the state by adopting a gendered discourse of nation reminiscent of that voiced by Thomas Nashe in *Pierce Penilesse* and echoed by English warriors throughout the *Henry VI* plays.[1] Like his predecessors, Richard expresses fears about an "effeminate" state in which once-valiant warriors are reduced to capering in "a lady's chamber" (1.1.12) and so defines his struggle for power as a quest to restore order to a world perverted by unnatural female domination. Of course, Richard is no chivalric hero but a "murtherous Machevil" who speaks a crass misogyny that, for the audience at least, belies his professed concern for Crown and country. But, however much the play discredits Richard, his gendered discourse nonetheless generates complex and even contradictory political effects on the Elizabethan stage.

Divergent critical opinion on the play points to one source for these complexities in the characterization of Richard and his female opponents. As many have argued, Richard may be a stage machiavel, but he is also a fully defined psychological subject.[2] And the fact that he forges his identity, as well as his ambition, in relation to women constitutes an important development in Shakespeare's handling of gender politics in the history plays. But if politics are complicated by questions about subjectivity and masculine identity, they are also complicated by the play's ambivalent presentation of women. What is perhaps most disarming about the women in *Richard III*, especially in comparison with

97

their counterparts in the *Henry VI* plays, is their seeming powerlessness, and as Richard's most visible victims, they offer persuasive testimony of his "unnatural" violence against the family and state. Even so, there has been a persistent critical tradition, beginning with Richard himself, of blaming the women, of seeing them as complicitous in their own victimization. As a result, many have concluded that the play—and Shakespeare—shares in Richard's misogyny. Most recently, Janet Adelman has persuasively argued the case in her study of masculine identity and "fantasies of maternal origin" in Shakespeare. In *Richard III*, she writes, Shakespeare "participates in Richard's violent unmaking of the maternal body that is the point of origin of his selfhood: though Richard's violence is always deplored, its action is nonetheless replicated in a dramatic structure that moves women from positions of power and authority to positions of utter powerlessness, and finally moves them off the stage altogether."[3]

This chapter is similarly concerned with masculine identity and with sorting out Richard's misogyny from Shakespeare's, but the focus here, as throughout this book, is less on questions of psychology than on questions of politics, especially those that bring Shakespeare's stage into conjunction with the Elizabethan state. By situating Richard's misogyny within a historical framework, marked at one end by Henrician versions of fifteenth-century history and at the other by the instabilities of the Elizabethan present, this chapter finds motives for the play's gender politics in the congruent sets of relations between past and present, stage and state. The point within the play on which these relations turn is constituted by Richard's dependence on women. It is the contradictory nature of this dependence, rather than Richard's misogyny alone, that may have spoken most powerfully to Elizabethans in the 1590s.

Doubly marginalized by his deformity and his subordinate place within the royal family as the king's youngest brother, Richard depends on his relations to women—as the enemy against which he forges his drive to power and, simultaneously, as the marriage partner who will strengthen his claim to the throne and guarantee its succession. We may understand his misogyny as both a proof and a consequence of his deformity. For his enemies, his outward form signifies what lies within: "As crooked in thy manners as thy shape"(5.1.158), Clifford declares in *2 Henry VI*. Of course, Richard sees it differently, attributing his war against women to the betrayal in his mother's womb:

> Why, love forswore me in my mother's womb;
> And for I should not deal in her soft laws,
> She did corrupt frail nature with some bribe,

To shrink mine arm up like a wither'd shrub,
To make an envious mountain on my back,
Where sits deformity to mock my body.

(3 Henry VI, 3.2.153–58)

But though Richard is "determined to prove a villain" (*Richard III,* 1.1.30) since he "cannot prove a lover" (1.1.28), his misogyny is more than just a symptom of his physical and moral deformity. Within the dynastic politics of Shakespeare's first tetralogy, Richard's attack on women also offers a telling measure of the weakness of his claim. In contrast to his father, who claimed the throne on the basis of consanguinity (witness the lengthy rehearsals of Yorkist genealogy in the *Henry VI* plays), Richard's "blood"—in the form of his older brothers— separates him from the Crown. Thus it is principally by warring with women that Richard authorizes his attack on his own family.

Yet Richard's need to legitimate his ambition by warring against women is complicated, and eventually compromised, by his simultaneous dependence on them as a means of consolidating power and ensuring his own lineage. This dependence signals the weakness not only of Richard's claim to the throne but of patriarchal structures in general, exposing the myth of patrilineal succession in which power is imagined as passing from father to son as if no women were involved. Confined to a closed economy of misogyny and marriage, Richard's relations with women indeed bring into relief the double bind of patriarchal structures of power and inheritance that seek to control, and suppress, women even as they depend on them to continue the father's name. Paradoxically, Richard would legitimate his bid for power by making his war against women and children. Yet, as his female opponents remind him, the succession depends ultimately on the "mother's womb." With Richard's contradictory dependence on women, the play registers, however equivocally, a dilemma of dynastic succession that resonates well beyond the confines of the Elizabethan theater.

Richmond's victory over Richard at the play's close does offer a solution of sorts to this dilemma by excluding women from history's stage and, at the same time, celebrating the figure of the independent heroic male whose legitimacy depends on relations with other men, not with women. Nowhere in the two tetralogies does the past come closer to the present than here, where Shakespeare stages the origins of the Tudor dynasty for his own monarch. And nowhere, perhaps, is the conjunction between past and present more unsettling. For however central the story of Richmond's triumph at Bosworth field was to the Tudor's own legitimating myth of history, to retell that story at the close of the century is to offer a perplexing tribute to the last Tudor monarch, the Virgin Queen who had no hope of continuing Richmond's line.[4] For Elizabethans in the 1590s, facing an uncertain future dictated by an aging queen who refused to settle the succession, Richmond's triumph may have appealed to the desire for a male monarch who would set things "right" after nearly fifty years of female rule. But against the concluding nostalgia for a stable patriarchy, figured in a monarch and nation that owed nothing to women, the play's more predominate economy of misogyny and marriage continues to remind its audience of current political concerns. In *Richard III*, as in the other plays of the tetralogy, women again figure centrally in interrogating the differences between past and present, between historical fictions and present realities.

Keen Encounters

Waged by a "murtherous Machevil" against the women of his brother's court, *Richard III*'s war against the Amazon parodies the classical narrative of patriarchal legitimacy and thereby deepens the critique of gender politics associated with the Yorkist drive to power throughout the *Henry VI* plays. Nowhere are the accusations against women more flagrant than when Richard attributes his deformity to a demonic alliance between Queen Elizabeth and her husband's mistress, Jane Shore. Dramatically displaying his withered arm as evidence to the court, Richard asks Hastings to condemn those who have "prevail'd / Upon my body with their hellish charms":

> Look how I am bewitch'd; behold, mine arm
> Is like a blasted sapling, wither'd up;
> And this is Edward's wife, that monstrous witch,
> Consorted with that harlot, strumpet Shore,
> That by their witchcraft thus have marked me.
>
> (3.4.68–72)

There is, of course, nothing new or surprising in Richard's assertion of a demonic and promiscuous female community that is destructive of male potency. But in his attempt to make women scapegoats for nature itself, Richard goes too far and in the process exposes both the absurdity and the danger of a gendered discourse that would consolidate the state by setting it against women. For Richard attempts not only to legitimate his aggression against his brother's family but also, and with a vicious irony, to invoke the bonds of brotherhood by aligning himself with other men in the fight against the women who supposedly conspire against them. Richard thus strives to become the "proper man" (1.2.254), one who is both legitimate and of "fair proportion" (1.1.18), by leading an attack on women. Those, like Hastings, who refuse to endorse Richard's misogyny, he declares traitors.

But however much Richard deploys the requisite ideologies of gender, he differs radically from his predecessors in the *Henry VI* plays, including his own father, in his outright rejection of what could be considered a corollary to the image of male dominance over women—that of a community of men, that "band of brothers" Henry V invokes before the battle of Agincourt. Though this community is rarely glimpsed in the *Henry VI* plays, and is even called into question, it nonetheless stands as an ideal against which we measure the "piteous spectacle" (*3 Henry VI,* 2.5.73) of civil butchery. Epitomized by his attack on his own brother, Richard's violence against the male community puts him at odds, then, with the patriarchal ideology he voices. Subverting the fundamental codes of chivalry and brotherhood, the misshapen Richard—who declares: "I have no brother, I am like no brother" (*3 Henry VI,* 5.6.80)— displays a destructive individualism that grotesquely parodies the noble Talbot, who, fighting against the French Amazon, dies a hero's death, his son in his arms. Rather than legitimating his desires, Richard's misappropriation of the gendered discourse of nation works instead to unmask him as a demonic imposter whose war against women is an attack on the nation itself. Indeed, as Hastings declares as he is being led away to his death: "Woe, woe for England" (*Richard III,* 3.4.80).

As misogyny becomes misanthropy and the scope of Richard's violence widens to include brothers and nephews, *Richard III* appears to simplify the gender wars of the *Henry VI* plays considerably. For one, the "sides" are more clearly defined in this play, which invites us to understand Richard's misogyny in opposition to Richmond's "true" patriarchy, as a demonic parody that reaffirms and validates the hero's sanctioned authority. Moreover, it is obvious from the start that the danger to the state resides in Richard, the "natural" brother, and not in the women he claims as enemies. Bearing little resemblance to aspiring women like Joan of Arc and Eleanor Cobham, Richard's opponents in this play are noble women who fight to protect the state and the succession—and who are of interest to Richard precisely for this reason. For the first time in the tetralogy, in fact, Shakespeare presents what many Elizabethans would have considered an acceptable model for female heroism with a string of lamenting women who grieve for their murdered husbands and sons.[5] Underscoring the unnaturalness of Richard's bloody war against family and state, these women reinforce orthodox values by exemplifying female vulnerability and suffering, which, in turn, persuasively argues for the need for a heroic male savior, like Richmond, who will protect the nation's women and children from "a bloody tyrant and a homicide" (5.3.246) like Richard.

But even as Shakespeare redefines the scene of gender confrontation in this play by setting the usurping misogynist against the grieving mother, the politics of gender are not without complication. For, while the women may be Richard's most visible victims, they are also his most outspoken opponents. In allowing the lamenting women a certain agency and power, Shakespeare again gives emphasis to the unsettling contradictions that arise when women appear on history's stage. And here, as in the *Henry VI* plays, these contradictions are powerfully displayed in scenes of gender confrontation. The play's three scenes of confrontation—between Richard and Anne (1.2), Richard and Margaret (1.3), and Richard and Queen Elizabeth (4.4)—all follow a similar pattern: each develops out of a scene of lamentation, and in each Shakespeare goes far beyond the script provided him by his sources. These confrontations, like those in the *Henry VI* plays, continue to reiterate a gendered discourse of nation while simultaneously exposing the dangers of this discourse. *Richard III* goes further than the previous plays, however, in allowing women a place in politics, one that offers a way out of Richard's misogynistic construction of women as either aggressors or victims.

Of the three scenes, Richard's encounter with Margaret is the least complicated, and in many ways it simply extends the critique of gender politics established in the *Henry VI* plays. Margaret's importance in the play is signaled, in part, by Shakespeare's decision to rewrite chronicle history, and the conclusion to *3 Henry VI*, in order to return the queen to England from her exile in France.[6] The play itself acknowledges the inconsistency of Margaret's appearance in Edward's court with Richard's own surprise upon seeing her: "Wert thou not banished on pain of death?" (1.3.166). Margaret's answer is that she has returned to exact vengeance on behalf of the Lancastrians:

> A husband and a son thou ow'st to me—
> And thou a kingdom—all of you allegiance.
> This sorrow that I have, by right is yours,
> And all the pleasures you usurp are mine.

> (1.3.169–72)

Although Margaret is only a shadow of her former self, her presence here in the enemy's court testifies to the vestiges of power she retains. She may no longer stand at the head of the royal army, but she does not passively wail her loss.

Like the attacks on women throughout the *Henry VI* plays, Richard's confrontation with Margaret in this scene continues to expose the political manipulation of familiar narratives of gender and to raise questions about the Yorkist claims to power. We have already seen in *3 Henry VI*, for example, how Richard and his brothers presented their rebellion as a necessary war against an aggressive, usurping female: as the boys explain to Margaret, because she refused to be "meek," to wear the "petticoat," "we set the axe to thy usurping root" (2.2.165). In *Richard III*, the Yorkists continue to attribute their crimes against the Lancastrians to Margaret's barbaric cruelty at Wakefield. And with their position now secure, the Yorkists fully engage in the legitimating politics of revisionist history, boldly rewriting the events Shakespeare staged in *3 Henry VI* to make Margaret, and not the avenging Clifford, bear responsibility for the death of Rutland, the schoolboy who is now remembered as a "babe" (1.3.182). According to the Yorkist version of history, Margaret's inhumane acts of murder at Wakefield not only give cause for Richard's vengeful murders of her son and husband—"So just is God, to right the innocent" (1.3.181), Queen Elizabeth moralizes—but they also set in motion the grisly cycle of vengeance being played out in *Richard III*.

Margaret is no helpless victim of Yorkist aggression, however. A precursor of those liminal figures on the borders of *Macbeth*, the ghostly Margaret succeeds in dominating this scene, rhetorically as well as visually, by uttering the string of curses that lends structure to the play's cycle of retribution. The effects of her power are immediately visible: the court "trembles" (1.3.159), Richard averts his eyes and "turn[s] away" (1.3.162) as if to deflect the power of her words, while Buckingham's "hair doth stand an end" (1.3.303) to hear her speak. Adopting the discourse of the marginalized, Margaret here engages in a kind of ritual cursing that, according to Keith Thomas, provided "a substitute for political action" for those cut off from power.[7] But as the Amazon comes face to face with the misogynist, there is, as Leslie Fiedler has remarked, "little to choose."[8] Natural opponents, each defines and justifies the other. Just as Margaret's so-called infanticide is said to authorize Richard's misogyny and, to some extent, his own acts of violence, so Richard's violent misogyny provokes Margaret's cruelty. The two opponents indeed begin to seem remarkably similar, as Queen Elizabeth herself remarks when she confronts Richard in act 4, pointing to the likeness between Margaret's bloody assault on the Yorkists at Wakefield and Richard's attempt to woo her daughter after he has already killed her sons:

> Therefore present to her—as [sometimes] Margaret
> Did to thy father, steep'd in Rutland's blood—
> A [handkercher], which, say to her, did drain
> The purple sap from her sweet brother's body,
> And bid her wipe her weeping eyes withal.
>
> (4.4.274–78)

Aligning Margaret and Richard, Shakespeare suggests an alignment of their political strategies as well: for just as Richard figures a parody of the legitimate patriarchal order of Richmond, so too does Margaret.[9]

If the scenes with Margaret replay the gendered confrontations of the *Henry VI* plays, the parallel wooing scenes of Anne (1.2) and Elizabeth (4.4) signal a shift in emphasis by bringing Richard's need to dominate women into conflict with his dependence on them as a means of consolidating power. Charting the trajectory of Richard's rise and fall, these two scenes document his complex and ultimately destructive dependence on women. Like his adoption of a misogynistic discourse, Richard's attempt to move up through marriage is well within the codes of established aristocratic practice. In marrying Anne, and thereby stepping into the place recently held by the Lancastrian crown prince himself, Richard attempts a union of York and Lancaster that anticipates the dynastic marriage at the play's close. But Richard's confession of a "secret close intent" (1.1.158) in marrying Anne also suggests other, "darker" purposes. The wooing of Anne provides a test case for Richard's strategy of exploiting gender politics and establishes the misshapen machiavel as "a marv'llous proper man" (1.2.254), in his own eyes if not in the court's, even as it documents his dangerous dependence on women. But in pointing as well to the ease with which women may be corrupted, the scene also voices fears about women who would betray their own blood.

The first woman to appear onstage in *Richard III*, "poor Anne" (1.2.9), as she calls herself, enters in obsequious lamentation, following the corpse of Henry VI. Dressed not in armor but in black, she offers a striking contrast to the aggressive women of the *Henry VI* plays and invites us, as the figure of the lamenting female will throughout the play, to pity the victims of Richard's bloody rise to power. It is remarkable, then, that by the end of the scene we have shifted our perspective. For Anne, who enters as a mourner, departs, some two hundred lines later, wearing Richard's ring. Her behavior is disturbing, and we are inclined to ask, along with Richard, "Hath she forgot already that brave prince, / Edward, her lord, whom I, some three months since, / Stabb'd in my angry mood at Tewksbury?" (1.2.239–41).[10] Transforming the victim into an accomplice, Shakespeare in this short scene constructs a model of female behavior that in many ways authorizes Richard's misogyny. The positive stereotype of the passive, long-suffering female, the central image *Richard III* teases us with, has been rendered suspect.

The scene of confrontation, or seduction, as it is more commonly called, has no counterpart in the play's chronicle sources, which provide the context but not the details for the encounter, ascribing the deaths of Prince Edward and Henry VI in 1471 to Richard and recording Richard's marriage to Anne a year later.[11] Shakespeare not only invents the greater part of this scene, then, he also compresses chronology to stage the seduction over the king's corpse. "With mirth in funeral, and with dirge in marriage," the play emphasizes the outrageousness of both Richard's wooing and Anne's capitulation—and thus gives motive to the play's misogyny. Geoffrey Bullough has suggested a possible literary source for the scene in Seneca's *Hercules Furens*, and whether Seneca was actually a source for the play, the differences between the two scenes are instructive.[12] For one, Seneca's text underscores the extent to which Shakespeare's version interrogates the "woman's part" as well as the man's. In Seneca, the invading tyrant Lycus, having murdered her father and brothers, woos Megara, the wife of the absent Hercules. In contrast to Richard, however, Lycus is not successful in his seduction of Megara, who vows to die before she will wed the usurper. Lycus's unsuccessful wooing of Megara thus provides a pattern by which we may evaluate Richard's wildly successful wooing of Anne. For Anne is measured, by Richard and audiences alike, against the mirror of the virtuous wife who nobly prefers death to family dishonor.

One critic has argued that Richard's triumph is "more of a rape than a seduction,"[13] an interpretation that places the blame on the villainous Richard and vindicates Anne, casting her as an innocent victim. The scene itself argues otherwise, however, and suggests instead that Richard brings Anne around by tempting her with the illusion of power, by holding out to her the belief that she has power over him. When Richard first enters, interrupting the funeral and taking control of the procession, Anne fiercely confronts him and proceeds to catalogue his demonic villainy with a string of accusations and curses. Richard takes control at once, however, by establishing the pattern for their exchange, a pattern Anne readily adopts.[14] Shifting into the Petrarchan idiom, Richard cleverly transforms this quarrel between innocent victim and willful murderer into a "keen encounter" (1.2.115) of wits between a cruel mistress and her lover. Demonically manipulating the courtly discourse, Richard pretends to empower Anne and place himself in the vulnerable position of the dejected lover, a redistribution of power that allows him to turn the tables and shift the blame for the murders away from himself and on to Anne. Once again, a Lancastrian woman becomes a scapegoat for Yorkist crimes against the Lancastrian state. Richard confesses that Anne's "beauty was the cause" (1.2.121) of his murder of her husband and father-in-law. Offering further confirmation of her hold over him, Richard compares the power of Anne's beauty with the death of his father. As Richard tells it, his "manly eyes did scorn an humble tear" (1.2.164) when he heard Warwick's "sad story" of his father's death. Anne's beauty, by contrast, has "made them blind with weeping" (1.2.165).[15]

Richard dramatically concludes his argument by kneeling before his cruel mistress, baring his breast to her, and offering her his sword. With the scene of Richard submissive before Anne, Shakespeare presents yet another version of the highly ambivalent figure of the Elizabethan court, that of the courtier kneeling before his queen. Whereas in *1 Henry VI* the scene of the dauphin "prostrate" before the armed and victorious Joan had exposed the figure's subversive potential by uncovering the power it gives to women, in *Richard III* Richard's kneeling to Anne restores power to the male by showing courtly submission to be a politic pose, adopted only as a means of dominance. The richly equivocating Petrarchan discourse likewise allows Richard to remain in control of the scene while at the same time offering Anne the illusion that she has power over men.[16] Professing that Anne's beauty has the power to transform murderer into mourner, Richard claims to be moved to repentance and begs to take her place in following Henry VI's corpse. Won over by her seducer's seeming transformation—and by her own power in effecting that change—Anne graciously grants his boon: "With all my heart, and much it joys me too, / To see you are become so penitent" (1.2.219–20). Miraculously transformed from "a dreadful minister of hell" (1.2.46) to Anne's "poor devoted servant" (1.2.206), Richard takes control of his prize.[17]

Celebrating his triumph in a self-congratulatory soliloquy, Richard directs the audience's attention to the weakness of Anne and, by extension, all women: "What? I, that kill'd her husband and his father, / To take her in her heart's extremest hate, / With curses in her mouth, tears in her eyes, / The bleeding witness of my hatred by. . . . / And yet to win her! All the world to nothing!" (1.2.230–33, 37). With this soliloquy Richard establishes the misogynistic politics that will characterize his subsequent confrontations with women and legitimate his own power. As Linda Charnes points out, by drawing on a misogynistic tradition, Richard "produces a viable public perception, however fragile, of himself as *ipso facto* a 'proper man' in relation to the women he designates as monstrous. The social recoding and redeployment of his deformity depend upon the motility of public misogyny."[18] But for Richard, Anne's attention is indeed transformative: he imagines that Anne sees him as a "proper man" (1.2.254) simply because she "abase[s]" (1.2.246) her eyes to look on him. To the extent that power within this relationship is reciprocal, Richard's marriage to Anne not only rehearses his drive to power, it also displays a dependence on women that will ultimately prove destructive.

The final confrontation between the sexes in the tetralogy comes with Richard's "wooing" of Elizabeth for her daughter's hand, a scene that is far less ambivalent than the wooing of Anne. Again Richard seeks marriage as a means of shoring up his power, but this time he acts defensively, knowing that "the Britain Richmond aims / At young Elizabeth, my brother's daughter, / And by that knot looks proudly on the crown" (4.3.40–42). If Richard's position is thus weakened, the queen's is strengthened, as Shakespeare here revises his chronicle sources to improve upon a woman's portrait. According to Hall, whose description of Elizabeth is especially harsh, Richard instructed his messengers to lure the queen and her daughters out of sanctuary with promises of "promocions innumerable and benefites." Easily tempted, the "avaricious" Elizabeth "delivered into kyng Richards handes her v. daughters as Lambes once agayne committed to the custody of the ravenous wolfe."[19] In misogynistic tones worthy of Richard himself, Hall draws the general lesson for his readers: "Surely the inconstancie of this woman were muche to be merveled at, yf all women had bene founde constante, but let men speake, yet wemen of the verie bonde of nature will folowe their awne kynde."[20]

Shakespeare, by contrast, deflects Hall's censure by emphasizing Elizabeth's strength in facing Richard, and the use of the source in this instance is not without irony. Borrowing the image of the lamb Hall had used to condemn Elizabeth, Shakespeare places it in the mouth of the grieving mother, who turns it back on Richard as an image of blood-sacrifice: "No doubt the murd'rous knife was dull and blunt / Till it was whetted on thy stone-hard heart / To revel in the entrails of my lambs" (4.4.227–29). In contrast to Hall's Elizabeth, Shakespeare's queen fights to protect her children, and though she may seem to yield at the end, her courage in standing up to Richard throughout most of this long confrontation associates her not with the misogynistic stereotype of the "monstrous" woman but with the heroic figure of a "natural" mother who fights not for herself but for her children, an image first associated with Margaret at the close of *3 Henry VI* that serves to counter the anxiety typically associated with female aggression.

Throughout most of this scene Elizabeth reacts to the tyrant's advances with admirable courage and outrage, and though Richard repeats the strategy that had been so successful with Anne, Elizabeth corrects the faults of her predecessor. When Richard explains that he murdered his niece's brothers and uncles "for love of her" (4.4.288), Elizabeth reacts as we wish Anne had: "Nay then indeed she cannot chose but hate thee, / Having bought love with such a bloody spoil" (4.4.289–90). As he did with Anne, Richard tempts Elizabeth with power, offering to advance her and her children. But the ultimate prize he holds out to her is the promise to give her daughter power over him and, by extension, the state itself:

> Bound with triumphant garlands will I come
> And lead thy daughter to a conqueror's bed;
> To whom I will retail my conquest won,
> And she shall be sole victoress, Caesar's Caesar.

> (4.4.333–36)

Elizabeth's biting answer—"What were I best to say? Her father's brother / Would be her lord? Or shall I say her uncle? / Or he that slew her brothers and her uncles?" (4.4.337–39)—exposes the blood ties that make Richard's extravagant offer of sexual power so grotesque. Significantly, when Elizabeth does appear to yield, it is out of a desire to protect the nation from Richard's threat of "death, desolation, ruin, and decay" (4.4.409).

Elizabeth's confrontation with Richard thus defines her as an exemplary woman, a heroic mother who fights not for herself but to protect the royal succession and the state. And although some critics have been troubled by the queen's apparent concession, they are less likely to agree with Richard's misogynistic assessment of Elizabeth—"Relenting fool, and shallow, changing woman!" (4.4.431)—than they were with his earlier condemnation of Anne.[21] Moreover, the report at the beginning of the next scene that "the Queen hath heartily consented" (4.5.7) that Richmond should marry her daughter would seem to put to rest fears about Elizabeth's capitulation to Richard's demands. Like another queen of the same name, this Elizabeth also engages in defensive policy-making, buying time with Richard but meanwhile arranging for her daughter's marriage to Richmond. But in contrast to Elizabeth I, this queen takes steps to ensure the succession.

As the tetralogy draws to a close, women would seem to have come full circle. No longer figuring a female enemy, the women of *Richard III*, and the two Elizabeths especially, come to be identified with the source of monarchical power. Indeed, with husbands and sons slaughtered by the usurping Richard, only women remain to transmit the "sacred blood" that will confer legitimacy on the play's "true" successor. Thus recognizing the importance of women within the royal succession, this play significantly revises the patriarchal genealogies that give shape and structure both to the great Tudor chronicles and Shakespeare's history plays.[22] But even as the play authorizes women's participation in politics, that participation is carefully circumscribed by its relation to the restoration of patriarchal order. Their role, as Barbara Hodgdon notes, "is to engender Richmond, to name a potential successor who will, eventually, cancel the entire 'monstrous regiment' of female 'misrule.'"[23] At the same time, however, in acknowledging the importance of women in the succession, the play continues to reinforce the double bind of patriarchy.

"Accursed womb, the bed of death"

As *Richard III* reminds its audience again and again, to acknowledge the importance of women in ensuring patrilineal succession is also to qualify the figure of the independent male warrior and with it the gendered discourse of nation. For Richard, who would be "myself alone," it is to admit a dangerous dependence. As the confrontations with Anne and Elizabeth make all too clear, Richard may cast women as his enemies, but he also depends on them to secure his own legitimacy and authority as monarch. The "mother's womb" may be a source of deformity and destruction for Richard, but it is also that mysterious "nest of spicery" (4.4.424) upon which the future depends. And it is in this sense that Richard's dependence on women is analogous to contemporary concerns about the Elizabethan succession.

In acknowledging the role of women in guaranteeing royal lineage, *Richard III* registers concerns that were felt, if not always voiced, by many in England in the last decade of the century. Like Richard, Elizabethans were acutely aware of their dependence on a woman to ensure the nation's present and future prosperity. The Elizabethan succession question had long haunted the reign, but in the 1590s the situation was exacerbated by the queen's age and her continued refusal to settle the question by naming an heir. Given the instabilities of the Elizabethan succession, epitomized by the mortal, aging body of the queen herself, the repetitive figure in *Richard III* of a queen whose womb is a "bed of death" (4.1.53) offers a timely image of the Tudor state, one that clearly opposes the images of eternal youth characterizing the portraits of the queen turned out by the court during this period.[24] Rather than registering general anxieties about "monstrous" female rule, Shakespeare's ambivalent representation of women as the source of both the destruction and the preservation of patriarchal lineage may speak instead to the more particular concerns of his nation in the 1590s, concerns prompted by an aging monarch who refused, officially at least, to provide for her own succession.

For the queen's critics, misogyny offered a convenient means of voicing these concerns. And, not surprisingly, in the last years of Elizabeth's reign, opposition to her rule again took a decidedly misogynistic turn as fears about the succession combined with the longstanding opposition to female rule.[25] As we saw in the previous chapter, attacks on the female Tudor body politic typically drew on a well-established misogynistic discourse to argue that female rule is contrary to the laws of God and nature and therefore, in John Knox's words, "the subversion of good order, of all equitie and justice."[26] Of particular interest in this chapter, however, is a less familiar passage in which Knox imagines a deformed and monstrous female body politic:

> For who wolde not judge that bodie to be a monstre, where there was no head eminent above the rest, but that the eyes were in the handes, the tonge and mouth beneth in the belie, and the eares in the feet. ... And no lesse monstruous is the bodie of that common welth, where a woman beareth empire.[27]

Knox's grotesque placement of the queen's tongue and mouth in the "belie"—a term that suggests both stomach and womb—anxiously equates a woman's sexual and verbal power and connects them both with an image of gross appetite. Knox thus renders suspect the one legitimate site of a woman's power in the patriarchy—the queen's womb. Catholic opponents to Elizabeth's reign likewise invoked images of female appetite to call the queen's legitimacy into question. Writing in his *Admonition to the Nobility and People of England* (1588), Cardinal Allen, for example, impugns the queen's chastity and with it the "cuntry" itself:

> She hath abused her bodie against God's lawes, to the disgrace of princely majestie, and the whole nation's reproache, by unspeakable and incredible variety of luste. ... [S]hamfully she hath defiled her person and cuntry, and made her court as a trappe, by this damnable and detestable art to intangle in sinne, and overthrowe the yonger sorte of her nobilitye and gentlemen of the lande.[28]

As Allen would have the English believe, the queen's sexual appetite endangers the nation, and the aristocracy especially, threatening to cut off the "true" succession by leaving the state to a "bastard-borne child of her own bodie."

Like those who spoke out against the Tudor queens, Shakespeare's Richard employs a misogynistic discourse in order to define female sexuality as a threat to the legitimacy and stability of the monarchy. In the play's opening scene, for example, Richard represents the female body as powerfully erotic, capable of seducing and thereby subverting masculine authority. He complains that the once-valiant warrior has become effeminate:

> And now, in stead of mounting barbed steeds
> To fright the souls of fearful adversaries,
> He capers nimbly in a lady's chamber
> To the lascivious pleasing of a lute.
>
> (1.1.10–13)

Rather than translating his aggressive horsemanship into the bedroom, the warrior is himself seduced and dominated, made "to strut before a wanton ambling nymph" (1.1.17). The political subtext for this passage, as Richard soon makes clear, is Edward IV's amorous affairs, his ill-advised marriage to Lady Grey and his liaison with Jane Shore. Richard thus shrewdly links the king's promiscuity with the contamination of the state.

After Edward's death, Richard extends his attack on his brother's sexuality as a way of undermining the legitimacy of the princes. Richard instructs Buckingham in speaking to the populace to "urge his hateful luxury / And bestial appetite in change of lust, / Which stretch'd unto their servants, daughters, wives" (3.5.80–82). Richard would have Buckingham insinuate not only that the lustful Edward has populated England with bastards but that the heirs to the throne are bastards as well. As Buckingham later explains to the citizens, because Edward was contracted to Lady Lucy and then to Lady Bona of France, his marriage to Elizabeth Grey is invalid. Their children, as a consequence, are bastards (3.7.5–6). But Richard's most outrageous attempt to steal the succession from his nephews is to declare Edward himself a bastard, a charge that requires him to impugn the virtue of his own mother. Again, he instructs Buckingham,

> Tell them, when that my mother went with child
> Of that insatiate Edward, noble York,

> My princely father, then had wars in France,
> And by true computation of the time,
> Found that the issue was not his begot;

(3.5.86–90)

but ironically offers this delicate coda: "Yet touch this sparingly, as 'twere far off, / Because, my lord, you know my mother lives."[29] Though Richard elsewhere traces his deformity to his mother's womb, here he acts to bolster his legitimacy by linking himself directly with his father, circumventing his mother altogether. As Buckingham reports: "Withal did I infer your lineaments, / Being the right idea of your father, / Both in your form and nobleness of mind" (3.7.12–14).

Richard's strategy of presenting the royal body and the women associated with it as sexually corrupt gains a certain topicality if we recall the propaganda generated against female rule in sixteenth-century England. In impugning his mother's virtue, Richard draws upon the one anxiety inherent in a patriarchal society where political and social order depend upon the purity of the queen's body to ensure the succession. When the queen is not merely a consort but a queen regnant, as in the case of the Tudor queens, and when she, like Elizabeth, also fails to marry and produce an heir, traditional anxieties about the queen's body and the succession naturally increase, as the seditious rumors that circulated during Elizabeth's reign dramatically demonstrate. Elizabeth, to be sure, worked to allay her nation's fears, cultivating an elaborate mythology of virginity and presenting herself as a kind of divinely sanctioned virgin-mother of England.[30] Yet while the queen presented her body politic as well as her own natural body as inviolable and sacred, court records indicate that others inverted the royal images to represent the queen's body as promiscuous and corrupt. In one notorious case, the queen was accused of having had four children by Robert Dudley. As Carole Levin has documented, persistent rumors detailing the queen's promiscuity and illegitimate children continued well past the queen's child-bearing years, fueled in the last decade of her reign by renewed anxieties about her failure to name a successor.[31]

Although the charges of bastardy and corruption in the body politic raised in *Richard III* have a topical resonance, Shakespeare in large part controls the play's potential for sedition by placing these slanders in the mouth of Richard, whose unbounded designs on the throne render all his accusations suspect. The play not only fails to authorize Richard's charges, it also demonstrates their ineffectiveness in stirring up rebellion. The multiple charges of bastardy, designed to win a cry of approval from the populace for Richard's election to king, summon only silence.

Buckingham reports: "they spake not a word, / But like dumb statuës, or breathing stones, / Star'd each on other, and look'd deadly pale" (3.7.24–26). That Richard's political misogyny takes on an Elizabethan cast may even work to reinforce the legitimacy of Elizabeth's monarchy, for if we associate Richard, even minimally, with opposition to the queen, then his defeat by Richmond in act 5 becomes a triumph not only for the Tudor dynasty but, more specifically, for Elizabeth Tudor as well. Yet, while *Richard III* discredits the spokesman of its decidedly misogynistic discourse, it does not necessarily discredit the discourse itself. The degree to which the play authorizes Richard's misogyny depends only in part upon the credibility of the tyrant's voice; it also depends upon the play's representation of women. Tellingly, when the women violate their supposedly natural roles as mothers, the play's censure is most resonant.

The idealized image of the queen as a chaste and fertile mother ensuring the patrilineal succession, epitomized in the play by Queen Elizabeth's fight for her children in act 4, provides a stable political and moral ground for a critique of those who would fall short of the maternal ideal. The most outrageous violator of the ideal, of course, is Richard himself. He attempts to rise to power by seizing control of the queen's body and her issue, with the charges of bastardy, the murder of her sons, and finally with his proposal of an incestuous union with her daughter, Elizabeth of York. Wooing Elizabeth for the hand of her daughter, Richard describes his plan to perpetuate the Yorkist succession, and though he admits to having killed the princes, he assures the former queen:

> But in your daughter's womb I bury them;
> Where in that nest of spicery they will breed
> Selves of themselves, to your recomforture.
>
> (4.4.423–25)

As Judith Anderson has pointed out, Shakespeare's use of a "nest of spicery" recalls the Garden of Adonis in *The Faerie Queene* but makes an important variation on its source.[32] In Spenser, Adonis lies hidden within the Mount, "lapped in flowres and pretious spycery," enjoyed by Venus who "possesseth him, and of his sweetnesse takes her fill" (3.6.46).[33] Beneath the Mount, imprisoned "in a strong Rocky Caue," is the "wilde Bore" (3.6.48). In Shakespeare's version, the white boar would gain access to the secret place of "spicery." Grotesquely desecrating the mystery of the source, Richard perverts its myth of regeneration into a figure of death, eroticism, incest, and even rape, as he takes possession of his niece's womb. If controlled by Richard, Princess

Elizabeth's womb, from which the Tudor succession will eventually originate, promises to become a place of death and destruction rather than of birth and regeneration.

Although Richard is principally responsible for perverting generation and the maternal role in this play, there is also the sense that the women themselves are responsible. "O my accursed womb, the bed of death!" (4.1.53), the duchess of York wails when she learns that Richard is about to be crowned king of England, locating the source of her son's and the nation's evil in her own body. Queen Elizabeth likewise reacts to the "unpleasing news" (4.1.36) of the coronation by blaming herself for the fate of her children. Indeed, as she warns Dorset, urging him to flee the country, "Thy mother's name is ominous to children" (4.1.40). As we have seen, Richard also blames women for his weaknesses when he displays his deformed body to the court as proof of the evil practice of women. The play makes it clear that Richard has been deformed from birth, but though that fact may exonerate Queen Elizabeth and Jane Shore from charges of witchcraft, it may also be used to implicate his mother in his monstrosity.

Not unlike Richard, who in *3 Henry VI* attributes his deformity to his "mother's womb," the avenging Margaret in *Richard III* also traces the origin of Richard's evil to this womb:

> From forth the kennel of thy womb hath crept
> A hell-hound that doth hunt us all to death:
> That dog, that had his teeth before his eyes
> ....
> Thy womb let loose to chase us to our graves.
>
> (4.4.47–49, 54)

More recent critics than Margaret have also implicated the duchess of York in her son's evil. Coppélia Kahn writes, for example, that the play "strongly suggests the importance of the mother, rather than the father, in the formation of masculine identity—but negatively, by showing how alienation from the mother helps turn a physical monster into a moral one."[34] Taking Richard's relation to his mother as a starting point for her discussion of "fantasies of maternal origins," Janet Adelman observes that in *Richard III*, "the womb takes on a malevolent power quite divorced from the largely powerless women who might be supposed to embody it, and divorced as well from the imagined particulars of Richard's psyche."[35] But it should be emphasized that though the play's women may appear to bear some responsibility for Richard's evil, they bravely attempt to reinstitute both the moral, and patriarchal, order

Richard would overturn.

As a way of righting the monstrosity they have engendered, the women actively seek control through destruction, the only choice left them. The play's most overt display of this strange inversion of maternal power occurs when the women come together in act 4, scene 4 to lament their losses and, led by Margaret, turn their grief into vengeance. Reversing the mother's blessing she had given her son earlier in the play, the duchess of York here urges a collective curse of her homicidal son:

> ... be not tongue-tied; go with me,
> And in the breath of bitter words let's smother
> My damn'd son that thy two sweet sons smother'd.
>
> (4.4.132–34)

When Richard enters on his way to battle, he does not recognize the changed women. Having abandoned her role as mother, the duchess now redefines herself as "she that might have intercepted thee, / By strangling thee in her accursed womb" (4.4.137–38). Yet, however heroic the duchess may be in attempting to restore the moral balance overturned by Richard, the figure of a death-bringing mother remains unsettling.

Like Richard's misogynistic politics, these ambivalent images of the female body as the site of both birth and death also have a counterpart in the Elizabethan debate about the succession. Elizabeth herself had appropriated the figure of motherhood early in her reign as a means of countering demands for her to marry and thereby ensure the Tudor succession.[36] In a speech to Parliament in 1563, for example, she presented herself as England's "natural" mother, thus combining the image of maternal care with the authority that comes with lineal succession: "And so I assure you all that, though after my death you may have many stepdames, yet shall you never have a more natural mother than I mean to be unto you all."[37] But the queen's subjects, as we have seen, sometimes gave Elizabeth's representations of herself as an unmarried mother a grotesque literalness. Some, like Cardinal Allen, feared that the queen's bastards would undermine the succession; others associated an unmarried queen and the possibility of illegitimate births with fears of murdering mothers. Rumors that the queen had given birth were often combined with gruesome tales of infanticide. The accounts are lurid: two peasants in Essex in the early 1590s, for example, alleged that Leicester had burned the children alive, stuffing them up a chimney;[38] another accusation recounts how the queen gave birth to a daughter and then ordered the child to be cast into a fire and the midwife who delivered her poisoned.[39]

More official voices than these also emphasized the discrepancy between expectations and the reality of Elizabeth's role as the nation's mother. Concerned about the instability of the succession in the early 1590s, the parliamentarian Peter Wentworth warned of the destruction implicit in the queen's failure to name an heir. A draft of a bold speech Wentworth had prepared to read before Parliament in 1593 seditiously inverts Elizabethan iconography by depicting the queen as an "unnatural" mother who withholds "nourishing milk" from the nation and so would destroy it:

> O England England how great ar thy sines towardes thy mercifull god, that he hath so alienated the harte of her that he hath sett over thee to be thy nource, that she should withold nourishing milk from thee, and force thee to drinke thyne one distruction. . . . Thes ungodly and unnaturall evills they cannot thinke or judg to be in your majestie as of your self and of your owne nature, but that your majestie is drawen unto it by some wicked charming spiritt of traiterous persuasion, or that your majstie is overcome by some feminine conceipt.[40]

Wentworth was silenced, imprisoned in the Tower before he was able to present his appeal.

In its place that year, Parliament heard a speech by the queen that, like the 1563 speech, sounded the key themes of her reign. Once again, the queen attempted to turn the weakness of her sex to advantage, emphasizing her maternal care for her subjects and hinting that a male successor might not be as "careful" of their "safeties" as she has been. The solicitor general Edward Coke delivered her words:

> And so much more with humblest thanks to be acknowledged, as that He enableth the weakest sex, and makes them to admire it that ere now were wont to doubt [women's] good success. . . . And though (she saith) you may have a wiser prince—for I must use her own words—she dare avow, you shall never have one more careful of your safeties, nor to give more even stroke among her subjects, without regard of person more than matter. And of such mind she beseecheth God ever send your prince.[41]

The queen's concern in this speech, however, was less with caring for her subjects than with asserting her authority over them. In fact, in this instance, she used her own speech to check the free speech of those in Parliament, warning them not to put forth "any bill that passeth the reach of a subject's brain to mention."[42] But if the queen might check her subjects' words, she could not control their desires, and many did indeed wish for a "wiser prince."

"Smiling plenty, and fair prosperous days"

Order is restored in the play—and in the tetralogy—with the death of Richard at Bosworth field and the subsequent crowning of the victorious Richmond. The figure of the heroic warrior-king that England had mourned at the beginning of *1 Henry VI* returns to the stage, and the cycle of history closes with a remarkably tidy resolution of the messy conflicts that have spanned the tetralogy. "Divided York and Lancaster, / Divided in their dire division" (5.5.27–28) are united in the marriage of Richmond and Elizabeth, "the true succeeders of each royal house" (5.5.30). With the restoration of the "true" successor, marriage appears to replace misogyny. Almost miraculous in its powers, the dynastic union indeed promises to resolve sexual as well as civil conflict and so ensure the nation's prosperous future. In the closing speech ushering in the Tudor state, Richmond links past, present, and future to evoke the familiar cadences of providential history: promising to heal the nation's wounds with his marriage to Elizabeth of York, he prays that his heirs will "enrich the time to come with smooth-fac'd peace, / With smiling plenty, and fair prosperous days" (5.5.33–34).

Richmond's epilogue thus neatly connects the past with the present age, inviting the audience to see the reign of their own queen as fulfilling her grandfather's prayer. But on the Elizabethan stage, this invitation may have worked to increase rather than diminish the audience's awareness of the gap between past and present, between the scene before them onstage and the world outside the theater.[43] In this instance, the Elizabethan context does not actually alter Shakespeare's staging of history's patriarchal narratives, as it does in the *Henry VI* plays, but it may have influenced the audience's understanding of those narratives. Figured by Richmond's silent invocation of Elizabeth I, the present times continue to qualify, and even rewrite, the Tudor history celebrated onstage. Again, as we have seen in earlier chapters, women are central to interpreting differences between past and present. But here, it is their absence, rather than their presence, that interrogates the differences between the patriarchal myth of Tudor origins and the political realities of the 1590s.

Given the prominent role of women elsewhere in Shakespeare's early histories, their exclusion from the resolution of *Richard III* is striking. Margaret had prayed that she would live to say "'the dog is dead'" (4.4.78), but it is Richmond who takes command at the end and announces: "The day is ours, the bloody dog is dead" (5.5.2). For all Richmond's talk of marriage, on Shakespeare's stage the Tudor beginnings are represented exclusively by the figure of the triumphant male warrior.

Elizabeth of York does not appear, either in this scene or elsewhere in the play. The absence of the royal bride is in striking contrast, of course, to the close of Shakespeare's second tetralogy where the promised union between Henry V and Katherine of France is represented onstage with a kiss; and though the epilogue of *Henry V* soon undermines the optimism of the royal marriage by looking ahead to the disastrous reign of Henry VI, the concluding image of the royal couple nonetheless figures Henry's conquest of France and England's increased power. By contrast, the union between Richmond and Elizabeth at the close of *Richard III* is only announced. "We will unite the White Rose and the Red" (5.5.19), Richmond promises, his ambiguous pronoun referring either to himself and Elizabeth or, as is more likely, his new authority as king. Elizabeth of York, whose lineage gives legitimacy to the Tudor claim, appears only through the agency of Richmond's voice, which names her but once.

If Shakespeare's decision to exclude Elizabeth seems at odds with a celebration of the Tudor monarchy written for the Elizabethan stage, her presence in other dramatizations of Richard III—where she is consistently linked with Elizabeth I—only increases the dissonance. In the anonymous *True Tragedy of Richard III* (1594), considered by many to be a source for Shakespeare's play, women are essential to the conclusion. In this version, the queen mother ceremoniously hands her daughter to Richmond and then, after a review of the Tudor dynasty, concludes the play with a lengthy compliment to Elizabeth I: "Worthie Elizabeth, a mirrour in her age, by whose wise life and civill government, her country was defended from the crueltie of famine, fire and swoord, warres, fearefull messengers."[44] Thomas Legge's *Richardus Tertius* (1579), though it does not include any women in its brief conclusion, does at least, in its epilogue, pay tribute specifically to "the mighty Princess Elizabeth, a daughter worthy of [her] father, and a maiden withstanding old age, who has happily ruled in peace the united English realms for so many completed courses of Phoebus, whom may the right hand of the supreme thunderer [always] defend, and may he protect her life by shielding [her]."[45]

Hall's *The Union of the Two Noble and Illustre Famelies of Lancastre and Yorke* (1548) also makes much of the royal marriage, as the title promises. Hall opens his chronicle with a lengthy paean to the sacrament of marriage in general and to the union of Richmond and Elizabeth in particular, a divinely sanctioned union to be fulfilled, he writes, in the peaceable rule of Henry VIII:

> By reason of whiche mariage peace was thought to discende oute of heaven into England, consideryng that the lynes of Lancastre and Yorke, being both

noble families equivalent in ryches, fame and honour, were now brought into
one knot and connexed together, of whose two bodyes one heyre might
succede, which after their tyme should peaceably rule and enjoye the whole
monarchy and realme of England.[46]

Hall then introduces the story of dynastic conflict with a lengthy
rehearsal of genealogy that extends from Henry III to Henry VII. To be
sure, women receive little mention in this litany of fathers and sons, but
they do merit attention when the line passes through them in the absence
of male heirs. In Hall's recitation, the Yorkist line depends on two
women—Phillipa (daughter to Lionel, duke of Clarence, who marries
Edmund Mortimer, third earl of March) and Anne (her granddaughter,
who marries Richard, earl of Cambridge, and whose great-granddaughter
Elizabeth of York marries Richmond).[47] On the Lancastrian side is
Richmond's mother, Margaret Beaufort, great-granddaughter to John of
Gaunt from his third marriage. Richmond's claim—and that of the
Tudors—thus depends on a number of women, most immediately on
Elizabeth of York (whose claim is clearly better than his) and on his own
mother, as well as the women within the Yorkist line.

The conclusion of *Richard III*, by contrast, all but suppresses
Richmond's dependence on women, as Shakespeare stages a myth of
Tudor history that is exclusively male. What Shakespeare's audience
actually witnessed at the play's close was not the dynastic kiss signifying
the union of families but a scene of single combat between men. As
Hodgdon has observed, "No other Shakespearean play so rigorously
schematizes the claims of a royal successor, constructing its close as
though to mask their absence."[48] At the tetralogy's conclusion, heroic
combat takes precedence over genealogy in determining the monarch, a
principle of succession reinforced by the fact that Stanley plucks the
crown from Richard's "dead temples" (5.5.5) and presents it to the
victorious Richmond with the simple words: "Wear it, enjoy it, and make
much of it" (5.5.7). With the crown now on Richmond's head, the
marriage hardly seems central to his claim. Rather than signaling his
dependence on women, Richmond's announcement of marriage instead
becomes his first proclamation, a sign not of his political weakness but of
his generosity and care in healing the nation's wounds. On Shakespeare's
stage, Richmond's "right" lies principally in his triumph over Richard, a
triumph that bears all the marks of providential design.

As critics have long noted, Tudor legitimacy in this play rests in large
measure on the play's structural opposition between Richmond and
Richard.[49] Restoring "fair proportion" to the body politic deformed by
the demonic Richard, the "courageous Richmond" (5.5.3) emerges from

battle as the seemingly divinely sanctioned warrior-king who will unify the divided nation. In contrast not only to Richard but all the heroic warriors of the tetralogy, Richmond is untainted by confrontations with women. Even his negotiations with Elizabeth for her daughter's hand take place discreetly offstage. If Richmond thus avoids depending on women—and so establishes his rule outside of an economy of misogyny and marriage—he also understands the importance of relations with men. In contrast to Richard, who "hath no friends but what are friends for fear" (5.2.20), Richmond makes his entrance hailing his "fellows in arms, and my most loving friends" (5.2.1). At the same time, Richmond's nationalistic discourse effectively suppresses anxieties about patriarchy's dependence on women by reinstituting hierarchical relations between men and women: "If you do fight in safeguard of your wives, / Your wives shall welcome home the conquerors" (5.3.259–60). The tetralogy thus comes to a close by restoring patriarchal authority to the heroic male warrior and returning women to their place, off the political stage.

In locating the Tudor state in Richmond alone, *Richard III* offers what is in many ways a more accurate representation of dynastic history than either the *True Tragedy* or *Ricardus Tertius,* for the historical Richmond based his title on his victory at Bosworth, not on his marriage to Elizabeth of York or his mother's lineage.[50] But as the opening of Hall's chronicle of the War of the Roses illustrates, the marriage nonetheless became a centerpiece of Tudor iconography, rounding out the story of civil conflict with the conventional resolution of comedy. The marriage also figured prominently in Elizabeth's coronation procession through London in 1559, set forth in the tableau at Gracechurch. This elaborate display represented the Tudor dynasty as ascending from the union of Henry VII and Elizabeth of York, signified by a joining of hands and a wedding ring, "out of the which two roses sprang two branches gathered into one."[51] Accompanying verses, delivered by a child, "opened" the meaning to the queen:

> The two princes that sit, under one cloth of state,
> The man in the red rose, the woman in the white:
> Henrie the seaventh, and queene Elizabeth his mate,
> By ring of marriage, as man and wife unite.
> . . . .
> Of whome as heire to both, Henrie the eight did spring,
> In whose seate his true heire thou queene Elizabeth doost sit.
> Therefore as civill warre, and shead of bloud did cease,
> When these two houses were united into one;
> So now that jarre shall stint, and quietnesse increase,
> We trust, o noble queene, thou wilt be cause alone.[52]

In striking contrast to Shakespeare's representation of dynastic origins, the verse associates both Elizabeth of York and Elizabeth I with the peace and prosperity of Tudor rule. Accounts of the scene went even further in linking the two queens. As Holinshed reports, since Elizabeth I was "the onelie heire of Henrie the eight, which came of both the houses, as the knitting up of concord: it was devised, that like as Elizabeth was the first occasion of concord, so she another Elizabeth, might mainteine the same among hir subjects."[53] In this prominent display of civic gratitude, the city's celebration of the Tudor dynasty affirms the queen's legitimacy; in return, it invites her to fulfill the genealogy's promise of peace and prosperity.[54]

When Shakespeare replays this scene of dynastic origins some thirty-five years later, the relationship between the past and present as represented in the body of Elizabeth I had changed considerably. Hardly evocative of the continuation of the Tudor dynasty, the figure of the aging queen now registered her failure to guarantee her father's and grandfather's line. Within the altered landscape of the 1590s, Shakespeare's choice to locate the Tudor body politic exclusively in the figure of the heroic male warrior—and to exclude the two Elizabeths altogether—suggests both the fears and desires of the nation itself. Like the rumors that surfaced again and again during Elizabeth's reign that her brother Edward VI was still alive, the play's closing image of a male savior may seem to resolve fears associated with aspiring women on Shakespeare's stage, and within the Elizabethan state, by enacting a myth of dynastic origins that frees the nation from its dependence on women.[55] The idealized figure of the warrior king, whose right lies in his heroic valor and not in a lineage traced through women, sweeps away anxieties about the queen's death-bringing womb by celebrating, at long last, the kind of reassuring myth of patriarchal history that had been withheld throughout the tetralogy.

But if the play's closing image of restored patriarchy registers the desires of Elizabethans "weary of an old woman's government,"[56] all that has come before—in the play, the tetralogy, and the Elizabethan state—invites skepticism rather than acceptance of this image. Again, as in the other history plays, contemporary political contexts rewrite the past and, in the process, call into question the efficacy of patriarchal narratives. In *Richard III*, however, the Elizabethan context does not directly interfere with the events onstage. It doesn't need to. For, as Elizabethans knew, the prosperous and fertile future of the Tudor patriarchy celebrated at the close of the tetralogy had already been contested by history itself. But if the Elizabethan present undermines the authority of this scene of Tudor origins, exposing its hollowness by reminding the audience that the future does indeed depend on women, Shakespeare's staging of patriarchal history also speaks to the present, reminding the nation of women's roles—and responsibilities—in ensuring the succession and, with it, the nation's welfare.

5
Refiguring the Nation:
Mothers and Sons in *King John*

When considered alongside the plays of the first tetralogy, the England of *King John* seems unusually diverse. In this play, marginal figures, not unlike Joan of Arc or Jack Cade in the earlier plays, fight *for* rather than *against* the nation as the army's ranks expand to include Amazonian women (5.2.155), bastards, and "all th' unsettled humors of the land" (2.1.66). The king himself rides into battle accompanied by his mother, "An [Ate,] stirring him to blood and strife" (2.1.63). One effect of this expanded military is to diminish the stature of the king and so to qualify dynastic myths identifying England exclusively with the monarch. This dynastic identity is further challenged by the succession conflict itself and the play's refusal to offer a clear choice between the contending heirs. By associating a contested succession with an expanded sense of national identity, *King John* suggests that when England is not figured exclusively in the monarch, a space opens up for the nation to reimagine itself in new and sometimes radical ways.

When Shakespeare interrupted his cycle of Lancastrian history to bring *King John* to the stage in the mid-1590s, Elizabethans themselves faced an unsettled succession. But if the succession question prompted anxieties, and even a resurgence of misogyny, as we have seen in the previous chapter, it also offered the nation an occasion to reimagine itself. Many Elizabethans, for instance, looked forward to the prospect of replacing their aging queen with a youthful king, idealized as "the perfection of strength and vigour both of bodye and mynde,"[1] whereas others hoped that the succession question would be resolved with a Catholic claimant and looked to Spain for a monarch. Still others may have been pushed to even more radical thoughts, imagining a nation

different from one identified exclusively with the monarch. Indeed, as
J. W. Allen has observed, the last years of Elizabeth's reign witnessed
significant changes in political thinking as people began to speculate
"about the origin of political authority and the nature of political
obligation, about the question as to the ideally best form of government
and the question as to where sovereignty lay in England and how much
was involved in it."[2] Undoubtedly, the late Elizabethan succession
question helped to create a climate for such speculation.

The succession conflict in *King John* may have offered more than a
general parallel to the succession problems of the Elizabethan state,
however. Furnishing legal precedents for many of the issues raised by the
Tudor succession, the thirteenth-century dispute between John and his
nephew Arthur entered directly into sixteenth-century disputes, from the
reign of Henry VIII to Elizabeth I. As a result, *King John* has long
invited topical readings.[3] While acknowledging the difficulties and
dangers of local readings, I too want to speculate about parallels between
the play's succession debate and the one being played out in the nation
itself. At the same time, however, I am also interested in the relationship
between an unsettled succession and changes in the nation's discourses
of identity, particularly when those changes involve a critique of the
institution of the Crown. The conflict between John and Arthur clearly
provides one point of entry into such considerations. Shakespeare's
representations of women provide another. As in the plays of the first
tetralogy, the figures of powerful women continue to play a central role
in interpreting relations between the stage and the state, and between past
and present.

Replaying many of the themes of *Richard III*, *King John*
acknowledges the dependence of the succession on women, but it also
points a way out of the double bind of misogyny and marriage with the
figure of the mother. In the prominent roles of Elinor and Constance,
King John foregrounds the positive image of women in power only
glimpsed in the previous plays, in Margaret's heroic fight for her son's
succession in *3 Henry VI*, for example, and in Queen Elizabeth's defense
of her daughter in *Richard III*. *King John* refigures the image of the
heroic, and independent, male monarch celebrated at the close of
Richard III by reminding the audience that kings have mothers, as well
as fathers. Indeed, mothers have a role in *King John* that is
unprecedented in Shakespeare's histories and comedies: each of the three
potential heirs to the throne of Richard Coeur-de-lion—John, Arthur, and
the Bastard—appears with his mother, and in the case of John and
Arthur, the mothers themselves become fierce contenders in the struggle
for succession. But, once again, women's participation in history

generates complex political effects on the Elizabethan stage. As *King John* illustrates, when mothers replace fathers in representations of the succession, their presence tends to raise rather than resolve questions about legitimacy and authority.

Like *Richard III*, *King John* also recognizes the importance of women in ensuring dynastic security: it is upon their fidelity and fertility, after all, that the succession depends. But, as Phyllis Rackin has persuasively argued of *King John*, to acknowledge the importance of women in history also has the effect of undermining traditional structures of patriarchal power.[4] Not unlike their counterparts in the earlier history plays, the women of *King John* call attention to the limitations of traditional patriarchal institutions as they freely raise their voices to question legitimacy and the law, right and possession. In the process, I argue, these outspoken mothers decenter representations of the monarchy itself, translating the traditional figure of the heroic warrior-king into a dependent son, whose power and authority rests with his mother. In its presentation of monarchical authority, *King John* extends the critiques of the earlier history plays to alter the appearance of the monarch himself and, at the same time, to undermine the authority of patrilineal succession. This analysis of women in *King John* thus goes beyond Rackin's not only in its privileging of succession questions within and outside the play but also, and more importantly, in arguing for a more radical Shakespeare whose critique of succession politics is not resolved by the play's seemingly conservative close.

Given the importance of the Elizabethan succession to the local politics of *King John*, this chapter begins by rehearsing the succession debate as it was framed in the 1590s, paying particular attention to the ways in which arguments shifted in the wake of Mary Stuart's execution. From there, the discussion turns to the play, to the questions about inheritance and succession raised in the opening scene with the parallel disputes between John and Arthur, on the one hand, and the Faulconbridge brothers, on the other. The final section takes up the political questions raised by the play's conclusion. With the coronation of the new monarch in *King John*, women are, once again, excluded from history's stage. But rather than reading this exclusion simply as a reiteration of patriarchy, as other critics have done, this chapter argues instead that even in its conclusion, the play invites a radical questioning of traditional structures of power.

The Elizabethan Succession

Like Henry VIII's obsessive attention to the Tudor succession, Elizabeth I's silence on such matters was also notorious. The queen's strategy may have been good politics, a sign of her "woman's wisdom,"[5] William Camden would later comment, but the official policy of silence was not without its liabilities. For in refusing to name an heir, Elizabeth invited her subjects to imagine the nation's future for themselves, and as the queen herself seemed to recognize, this liberty posed a potential challenge to the Crown's authority and autonomy. The Crown, for its part, attempted to inhibit such imaginings by extending the scope of treason to include matters of succession; and in the statute of 1571 (13 Eliz. c. 1), the injunction against "imagining" the death or destruction of the monarch, which had been in place since 1352 (25 Edw. III. c. 2), was extended to include imagining the monarch's successor.[6] It was now considered treason to print or disseminate any claim for the queen's successor. The succession could only be discussed in Parliament, and then only with the queen's approval. But in spite of the suppression of public debate, discussion continued, most often and most safely in private, among friends, but sometimes more openly, with the circulation of manuscripts and tracts printed by foreign presses. As John Harington was to write in his unpublished succession tract of 1602, the issue was "so neerly concerning every one of us in his particular as no man almost can be found so symple never to have thought of it, or so subtill as to cleere all doubtes and daungers incident to the Question."[7]

In the 1590s, the question of the Elizabethan succession, which had previously haunted the reign in the figure of the Catholic Mary Stuart, now returned with particular urgency as England experienced a growing sense of vulnerability, visibly figured by the aging queen but exacerbated by renewed tensions with Spain and more frequent attempts on Elizabeth's life. With the Protestant James now the principal claimant—his Catholic mother safely out of the way—many in England, including parliamentarian Peter Wentworth, became emboldened and began to press for a settlement to the succession question once and for all. In an undelivered speech addressed to his monarch, posthumously published under the title *A Pithie Exhortation to Her Majestie for Establishing Her Successor to the Crowne* (1598), Wentworth warned of the dire effects of an unsettled succession and urged Elizabeth to summon a parliament on the matter.[8] When the queen did convene Parliament in 1593, Wentworth "took it for a sign" and launched his campaign, gathering supporters, polishing his speech, and even going so far as to draw up a bill "with blanks" to be filled in once the heirs had been determined.[9] Before the session began, however, word of the campaign got out and Wentworth ended up in the Tower, where he remained until his death in 1597.

It was in this already charged atmosphere that one of the most provocative and dangerous tracts on the Elizabethan succession was printed in Antwerp in 1594. Written by the Jesuit Robert Parsons, and published under the pseudonym R. Doleman, *A Conference About the Next Succession to the Crown of Ingland* (1594) claimed to be occasioned by the failure of the 1593 Parliament to take up the matter. Parsons ensured that his prolix tract would receive immediate attention by dedicating it to the earl of Essex—"for that no man is in more high and eminent place or dignitie at this day in our realme . . . and consequently no man like to have a greater part or sway in deciding of this great affaire"—and then arguing at length for the claim of the Spanish Infanta.[10] But what made *A Conference* especially incendiary was its attack on the principles of hereditary right based exclusively on bloodlines. Contending that succession based on "neernes of blood" was sanctioned neither by divine nor natural law, "but only by humane and positive lawes of every particuler common wealth," Parsons boldly asserted that it "may uppon just causes be altered by the same" (sig. B6).

For Elizabeth, Parson's call to alter primogeniture was inevitably complicated by the legal and political issues surrounding Henry VIII's unprecedented attempts to control the succession earlier in the century, issues that affected her own claim to power. As supporters of Mary Stuart had been quick to point out, Elizabeth's status as bastard had never been legally altered. As a result, her right to the throne rested not on blood but on an act of Parliament, passed in 1543, which provided that the Crown would pass first to Henry's male heirs and then to his daughters. Moreover, this act also gave the king "full and plenar power" to designate the succession further, either by "letters patents" or by his "last will."[11] The Crown could now be bequeathed by the monarch at his death, as if it were property. In a handwritten will, Henry did exactly that, excluding the Stuarts, who as descendants of Henry VII's elder daughter held the better title, and naming in their place the Suffolks, the descendants of the younger daughter. The right of succession based exclusively on "neernes of blood" had been altered, on paper at least, and the title to the English throne became subject to the monarch's will and the consent of Parliament. In the eventual succession of the Stuart line, history would appear to nullify these wishes. But with the legal complications of Henry's tampering with the succession not yet fully untangled in the 1590s, the publication of Parsons's tract no doubt caused a stir, particularly in its assertion that when it was in the interest of the commonwealth, the right to the throne based on "neernes of blood" might be altered.

That Parsons found precedent for his argument in the reign of King John only made matters worse for the Elizabethan government. Long associated with the Tudors, who found in his reign a useful analogue for Henry VIII's conflict with the church, John had been transformed by Protestant writers like William Tyndale, John Bale, and John Foxe from a medieval tyrant into a proto-Protestant martyr. As a result, his reign furnished useful precedents for Tudor propagandists. Indeed, as John Elliott succinctly puts it: "John became firmly identified with a set of religious-political doctrines that were at the heart of official Tudor policy: hatred of the Pope, obedience to the King, resistance to foreign intervention, and intolerance of all forms of civil dissension."[12] The example of John also proved useful to Elizabeth in her own battles with the Catholic opposition. In the wake of the Northern Rebellion in 1569 and the papal bull of excommunication in 1570, for example, the Crown pointed to John's reign in the *Homilie Against Disobedience and Wylfull Rebellion* (1571) to exemplify the dangers of disobedience and foreign intervention.[13] In the 1580s, John again appeared in anti-Catholic propaganda, this time in response to growing tensions with Spain and Mary Stuart's renewed claim to the throne.[14]

But if John's conflict with Rome figured importantly in Tudor ideology, questions about the legitimacy of his claim were at the heart of the legal issues raised by Henry VIII's will and the exclusion of the Stuart claim. Significantly, Richard's will furnished the *only* precedent for Henry's controversial act of willing the succession.[15] And it is in this connection that the reign of John became so vexing for the Elizabethans. For while John's claim depended on the will of Richard I, Arthur's claim rested on primogeniture. Henry VIII, for his part, had taken measures to ensure the authority of his will, and to preempt a Stuart claim, by gaining the approval of Parliament (and in the process established a precedent for parliamentary involvement in the succession that would end up limiting Elizabeth's prerogatives in these matters).[16] But his manipulation of the succession did not go uncontested.

For while the Tudors suppressed questions about John's right to the throne and cited Richard's will as precedent for Henry VIII's will, the Stuarts countered by calling John a usurper and raised questions about his legitimacy as a way of restoring their own claim based on nearness of blood. In addition to arguing against both the legality and the authenticity of Henry's will, the Stuart argument centered on two key points—that their claim was superior to that of the Suffolk line on the basis of primogeniture and that the common law rule against inheritance by aliens did not apply to the succession. The case of Arthur supplied precedents for both points. Arguing that John succeeded to the throne by "might and usurpation," not because Arthur was excluded on the basis of his French birth, Stuart supporters moved to eliminate the objection to alien rule that was being used against Mary.[17] In an argument typical of Stuart succession tracts, Edmund Plowden brings these two arguments together: "King John toke the kingdome upon him unjustly . . . and would never ceasse untill he had founde the meanes to distroy Arthure . . . whiche he neded not so diligently to have practised if Arthure had ben an alien and disabled to the kyngdome by Lawe."[18]

With the execution of Mary Stuart in 1587, and her Protestant son James now the principal claimant on the basis of primogeniture, the debate over the Elizabethan succession suddenly took a radical turn. Because James's claim was primarily through his mother, his Protestant supporters in England found themselves in the awkward position of having to defend the son against many of the same arguments they had marshalled against his mother only a few years before. Those who had vehemently argued against Mary's claim on the basis that she was of foreign birth, for example, now began to sound like the Catholics before them, claiming that the rule against alien inheritance did not apply to the Crown and that Scotland was not a foreign land. Since historical precedent for the alien argument rested principally with Arthur, Protestants who had once supported John's right on the basis that Arthur had been born in France now reversed their position to argue for Arthur's right on the basis of primogeniture and to question John's as authorized by Richard I's will. Writing in support of James's claim in his 1602 succession tract, Harington makes much of the wrong done to Arthur— his uncle, "John, most tirannouslie tooke both his kingdome and his life frome him, for which notable injustice he was detested of all men, both abroad and at home, and most apparantlie scourged by God with grevous and manifold plagues both upon himself and upon the realme which yealded to his usurpation"[19]—and in the process overturns the arguments long central to Tudor policy.

Catholic writers in the 1590s likewise did an about-face, embracing the arguments previously used against them by their Protestant opponents. In a particularly shameless appropriation of the radical Protestant position, Parsons invoked the 1585 Bond of Association—one of the most notorious measures the English had undertaken to ensure Mary Stuart's exclusion from the succession—as the basis for why James should be excluded from succeeding Elizabeth at her death.[20] John's reign thus took on new meaning for Catholics like Parsons who hoped to bar the Protestant James from the English succession. Appropriating a centerpiece of Protestant Tudor propaganda, Parsons boldly set forth the reign of King John, along with that of Henry IV, as precedent for his argument that the succession "may uppon just causes be altered by the same." Parsons begins by arguing that Arthur, as "sonne and heyre to Geffery (that was elder brother to John) was against the ordinarie course of succession excluded" (sig. O6v) and from there builds an unusual case for John's rule. For, as Parsons would have his readers believe, the fact that John murdered his nephew and still kept the Crown offers proof that "god did more defend this election of the common wealth, then the right title of Arthur by succession" (sig. O6v). Therefore, Parsons concludes, a monarch may rightfully be chosen for office. By the same token, he may also be removed, for if relations between the monarch and his subjects are contractual, as Parson's argues, then when one party "wickedly" breaks the contract, "the other were not bound to kepe his oth towards that party" (sig. G2v).

By the mid-1590s, then, when Shakespeare brings *King John* to the Elizabethan stage, the example of John's reign had not merely lost much of its political efficacy for the Tudors, as some studies of the play have claimed.[21] Rather, it had become a highly volatile figure for the problems surrounding the Elizabethan succession. The about-face in Catholic and Protestant positions during this period turned upside down the familiar parallels between John and Arthur and Elizabeth and Mary that had figured in the succession debate for more than a quarter of a century. More seriously, however, this radical shift threatened to compromise the very principles that governed the English succession. In the end, it seems, politics rather than principle or custom ruled. In this sense, the reversals in the succession argument after Mary Stuart's execution offer support for Parson's assertion that the succession is authorized not by divine or natural law "but only by humane and positive lawes of every particuler common wealth."

Considered within this context, Shakespeare's decision to take up the succession struggle between Arthur and John in the mid-1590s invites comparison between the play and the debate about the succession taking place outside the theater. The play, indeed, turns on many of the same issues plaguing the Tudor succession as it pits Arthur's claim based on primogeniture against John's based on a monarch's will. But, as many have noted, in contrast to Elizabethan succession tracts, or even to a "succession play" like *The Troublesome Raigne of King John*, *King John*'s position on the rights of John and Arthur is not so easy to determine: on the one hand the play appears to validate Arthur's claim, supporting primogeniture over a monarch's will and minimizing the issue of Arthur's foreign birth, but on the other it is not clear, at least not until

Arthur's death, that he and not John should be England's king. As A. R. Braunmuller has suggested, we may understand the play's ambivalent, if not contradictory, presentation as Shakespeare's politic response to the succession debate of the 1590s.[22] But if the shifting terms of the debate weakened the authority of patrilineal succession, as I want to argue, we might push this argument further, reading the play's ambiguity and "verbal obfuscation," in part, as laying the groundwork for a potentially radical rethinking of monarchy and nation.

Significantly, it is John's own mother who first raises questions about legitimacy and the succession in *King John*. Quick to defend John in public, in private she criticizes him for not handling his nephew Arthur in a politic manner. And when John attempts a defense, arguing that his claim lies in "our strong possession and our right for us" (1.1.39), she tersely corrects him:

> Your strong possession much more than your right,
> Or else it must go wrong with you and me;
> So much my conscience whispers in your ear,
> Which none but heaven, and you, and I, shall hear.
>
> (1.1.40–43)

Although neither Elinor nor her son will heed her whisper of "conscience," the passage is nonetheless important in asserting primogeniture as a moral principle in the play. It is also important in undermining expectations for the kind of nationalistic defense of John's troublesome reign typical of Shakespeare's Tudor sources.

In spite of what might seem to us to be obvious questions about John's right to the throne, the play's sources generally concur in accepting the legitimacy of his rule. John Foxe, as we might expect, presents John's claim as indisputable: saying nothing about Richard's will, Foxe focuses instead on France's exploitation of Arthur as a means of justifying an attack on England.[23] Holinshed's *Chronicles* also endorses John's claim, although the account does note that there were questions surrounding Richard's will: Richard first "named (as some suppose) his nephew Arthur . . . to be his successor" but then before he died "reformed" his will, this time leaving "unto his brother John . . . the crowne of England, and all other his lands and dominions."[24] The Holinshed account further suggests the rightness of John's claim by emphasizing Elinor's efforts on her son's behalf: the powerful queen "left no stone unturned to establish him in the throne, comparing oftentimes the difference of governement betweene a king that is a man, and a king that is but a child."[25] Although it may not have been a source for Shakespeare, the anonymous play *The*

Troublesome Raigne of King John likewise emphasizes Elinor's active support for John.[26] The play opens with the queen celebrating John's accession in a speech that directly links him with Richard in the fraternity of the royal womb:

> Yet give me leave to joy, and joy you all,
> That from this wombe hath sprung a second hope,
> A King that may in rule and vertue both
> Succeede his brother in his Emperie.[27]

Constructing a genealogy that omits Geffrey altogether, the queen in *The Troublesome Raigne* thus moves to suppress Arthur's claim even before it is made and, in the process, simplifies the dispute considerably.

Shakespeare's Elinor, by contrast, immediately puts the audience on guard as she undermines both Tudor history and her own impassioned defense of her son at the start of the play. But rather than simply subverting the orthodox Tudor defense of John's reign, Elinor's mixed signals may instead register, and even negotiate, the dangerously shifting terms of the Elizabethan succession question in the 1590s. Elinor actively supports John's rule and defends England against foreign intervention, but at the same time she acknowledges primogeniture as a moral and legal principle. Not unlike England's ruling queen, this proto-Volumnia appreciates, as her son never does, the issues at stake in the succession struggle, and the difference between principles and power. But in supporting John's claim even as she recognizes that it rests more on "possession" than "right," Shakespeare's Elinor also begins to sound a little like Parsons in his claim that succession based on "neernes of blood . . . may upon just causes be altered."

"Vulgar circumstances"

If the queen-mother's distinction between "possession" and "blood" initiates the play's critique of succession, the intervening Faulconbridge episode extends this critique to its radical end by calling into question the very blood on which the right of patrilineal succession customarily depends. Appearing in both *The Troublesome Raigne* and *King John*, the incident is largely fictitious, growing out of a passing reference in Holinshed to "Philip bastard sonne to king Richard" who "killed the vicount of Limoges, in revenge of his fathers death."[28] Because it is located outside the constraints of chronicle history, the Faulconbridge conflict allows an important perspective on the questions of inheritance and legitimacy raised in the opening scene. In both plays, the Faulconbridge dispute replays the dynastic conflict on the familial level, and in both, the debate turns on questions of primogeniture and legitimacy. *King John*, however, heightens the parallels between the two conflicts by adding the matter of a father's death-bed will that would overturn primogeniture by favoring the younger son. The play also goes beyond *The Troublesome Raigne* in its concern for the role of women in guaranteeing the legitimacy of patrilineal inheritance. In its attention to women, this scene indeed exposes the unsettling contradictions at the heart of English inheritance law and, by extension, the principles of patrilineal succession.

Staged as a trial, the Faulconbridge controversy foregrounds legal issues, taking up many of the same questions about legitimacy and inheritance raised in the opening scene but submitting them to the scrutiny of the law. Acting now as adjudicator rather than defendant, John here follows the law to the letter, with paradoxical results. For rather than ensuring justice, his ruling instead exposes the limitations of inheritance law by opening up a disturbing gap between legal principles and the truths they purport to uphold. The case begins with the entrance of the two brothers, each claiming to be the eldest son and heir of Robert Faulconbridge. As the younger son, Robert's claim rests on the authority of his father's will, which declares the elder son, Philip, a bastard and bequeaths the lands to Robert. Robert attempts to confirm the will's assertion by citing the standard legal proofs of bastardy: his father had been separated from his mother by "large lengths of seas and shores" (1.1.105) at the time of conception, a fact confirmed by Philip's birth "full fourteen weeks before the course of time" (1.1.113). After the conclusion of Robert's detailed accusation, John issues his judgment: because Philip was born after wedlock, he is legitimate and by rights must inherit his father's lands.

John's ruling succinctly addresses two legal questions that were of concern to Elizabethans—the status of wills in matters of inheritance and the proof of bastardy—questions that, as we have seen, also have a bearing on the larger succession conflicts both within and without the play. In both instances, John's ruling accords with English law. That John says nothing about the father's death-bed will may in part reflect his attempt to suppress connections between this dispute and his own quarrel with Arthur. But his neglect of the will is also in keeping with inheritance law that held, from the twelfth to the sixteenth century, that a last will could not overrule the inheritance of land based on primogeniture.[29] As the law requires, John's decision turns instead on the question of Philip's legitimacy, and here John offers a detailed explanation of the assumption behind his ruling: women and children, like livestock, are to be treated as the husband's property:

> In sooth, good friend, your father might have kept
> This calf, bred from his cow, from all the world;
> In sooth he might; then if he were my brother's,
> My brother might not claim him, nor your father,
> Being none of his, refuse him. This concludes:
> My mother's son did get your father's heir;
> Your father's heir must have your father's land.
>
> (1.1.123–29)

However disturbing John's ruling is to our own ideas of justice, his argument is commonplace and the comparison with livestock a textbook example that Elizabethans might have read for themselves in Henry Swinburne's *A Briefe Treatise of Testaments and Last Willes* (1590): "He which maried the woman, shall bee saide to bee the father of the childe, and not hee which did beget the same . . . for whose the cow is, as it is commonly said, his is the calfe also."[30] As both Swinburne and John make clear, children born within wedlock were presumed legitimate, and proving them bastards in a court of law was nearly impossible.[31]

What is troubling about John's ruling is that it accepts and even sanctions a contradiction between an heir's legal status and his biological identity. In this case, primogeniture is cynically upheld as a legal principle in inheritance even when the heir's true paternity undermines the rationale authorizing such law. The social and political implications are significant. As Rackin observes, "by admitting that the relationship between father and son is finally no more than a legal fiction, John attacks the very basis of patriarchal history."[32] A comparison with *The Troublesome Raigne* further underlines the extent to which *King John* anatomizes the legal inequities of inheritance. In *The Troublesome Raigne*, John settles the dispute not by recourse to legal arguments but by attempting to find out the truth by asking "them that know."[33] In this version, the mother answers as expected and politely lies, but when the question is put to Philip, he falls into a trance in which the truth is revealed. As if possessed by the vision, Philip volunteers to give up his "land and living" to his brother. In contrast to *King John*, there is no discrepancy here between justice and the law, but then the law is never actually put to the test since justice comes, finally, not from positive law but from divine revelation. *King John*, by contrast, follows the law to the letter with unsettling results. Furthermore, because it is John himself who articulates the law, political ironies abound. In asserting primogeniture and in disregarding a death-bed will, John clearly undermines his own claim to the throne, but in acknowledging a discrepancy between the form and substance of patrilineal descent, he also exposes the weakness of any judgment based solely on bloodlines.

In *King John*, in marked contrast to *The Troublesome Raigne*, Lady Faulconbridge does not appear onstage until after the hearing, when she arrives in haste "in riding-robes" (1.1.217), too late to prevent her son from chasing her honor "up and down" (1.1.223). As the central figure in Robert's suit, and the only one who actually knows the truth of Philip's paternity, her absence from the hearing is noticeable in *King John*, and Shakespeare's omission here seems provocatively overdetermined. In one way, her absence spares her the taint of having to lie before the court as her counterpart did in *The Troublesome Raigne*. But her absence may also be read in terms of the contradiction between the power women actually possessed to subvert patrilineal inheritance by conceiving another man's child and the place accorded them in historical and legal records. In cases involving legitimacy and inheritance, a woman could speak out in a court of law only to confirm her husband's paternity; testifying against the legitimacy of her child was strictly forbidden.[34] "Albeit the mother doo confesse that the adulterer did beget the childe, yet her sole confession dooth not hurt the childe," Swinburne writes. If the charge of bastardy acknowledges the fact that otherwise powerless women have the power to subvert the structure of patriarchal order by transforming the succession from father to son into a lie, then sixteenth-century law worked to suppress that power.[35] Similarly, John's ruling admits the subversive power of a wife's infidelity, but it simultaneously eradicates that power by treating women as chattel and pretending that one man's "calf" is the same as another's. Women's power is also both evoked and displaced by the misogynistic banter that erupts during the hearing, in John's jocular advice to young Robert on the proverbial power of wives to "play false" (1.1.118) and in Philip's playful remark that "all men's children" (1.1.63) may doubt their legitimacy.

Lady Faulconbridge does speak against her son's legitimacy but only after she learns that Philip has already "disclaim'd" his land and name. Like Elinor's whisper of "conscience," Lady Faulconbridge's testimony is spoken in private to her son and witnessed by "heaven" (1.1.256) and thus sanctioned by its confessional status. Like the earlier critique of a son's legitimacy, this mother's statement does not affect the outcome of legal or political disputes within the play, but it may have affected the way Shakespeare's audience understood these disputes. Again, the signals are mixed. On the one hand, Lady Faulconbridge affirms the power of women in matters of paternity. Her direct statement to her son—"King Richard Cordelion was thy father" (1.1.253)—boldly confirms the rupture in patrilineal descent that John's ruling would have denied. On the other hand, her testimony also works to translate that power into a more acceptable form. In direct contrast to the mother in *The Troublesome Raigne*, who admits both fault and pleasure, this mother pleads her innocence, begging her son: "lay not my transgression to my charge" (1.1.256). Presenting herself as a victim, won over by a king's "long and vehement" seduction, she depicts her "dear offense" as a kind of rape "so strongly urg'd past my defense" (1.1.258). The adulterous wife has become a passive object of male desire.

Taking the cue from his mother, the Bastard now mythologizes his own making as a royal conquest, one that sexually enacts "right" relations between England's subjects and their warrior-king:

> Needs must you lay your heart at his dispose,
> Subjected tribute to commanding love,
> Against whose fury and unmatched force
> The aweless lion could not wage the fight,
> Nor keep his princely heart from Richard's hand.
>
> (1.1.263–67)

As it glorifies the monarch's sexual power, the Bastard's heroic discourse may assuage fears about the power of women to subvert patrilineal inheritance, but in discovering the offender in the figure of the monarch, it shifts attention from domestic to dynastic disputes and thereby provokes a deeper set of anxieties about bloodlines. Adulterous wives may threaten social order, but as the Tudor subjects knew well, sexual openness on the part of the royal family threatened the security and power of the nation itself.

Although these problems never come to pass in the fictive Faulconbridge plot, the Bastard's paradoxical status powerfully displays the limitations of patrilineal succession. Based on "neernes of blood" alone, the Bastard has a better right to the throne than either Arthur or John: even John recognizes him as "perfect Richard" (1.1.90). But because his status as the king's bastard is never legally determined—John's ruling indeed leaves him as Faulconbridge's heir—he poses no threat to the competing claims of nephew and uncle. In this regard, Elinor's intervention in the dispute negotiates a resolution that is both politic and certainly more equitable than John's strict adherence to legal principle. Having recognized the "tokens" of Cordelion in the "madcap" Philip even before the two are linked by the specifics of Robert's charges, Elinor overrides

John's verdict—and the limitations of patriarchal law—by encouraging the Bastard to give up his land and become "the reputed son of Cordelion, / Lord of thy presence and no land beside" (1.1.136–37). Cashing in his land for a promotion in rank, Philip becomes a knight in service to his queen. As it moves outside the constraints of positive law and legal history, Elinor's solution resolves the legal dilemma by evoking the world of heroic romance. In this world, a king's bastard, his "living blood," poses no threat to the succession. Instead, he is embraced by the royal family and becomes their most ardent supporter.

History provided few such happy endings, to be sure, as *King John* itself suggests, for when charges of bastardy erupt within the dynastic dispute, as they do with the so-called "slanging match" between Elinor and Constance at the beginning of act 2, anxieties are not so easily alleviated. The conflict, now waged by mothers rather than sons, replays many of the arguments aired in the previous disputes. And, once again, women's voices serve to expose the limitations of patrilineal inheritance. The dispute begins with Elinor calling Arthur a "bastard" in response to Constance's attack on her "usurping son" (2.1.121). Constance's unrestrained rebuttal, not unlike Richard of Gloucester's attack on his brother Edward, illustrates the danger of raising questions about illegitimacy within the royal family. For in her desire to impugn Elinor's fidelity and John's legitimacy, Constance goes too far. She argues that her son is more legitimate than his own father and so, in effect, undermines Arthur's claim:

> My bed was ever to thy son as true
> As thine was to thy husband, and this boy
> Liker in feature to his father Geffrey
> Than thou and John in manners, being as like
> As rain to water, or devil to his dam.
> My boy a bastard? By my soul I think
> His father never was so true begot—
> It cannot be, and if thou wert his mother.

>   (2.1.124–31)

Constance's tactical error is noted at once by Elinor, who wryly points out to Arthur: "There's a good mother, boy, that blots thy father" (2.1.132).[36]

The circularity of Constance's accusation calls attention to the double edge of bastardy charges within an endogamous royal family and may have prompted some in Shakespeare's audience to recall the troublesome politics of the Henrician succession. Adultery on the part of the queen consort, after all, constituted treason against the monarch and was punishable by death. Elizabeth had herself been declared a bastard by the Succession Act of 1536 on the basis that her mother had committed both adultery and incest and had, therefore, as one of the charges against Anne Boleyn read, slandered "the issue that was begotten between the king and her."[37]

Perhaps more to the point in the mid-1590s, however, was the way in which questions about legitimacy played into the hands of those like Parsons who wanted to argue against a succession based exclusively on "neernes of blood."[38] *A Conference* begins, for example, with one lawyer declaring that determining the English succession should not be a problem because "it was an easy matter to discerne, who was next in discent of blood, and who not" (sig. B2). "Not so easy," the other responds, citing the "vulgar circumstances" that must be considered in discerning the best title: "The right of the first stock, whereof ech part doth spring, the disabling of the same stock afterwards by attainders or otherwise: the bastardies or other particular impediments that may have fallen uppon ech discent or branch therof" (sig. B2). On the basis of these and other objections, Parsons then concludes that succession should not be determined solely on "neernes by blood," that "bare propinquity or ancetrie of blood may justly be rejected, and he that is second, third, fourth, fifth or last, may lawfully be preferred before the first, and this by al law both divine and humane, and by al reason, conscience, and custome of al nations, christian" (sig. B4). Although *A Conference* thus accepts the institution of the Crown and the general principle of succession based on bloodlines, it rejects primogeniture as the determining condition.

In *King John*, women rather than lawyers initiate the critique of patrilineal succession, but they too raise questions about legitimacy. By their presence alone, these women remind the audience of what patriarchal history would deny—that bloodlines depend on mothers as well as fathers and that patrilineal inheritance may therefore be undermined by an unfaithful wife. Like Parsons, the play's women also speak out against the authority of the law. As Constance explains to the papal legate after he invokes the law against her: "Law cannot give my child his kingdom here, / For he that holds his kingdom holds the law" (3.1.187–88). Here, as elsewhere in the play, the laws governing succession and inheritance do not ensure justice. Indeed, as both Constance and Parsons would argue, positive law, in distinction from natural law, is not based on absolute authority. And, as the Faulconbridge case dramatically illustrates, man's law allows bastards to become heirs.

In contrast to Parson's tract, however, *King John*'s critique of the principles of patrilineal inheritance and royal succession does not direct the audience to a clear solution. Most problematic is the absence of any locus of authority in *King John*: not the law, the Crown, or the church offers a place from which to judge. Neither does the play endorse the authority of the populace, as witnessed by the failed attempt to "elect" a monarch before the gates of Angiers: "Both are alike, and both alike we like" (2.1.331), Hubert explains, speaking for the people. In *King John*, the process of election demeans all the participants: the kings become mere actors, flouted by the "scroyles of Angiers" who, as the Bastard describes them, "stand securely on their battlements / As in a theatre, whence they gape and point / At your industrious scenes and acts of death" (2.1.374–76).[39] Even the traditional resolution of political marriage—so successful at the conclusion of *Henry V*—unravels here before the festivities are over.

"If England to itself do rest but true"

In the end, *King John* does offer a conclusion to the questions of legitimacy and inheritance, one that promises a return to a nation figured in the monarch with the succession of John's son, Henry III. Once both John and Arthur are dead, Prince Henry is by all rights the true successor to Richard Coeur-de-Lion, and as a child and a newcomer to history's stage, Henry bears none of the responsibility for Arthur's death, and none of the guilt. As in *Richard III*, the restoration of "the lineal state" (5.7.102) in this play is also marked by the absence of women. Constance and Elinor have died, and the dismembered Blanch is reconstituted only in her husband's speech, objectified as the "marriage-bed" (5.2.93) whose "honor" now authorizes France's incursion into England. Patrilineal succession has been restored, "the lords are all come back," and the Bastard, John's most obedient subject, closes the play with a patriotic appeal to national unity: "Nought shall make us rue, / If England to itself do rest but true" (5.7.117–18). Once again, the nation's strength is cast in martial terms, but here the ranks appear to close around its "princes" (5.7.115).

While this closing of ranks has prompted much discussion over the years, critics have only recently begun to consider the politics of excluding women from the play's conclusion. Rackin, for example, suggests that the exclusion is prerequisite to the restoration of patriarchy, "that before this reconstruction can take place, the women's voices must be stilled."[40] Similarly, Janet Adelman argues that Shakespeare "kills" the outspoken mothers "in order to recuperate masculinity at the end of the play." "Mothers and sons cannot coexist in his psychic and dramatic world," she writes, "and his solution is to split his world in two, isolating its elements . . . from each other and from the maternal body that would be toxic to both."[41] The play does indeed separate mothers from sons before moving to the restoration of patrilineal succession, and the play's one "true" successor is the only heir in the play who appears without a mother. But does *King John* necessarily encourage us to regard the closing scene of the nation-without-mothers as the ideal, or even normative, state?

We might also see the women's absence as a loss, a loss that is most poignantly evoked by the play's closing figure of the male monarch as a boy of tears: "I have a kind soul that would give thanks, / And knows not how to do it but with tears" (5.7.108–9), the prince confesses to his subjects at the end of the play. The absence of women from the closing scene might function, as their presence does earlier in the play, to call attention to the limitations of a patrilineal succession that would suppress the role of women in determining the nation's heirs. In its closing moments, one could argue, *King John* does more than simply reiterate the patriarchal myth of succession inscribed in chronicle history. Instead, it registers the nation's dependence on women even as it stages a scene in which the Crown passes from father to son.

As Braunmuller has noted, Shakespeare's emphasis on mothers and sons in this play is unusual within the context of the history plays and offers a striking contrast to the dominant pattern of the *Henriad,* in which the son must work out his identity and legitimacy in relation to his royal father.[42] There is, to be sure, much talk of fathers and sons in *King John,* as heirs struggle to assert their legitimacy in relation to fathers. King Philip, for example, notes Arthur's resemblance to his father as a way of pushing the boy's claim—"These eyes, these brows, were moulded out of his; / This little abstract doth contain that large / Which died in Geffrey" (2.1.100–102). The Bastard is said to have "a trick of Cordelion's face" (1.1.85), his "large composition" (88), and "the very spirit of Plantagenet" (167). But in contrast to the plays of the *Henriad,* in *King John* the fathers are all dead, and patrilineal inheritance is complicated by the presence of dominating mothers. The haunting figure of young Arthur—who claims the throne through his father but whose "powerless hand" (2.1.15) now depends on his mother—exemplifies the importance of the son's relation to the mother in *King John.* The pattern is also repeated with John himself. During the first three acts, neither John nor Arthur appears onstage without his mother. Even the French king, whose repeated appearances with his son would seem to offer a counterexample to the English royal family, in the end submits to a mother's authority, breaking his manly oath to England when the church breathes "a mother's curse, on her revolting son" (3.1.257).

Central to the questions of succession and authority, the presence of mothers in *King John* is richly ambivalent, for these dominating women are at once a political asset and a liability to their sons. Both Arthur and John depend upon the political support of their mothers, and once they become separated from them at the end of act 3, their fortunes fall dramatically. But the dominating presence of women onstage for the first half of the play is also, as Juliet Dusinberre has argued, "a cause of extreme embarrassment to the men on stage."[43] Elinor's intervention in national affairs may help to bolster John's power, for example, but in the process it points up the failure of his authority. Similar contradictions appear in Arthur's relation to Constance: although dependent on his mother's success in wooing France, Arthur, like John, also reveals his discomfort over his mother's aggressive support—"Good my mother, peace" (2.1.163)—in words that curiously echo John's "Silence, good mother" (1.1.6) at the start of the play. But in *King John*, in contrast to the plays of the first tetralogy, it is the French, and not the English, who interpret dependence on women solely as a sign of weakness and a perversion of masculine authority. Describing "the Mother Queen" as "An [Ate,] stirring him to blood and strife" (2.1.63), the ambassador Chatillion adopts the kind of gendered nationalistic discourse voiced by the English against the French in the *Henry VI* plays. Elinor herself recalls the strong women of the earlier plays: like Joan of Arc and Margaret of Anjou, she too becomes a "soldier" (1.1.150), leading her nation in war, and like them she may even have appeared onstage in armor.

King John's attention to the son's dependence on his mother clearly anticipates later plays like *Hamlet* and *Coriolanus*, but it also suggests a counterpart in the family politics being played out within the Elizabethan state. Like the heirs in *King John*, James VI was in the unusual position of having to establish his identity and legitimacy in relation to dominant mothers. James's right to the English throne literally depended upon his mother—it was through her line that he traced his claim—and as the succession debate in the 1590s persuasively documents, in the nation, as in the play, dependence on the mother may be a political necessity but it is also something of a liability. In addition to the legal liability posed by his relation to Mary, James's situation, like that of the heirs in *King John*, underscored the difficulties of legitimating male authority within the presence of a powerful mother. For when mothers replace fathers in representations of succession, the substitution tends to complicate questions of legitimacy and authority with fears of female dominance and

male dependence. This is dramatically illustrated by the 1583 double
portrait of James and Mary Stuart. What is most striking about this
portrait, as Jonathan Goldberg has observed, is the likeness between
mother and son: James's face is, in fact, an exact copy of Mary's, and "as
mirror of his mother, the king [is] in an essential position of dependence
and obligation."[44]

James's situation was further complicated by his dependence on
Elizabeth. James was, as Harington wrote, "by birth her kinsman, by
adoption as it were her sonne, and indeed her godsonne, and by age
might be her grandsonne."[45] The king, for his part, played the dutiful son
when occasion called for it, referring to Elizabeth as "mother" and
"sister" and himself as her "most loving and devoted brother and son."[46]
Elizabeth, by contrast, usually referred to herself as "sister," but she
readily stepped into the mother's part when it would serve her interests.
After the discovery of a Spanish conspiracy in Scotland in 1593, for
example, Elizabeth adopted the role of devoted mother in order to
upbraid James as an ungrateful son. In the process, she shrewdly asserted
her authority over the king by reducing him to a dependent child:

> You know, my dear Brother, that, *since you first breathed, I regarded always
> to conserve it as my womb it had been you bear.* Yea, I withstood the hands
> and helps of a mighty King to make you safe, even gained by the blood of
> many my dear subjects' lives. I made myself the bulwark betwixt you and
> your harms when many a wile was invented to steal you from your land, and
> making other possess your soil. When your best holds were in my hands, did
> I retain them? Nay, I both conserved them and rendered them to you.[47]
> (emphasis added)

It was upon this mother's will that James's succession ultimately rested,
and Elizabeth's refusal to settle the succession was designed in part to
keep James in a position of continued dependence: like a child he was to
be rewarded or denied the English throne, depending on his behavior.[48]

But however much the son may chafe against his dependence, the
death of the mother is accompanied by an unsettling ambivalence. As
Steven Mullaney has recently observed of the Elizabethans faced with
the prospect of their queen's death, the mother's death dramatically
focuses the contradictions of the son's relation to his mother, offering
him the possibility for independence while simultaneously reminding
him of his loss, and his dependence.[49] Much of the ambivalence in *King
John* is generated by the messenger's brief report of the deaths of Elinor
and Constance in act 4, a report that unhistorically compresses the time
between their deaths from three years to three days. In one way, of

course, this odd report efficiently, and rather coldly, marks the "containment" of powerful women that precedes the restoration of patrilineal succession at the close. But while the play teases its audience with a misogynistic dismissal of powerful mothers—Shakespeare kills them off "with an abruptness that borders on the ludicrous,"[50] Adelman remarks—it simultaneously evokes the enormity of their loss, both for their sons and for England. Rather than diminishing the importance of these women, the messenger's brief report—particularly as it is punctuated by John's halting response, "What? mother dead?" (4.2.127)—might be seen as intensifying the psychological and political import of their deaths. The loss of these mothers turns out to be catastrophic not only for young Arthur and John but for England as well: the act closes with Arthur's limp body being carried off the stage only to be followed by the scene of John yielding up the English crown to the pope.

After the deaths of Elinor and Constance in act 4, the maternal figure reappears, but in a more traditional and passive role associated with the land and, therefore, with England itself. The weeping Salisbury, for example, underscores the unnaturalness of his rebellion by representing the subject's duty to country in familial terms:

> And is't not pity, O my grieved friends,
> That we, the sons and children of this isle,
> [Were] born to see so sad an hour as this,
> Wherein we step after a stranger, march
> Upon her gentle bosom, and fill up
> Her enemies' ranks—I must withdraw and weep
> Upon the spot of this enforced cause—
>
> (5.2.24–30)

The Bastard also evokes the son's complex relation to his mother when he castigates the rebellious barons: "You bloody Neroes, ripping up the womb / Of your dear mother England, blush for shame" (5.2.152–53). To betray the state is to violate one's mother and, the Bastard's comparison suggests, to engage in a kind of incestuous self-destruction.

Given the importance of "right" relations between mothers and sons to the strength of the nation-state, what should we make of the play's conclusion where an England "true" to itself is represented exclusively in terms of bonds between men, as the Bastard and Salisbury kneel before their prince in "true subjection"? In this context, the figure of a weeping prince, grieving for the death of his father, might anticipate the family relations of the *Henriad*, where the scene of the son mourning the death of his father is prelude to his taking his father's place on the throne. And we might compare Prince Henry's weeping here with Hal's tears over what he believes is his father's death in *2 Henry IV*:

> Thy due from me
> Is tears and heavy sorrows of the blood,
> Which nature, love, and filial tenderness
> Shall, O dear father, pay thee plenteously.
> My due from thee is this imperial crown,
> Which as immediate from thy place and blood,
> Derives itself to me. [*Puts on the crown.*]
>
>   (4.5.37–43)

As this passage illustrates, for Hal, the son's mourning for the father is part of the bargain of patrilineal succession: if the son gives his father his due, displaying grief and "filial tenderness" at his death, then the father must give the son his due, paying him back with the "imperial crown." By contrast, the weeping prince in *King John* is unable to translate his grief into power, a failure underscored by its contrast with the parallel scene in *The Troublesome Raigne* where a tearful Henry quickly resolves his grief with an act of violence, ordering the Bastard to pull the stones of Swinsted Abbey down "about the Friers eares: / For they have kilde my Father and my King."[51] *The Troublesome Raigne*'s young monarch then proves his, and England's, strength by facing down the French dauphin in open confrontation.

King John, by contrast, locates masculine strength in the figure of the Bastard, in the fictive rather than the historical plot. In *King John*, it is the Bastard, and not the crown prince, who voices the heroic cry for "revenge" (5.7.71) that will rally the English "to push destruction and perpetual shame / Out of the weak door of our fainting land" (5.7.77–78). That it is the Bastard, and not Henry, who closes the play suggests a radical refiguring of England embodied in the illegitimate son whose mixed blood brings kings together with commoners in communal service to the nation-state.[52] Indeed, the heroic figure of the Bastard would seem to rewrite the orthodox discourse of nation figured in the aristocratic male warrior, and so clearly illustrated by Thomas Nashe in his description of "brave *Talbot*" in the English history play. But yet the play hesitates in actually voicing these sentiments, in contrast to *The Troublesome Raigne*, where the Bastard closes the play with a vision of national strength that depends upon a merging of all peoples into one: "If *Englands* Peeres and people joyne in one, / Nor Pope, nor *Fraunce*, nor *Spaine* can doo them wrong."[53]

As the Arden editor tells us, the Bastard's call for unity at the close of *King John* resonates with watch words popularized by the Armada pamphleteers, and we may wonder whether such brave words weren't starting to sound a little hollow as England again found Spain on her borders in the mid-1590s.[54] As David Kastan has argued, if we compare the Bastard's heroic rhetoric at the play's close with his inflated descriptions of John only a few scenes earlier, "the vision of England 'true' to itself is no less a fiction than his vision of England's dauntless king."[55] The comparison with *The Troublesome Raigne* only reinforces the hollowness of *King John*'s staging of the patriarchal nation-state at its close. In place of England's clear victory over France, figured in *The Troublesome Raigne* by the direct confrontation between Henry and Lewis, *King John* offers yet another deal brokered by the Cardinal Pandulph, one that seems as tenuous as those that have come before. And where *The Troublesome Raigne* closes by celebrating Henry's coronation, *King John* offers its audience a weeping prince, a figure that recalls the powerless and tearful Arthur earlier in the play. Evoking the nation's desire for a mother even as it voices a nostalgic yearning for a patriotic and patriarchal past, *King John* may also register both the anxieties and the possibilities prompted by the unsettled Elizabethan succession.

Epilogue

The nation, Benedict Anderson writes, is "an imagined political community." It is imagined "because the members of even the smallest nation will never know most of their fellow-members, meet them, or even hear of them, yet in the minds of each lives the image of their communion."[1] As recent discussions of national identity in early modern England emphasize, this "imagined community" was shaped in part by the dominant institutions of the Crown and church, but also by a host of other influences—chronicles, travel writing, legal discourse, literature, drama—all of which were related to but not identical with the interests of the monarch.[2] Strictly speaking, Tudor England was dynastic rather than national. Indeed, as Anderson defines it, the concept of "nation" emerges out of, and even against, the religious and dynastic structures that dominated Europe in the years before the Enlightenment. It was only when these "cultural systems" began to lose their power, Anderson argues, that it became possible to imagine "the nation." But as sixteenth- and seventeenth-century English history amply documents, spaces did open up in these "cultural systems," making it possible for the English to begin to think about their community in new ways.

While the reigns of the Tudor queens did not overturn patriarchal structures of dynastic power, they nonetheless undermined the authority of these structures, at least temporarily, by requiring England to refigure orthodox representations of the nation-state as a powerful male monarch. Working within the new genre of the national history play at the start of his career, Shakespeare may have drawn on these weaknesses to raise questions about monarchical authority and national identity. One of the central questions the early history plays ask is, How does the nation-state redefine itself in the absence of a strong, patriarchal monarch? If these plays can be said to answer that question, the response is in some ways radical, but it is also characterized by skepticism and caution. The plays move toward including women in the political community, for example, but they are certainly not proto-feminist in their sentiments. *Richard III* and *King John* both recognize, and even celebrate, the importance of women in ensuring the succession but, at the same time, limit women's participation in politics to their role as mothers. Similarly, the *Henry VI* plays, and *2 Henry VI* especially, endorse the importance of commonwealth but stop short of endorsing a radical expansion of nation, one that includes, say, "all th' unsettled humors of the land" (*King John*, 2.1.66). But however conditional, and tentative, these answers may appear, they do not offer support for reading Shakespeare's history plays as orthodox texts "concerned above all with the consolidation and maintenance of royal power,"[3] as Richard Helgerson has argued.

The image of the patriarchal monarch, and a unified Crown, exists in these plays as a kind of ghostly ideal. When it actually materializes onstage—with the accessions of Henry VII and Henry III—the image does not stand without qualification or without question. Shakespeare's early histories, as this book has argued, are concerned less with propagandizing a particular image of authority than with examining the processes by which these images are constructed. The plays offer a sustained critique of the politics of state power and national identity, one that calls for a skepticism about representations of authority, both past and present. Refusing to close on a single locus of authority in the *Henry VI* plays, Shakespeare requires his audiences to reconsider the legitimacy of traditional figures of state power even as he offers *them* power in adjudicating the contentions displayed before them onstage. And throughout, as we have seen, women are key to the political resonance of this critique on the Elizabethan stage.

If the early histories widen the political community by acknowledging the importance of women in conferring power and legitimacy and, at the same time, decentering the image of the powerful male monarch, the second tetralogy would seem to narrow that community by celebrating a nation-state in which legitimacy and stability depend on the exclusion of women. No longer participating in the masculine domains of court and battlefield, women all but disappear in these plays. Those who remain inhabit either enclosed, and controlled, spaces—gardens or domestic interiors shut off from the court and its politics—or the marginal terrain of borders and foreign lands. It may be tempting to conclude, as Leah Marcus does, that Shakespeare's history plays, when seen in order of their composition, offered audiences in the 1590s "a gradual conquest over deviant female rule," replacing the "monstrous regiment of women" with the strong Lancastrian monarchs of the *Henriad*.[4] But the "grand narrative" of these plays offers other possibilities as well. If we understand the first tetralogy as critiquing, as well as enacting, patriarchal

fictions of power, then the marginalization of women in the second
tetralogy gains a complex resonance. We might understand the staging of
power in the *Henriad*, then, much as we did the conclusion of *Richard III*
and *King John*, as registering a skepticism not only toward representations of ruling women but also to the figure of the independent male
monarch who would, as Shakespeare would later put it, be "author of
himself" (*Coriolanus*, 5.3.36).

To be sure, the England of the second tetralogy is, in many ways, as
the revered Lancastrian patriarch imagines it, a "throne of kings"
(*Richard II*, 2.1.40), a dynastic realm rather than a national community
that includes women. As John of Gaunt mythologizes the land, patrilineal
succession owes nothing to women; generation itself, in fact, takes place
outside the woman's body as "this earth, this realm, this England"
becomes a "teeming womb of royal kings" (2.1.50–51). True to Gaunt's
vision, the Lancastrian monarchs would define their own identity, and the
nation's, exclusively in terms of relations between men: in a vertical
succession, in which Hal discovers his own identity by becoming his
father, and in a horizontal comradeship figured in Hal's relations with
Falstaff and his tavern mates in *2* and *3 Henry IV* and in his relation to
his troops in his heroic paean to English fraternity before Agincourt in
Henry V:

> We few, we happy few, we band of brothers;
> For he to-day that sheds his blood with me
> Shall be my brother; be he ne'er so vile,
> This day shall gentle his condition.

> (4.3.60–63)

But if Shakespeare's insistence on representing the Lancastrian
monarchs in relation to other men avoids the unsettling politics of the
gendered conflicts of the first tetralogy, questions of authority and
legitimacy have not disappeared. Located most immediately in the
Lancastrian usurpation of the Crown in *Richard II*, but reaching back to
the death of Woodstock, these questions provide the cause and motive for
the cycle of conflict and violence played out between men in the
Henriad. When women do appear in these plays, their presence is once
again ambiguous and disruptive. While there are few mothers in these
plays, fears about dependence on women continue to surface in relation
to genealogy and patrilineal rights, first in *1 Henry IV* with "the foolish
Mortimer" whose claim to the throne is doubly circumscribed—both
enabled and prevented—by his relations to women. Disruption comes
again at the start of *Henry V* with the strangely mediated rehearsal of

Henry's claim to France, a claim that depends on a number of women. And though Henry's martial discourse of fraternity would seem to erase the women who underwrite his aggression against France, confusing questions about legitimacy and right remain.[5]

But if these examples offer versions, in small, of the complex politics of gender set forth in the first tetralogy, the women of the Boar's Head Tavern open up new possibilities for thinking about gender and the nation.[6] In many ways, of course, these women simply replay the double bind of male dependency on a lower level. A source of desire, their wombs too are a "bed of death." "We catch of you, Doll, we catch of you" (2.4.44–46), as Falstaff puts it in *2 Henry IV*. But while these women are duly punished for profiting from male desire—Quickly and Doll are apprehended at the close of *2 Henry IV* for beating a man to death, and in *Henry V*, we hear that Doll died "i' th' spittle" from venereal disease—their presence in the plays blurs the demarcation between past and present, history and comedy. As the clearly defined borders of history's stage begin to open out onto the London streets and taverns, the plays offer a glimpse of a public sphere that touches on the world outside the stage of England's dynastic history, the world of the early modern nation-state whose identity was already being redefined in an urban and commercial space that included the theater itself. This image of a more inclusive nation-state is hardly idealized, to be sure, and its fleeting presence in these plays does not constitute an alternative to the dynastic realm of the earlier plays. But it nonetheless works to qualify the image of patriarchal order closing out Shakespeare's two cycles of English history.

With the betrothal of Henry V and Katherine of France celebrated at the close of *Henry V*, and at the close of the sixteenth century, Shakespeare offers what at last appears to be an unapologetic scene of patriarchal triumph: Katherine of France stands before the heroic Henry barely able to protest, a possession to be colonized by the victor. But if the instabilities of gender playing across the history plays contest the authority of this closing scene of dynastic conquest, so does history itself. Reminding the audience of the *Henry VI* plays, "which oft our stage hath shown," the Epilogue to *Henry V* undermines this celebration of male triumph by taking the audience back full circle to the reign of Henry VI, "Whose state so many had the managing, / That they lost France, and made his England bleed" (Epilogue 11–12). At the same time, the Epilogue takes its Elizabethan audience out of the past, and the theater, inviting them to regard "our bending author" at work, "in little room confining mighty men, / Mangling by starts the full course of their glory" (3–4), an image that, if only for a moment, replaces the figure of the

imperial monarch with that of a common playwright as the one who
speaks the nation.

Notes

Introduction

1. All quotations from Shakespeare's plays follow *The Riverside Shakespeare*, ed. G. Blakemore Evans (Boston: Houghton Mifflin, 1974); the reference to Elizabeth is complicated, of course, by its subordinate position within the Chorus's praise of Essex, "the general of our gracious Empress" (5.Chorus.30).

2. Katherine Eggert, "Nostalgia and the Not Yet Late Queen: Refusing Female Rule in *Henry V*," *ELH* 61 (1994): 528; see also Alan Sinfield, written with Jonathan Dollimore, "History and Ideology, Masculinity and Miscegenation: The Instance of *Henry V*," in *Faultlines: Cultural Materialism and the Politics of Dissident Reading* (Berkeley: University of California Press, 1992).

3. Joan W. Scott, "Gender: A Useful Category of Historical Analysis," in *Coming to Terms: Feminism, Theory, Politics*, ed. Elizabeth Weed (London: Routledge, 1989), 94.

4. Graham Holderness, *Shakespeare's History* (New York: St. Martin's, 1985), 25.

5. Louis Adrian Montrose, "'Shaping Fantasies': Figurations of Gender and Power in Elizabethan Culture," *Representations* 1 (1983): 77.

6. Montrose, "The Elizabethan Subject and the Spenserian Text," in *Literary Theory/Renaissance Texts*, ed. Patricia Parker and David Quint (Baltimore: Johns Hopkins University Press, 1986), 310.

7. I take this phrase from Walter Cohen, *Drama of a Nation: Public Theater in Renaissance England and Spain* (Ithaca: Cornell University Press, 1985).

8. Exceptions include David M. Bevington, "The Domineering Female in *1 Henry VI*," *Shakespeare Studies* 2 (1966): 51–58; Madonne M. Miner, "'Neither mother, wife, nor England's queen': The Roles of Women in *Richard III*," in *The Woman's Part: Feminist Criticism of Shakespeare*, ed. Carolyn Ruth Swift Lenz, Gayle Greene, and Carol Thomas Neely (Urbana: University of Illinois Press, 1980); Irene G. Dash, *Wooing, Wedding and Power: Women in Shakespeare's Plays* (New York: Columbia University Press, 1981); Marilyn L. Williamson, "'When Men Are Rul'd by Women': Shakespeare's First Tetralogy," *Shakespeare Studies* 19 (1987): 41–59; Gabriele Bernhard Jackson, "Topical Ideology: Witches, Amazons, and Shakespeare's Joan of Arc," *English Literary Renaissance* 18 (1988): 40–65; Leah S. Marcus, *Puzzling Shakespeare: Local Reading and Its Discontents* (Berkeley: University of California Press, 1988); Phyllis Rackin, *Stages of History: Shakespeare's English Chronicles* (Ithaca: Cornell University Press, 1990); Barbara Hodgdon, *The End Crowns All: Closure and Contradiction in Shakespeare's History* (Princeton: Princeton University Press,

1991); and Theodora A. Jankowski, *Women in Power in the Early Modern Drama* (Urbana: University of Illinois Press, 1992).

9. For arguments of multiple authorship, see Edmond Malone, "A Dissertation on the Three Parts of *Henry VI*," in *The Plays and Poems of William Shakespeare*, ed. James Boswell (1821; reprint, New York: AMS, 1966), 18:557–97; and Dover Wilson, ed., *The First Part of "King Henry VI"* (Cambridge: Cambridge University Press, 1952). For a review of authorship questions, see David V. Erdman and Ephim G. Fogel, *Evidence for Authorship: Essays on Problems of Attribution* (Ithaca: Cornell University Press, 1966), 438–50.

10. Bevington, "Domineering Female," 51.

11. David Scott Kastan, "Shakespeare and 'The Way of Womenkind,'" *Daedalus* 111 (1982): 116.

12. See, for example, Bevington, "Domineering Female."

13. Marcus, *Puzzling Shakespeare*, 53.

14. Rackin, *Stages of History*, 197.

15. In *End Crowns All*, Hodgdon offers what is perhaps the most nuanced negotiation of this binary, for though, like Rackin, she tends to come down on the side of "containment," her readings also attend to contestation and disruption.

16. In defining the shape of Elizabethan contexts on the plays' dramatic structures, my analysis of the early histories concurs with Eric S. Mallin's recent work on late Elizabethan plays like *Hamlet* and *Twelfth Night* in *Inscribing the Time: Shakespeare and the End of Elizabethan England* (Berkeley: University of California Press, 1995). Taking topicality "not only as referent but as literary *structure*," Mallin contends that "the contemporary history materially shapes and misshapes the drama" (2). To make this argument for the history play, however, is to generate a complex dynamic of textual and political play in which Elizabethan contexts write and rewrite Tudor sources, which are themselves constituted by the contextual writing and rewriting of their own sources. See also Hodgdon, who examines scenes of closure in these plays within multiple historical contexts, past and present. Although Hodgdon privileges the figure of the monarch as a "single constant" within the interplay of text and context, in seeing Shakespeare's histories as places of confrontation and conflict, where "multiple, contradictory positions can interact" (*End Crowns All*, 12), her work corroborates an assumption central to my own thinking about these plays.

17. Rackin, *Stages of History*, 142.

18. See E. M. W. Tillyard, *Shakespeare's History Plays* (London: Chatto and Windus, 1944); and Lily B. Campbell, *Shakespeare's "Histories": Mirrors of Elizabethan Policy* (San Marino: Huntington Library, 1947). For more recent discussions of humanist historiography, see F. J. Levy, *Tudor Historical Thought* (San Marino: Huntington Library, 1967), 33–78; and Rackin, *Stages of History*, 1–39.

19. *The Works of Thomas Nashe*, ed. Ronald B. McKerrow (Oxford: Basil Blackwell, 1958), 1:212.

20. Cited in Peter Ure, ed., *King Richard II* (1956; reprint, London: Methuen, 1987), lix.

21. Holderness, *Shakespeare's History*. For a more recent discussion of Shakespeare as historiographer, see Paola Pugliatti, *Shakespeare the Historian* (New York: St. Martin's, 1996).

22. Richard Helgerson, *Forms of Nationhood: The Elizabethan Writing of England* (Chicago: University of Chicago Press, 1992), 11. For a discussion of the popularity of chronicles in the sixteenth century, see D. R. Woolf, "Genre into Artifact: the Decline of

the English Chronicle in the Sixteenth Century," *Sixteenth Century Journal* 19 (1988): 321–54.

23. Rackin, *Stages of History*, 147.

24. John Stow, *The Chronicles of England* (London: Ralphe Newberie, 1580), sig. iiii.

25. Annabel Patterson, *Reading Holinshed's "Chronicles"* (Chicago: University of Chicago Press, 1994), 7–8. Although Patterson's observations may not hold true for all sixteenth-century chronicles, her attention to the multivocal nature of these texts offers an important corrective to the tendency to read them primarily as a form of Tudor propaganda.

26. See, for example, articles by Montrose, especially "Elizabethan Subject," and Susan Frye, *Elizabeth I: The Competition for Representation* (Oxford: Oxford University Press, 1993). Other important discussions of Elizabethan strategies of power include Allison Heisch, "Queen Elizabeth I: Parliamentary Rhetoric and the Exercise of Power," *Signs* 1 (1975): 31–55, and "Queen Elizabeth I and the Persistence of Patriarchy," *Feminist Review* 4 (1980): 45–56; Marie Axton, *The Queen's Two Bodies: Drama and the Elizabethan Succession* (London: Royal Historical Society, 1977); Leah S. Marcus, "Shakespeare's Comic Heroines, Elizabeth I, and the Political Uses of Androgyny," in *Women in the Middle Ages and the Renaissance: Literary and Historical Perspectives*, ed. Mary Beth Rose (Syracuse: Syracuse University Press, 1986); Constance Jordan, "Representing Political Androgyny: More on the Siena Portrait of Queen Elizabeth I," in *The Renaissance Englishwoman in Print: Counterbalancing the Canon*, ed. Anne M. Haselkorn and Betty S. Travitsky (Amherst: University of Massachusetts Press, 1990); and Carole Levin, *"The Heart and Stomach of a King": Elizabeth I and the Politics of Sex and Power* (Philadelphia: University of Pennsylvania Press, 1994).

27. Studies of Elizabethan iconography include Elkin Calhoun Wilson, *England's Eliza* (Cambridge: Harvard University Press, 1939); Frances A. Yates, *Astraea: The Imperial Theme in the Sixteenth Century* (London: Routledge and Kegan Paul, 1975); Roy Strong, *The Cult of Elizabeth: Elizabethan Portraiture and Pageantry* (London: Thames and Hudson, 1977) and *Gloriana: The Portraits of Queen Elizabeth I* (London: Thames and Hudson, 1987); and John N. King, *Tudor Royal Iconography: Literature and Art in an Age of Religious Crisis* (Princeton: Princeton University Press, 1989).

28. Strong, *Gloriana*, 20. For other discussions of attitudes toward the queen in the 1590s, see Christopher Haigh, *Elizabeth I* (London: Longman, 1988), 164–74; Frye, *Elizabeth*, 97–147; and John Guy, ed., *The Reign of Elizabeth I: Court and Culture in the Last Decade* (Cambridge: Cambridge University Press, 1995).

29. André Hurault, Sieur de Maisse, *A Journal of All That Was Accomplished by Monsieur de Maisse Ambassador in England from King Henry IV to Queen Elizabeth Anno Domini 1597*, trans. and ed. G. B. Harrison and R. A. Jones (London: Nonesuch, 1931), 11–12.

30. Steven Mullaney, *The Place of the Stage: License, Play, and Power in Renaissance England* (Chicago: University of Chicago Press, 1988), viii.

31. For discussions of the politics of these plays prior to the new historicist and cultural materialist criticism of the 1980s, see Tillyard, *Shakespeare's History*; Campbell, *Shakespeare's "Histories"*; Irving Ribner, *The English History Play in the Age of Shakespeare* (Princeton: Princeton University Press, 1957); M. M. Reese, *The Cease of Majesty: A Study of Shakespeare's History Plays* (New York: St. Martin's, 1961); Ernest William Talbert, *Elizabethan Drama and Shakespeare's Early Plays: An Essay in Historical Criticism* (Chapel Hill: University of North Carolina Press, 1963); A. C. Hamilton, *The Early Shakespeare* (San Marino: Huntington Library, 1967); David Bevington, *Tudor*

Drama and Politics: A Critical Approach to Topical Meaning (Cambridge: Harvard University Press, 1968); and Emrys Jones, *The Origins of Shakespeare* (Oxford: Clarendon Press, 1977).

32. Stephen Greenblatt, "Introduction," in *The Power of Forms in the English Renaissance*, ed. Stephen Greenblatt (Norman, Okla.: Pilgrim Books, 1982), 3–6.

33. Norman Rabkin, "Rabbits, Ducks, and *Henry V*," *Shakespeare Quarterly* 28 (1977): 279–96.

34. Most editions of the plays provide a full discussion of problems of dating these early plays. For a concise overview of the debate on the composition of the *Henry VI* plays, see Hanspeter Born, "The Date of *2, 3 Henry VI*," *Shakespeare Quarterly* 25 (1974): 323–34.

35. Marcus, *Puzzling Shakespeare*, 94.

1. The Politics of Chivalry in *1 Henry VI*

1. George Lyman Kittredge, ed., *The Complete Works of Shakespeare* (Boston: Ginn, 1936), 665.

2. David Riggs, *Shakespeare's Heroical Histories: "Henry VI" and Its Literary Tradition* (Cambridge: Harvard University Press, 1971), 105.

3. Barbara Hodgdon, *The End Crowns All: Closure and Contradiction in Shakespeare's History* (Princeton: Princeton University Press, 1991), 55.

4. Leah S. Marcus, *Puzzling Shakespeare: Local Reading and Its Discontents* (Berkeley: University of California Press, 1988), 53.

5. Marcus, *Puzzling Shakespeare*, 76. It needs to be pointed out, however, that while the association between Joan of Arc and Elizabeth was hardly commonplace during Elizabeth's reign, it was not without precedent and not necessarily seditious. Both figures appear in Elizabethan catalogues of women worthies, and Joan was directly linked with Elizabeth on at least one occasion when John Aylmer referred to her in his defense of Elizabeth to show that a woman ruler had the capability to bear arms and lead her troops into battle (J. Aylmer, *An Harborowe for Faithful and Trewe Subjectes* [1559], facsimile ed. [New York: Da Capo, 1972], sig. F4).

6. Notable exceptions to this tendency to privilege Joan and Talbot include M. M. Reese, *The Cease of Majesty: A Study of Shakespeare's History Plays* (New York: St. Martin's, 1961); and Ernest William Talbert, *Elizabethan Drama and Shakespeare's Early Plays: An Essay in Historical Criticism* (Chapel Hill: University of North Carolina Press, 1963).

7. In emphasizing the critique of the aristocracy in *1 Henry VI*, my argument not only extends discussions centered on the Talbot-Joan conflict to include the feuding nobles, it also qualifies the argument set forth by Richard Helgerson, *Forms of Nationhood: The Elizabethan Writing of England* (Chicago: University of Chicago Press, 1992), 193–246, 295–301, that Shakespeare's representation of the nation-state in the history plays is aristocratic and "inclusive."

8. Discussions of *1 Henry VI*'s topicality arose initially in reference to problems of dating as editors noted parallels between the play's French sieges and Essex's French campaigns of 1591–92. See John Munro, "Some Matters Shakespearian—III," *TLS* 11 October 1947; J. Dover Wilson, ed., *The First Part of "King Henry VI"* (Cambridge: Cambridge University Press, 1952), xvi; Geoffrey Bullough, *Narrative and Dramatic*

Sources of Shakespeare (London: Routledge and Kegan Paul, 1960), 3:23–25. David Bevington, *Tudor Drama and Politics: A Critical Approach to Topical Meaning* (Cambridge: Harvard University Press, 1968), 202, by contrast, cautions against identifying the play too closely with Essex's campaign but acknowledges the political valence of the association.

9. Reprinted in John Nichols, *The Progresses and Public Processions of Queen Elizabeth* (1823; reprint, New York: AMS, 1966), 3:42–43.

10. Richard C. McCoy, *The Rites of Knighthood: The Literature and Politics of Elizabethan Chivalry* (Berkeley: University of California Press, 1989), 2–3. Previous studies of Elizabethan chivalry include Frances A. Yates, *Astraea: The Imperial Theme in the Sixteenth Century* (London: Routledge and Kegan Paul, 1975); and Roy C. Strong, *The Cult of Elizabeth: Elizabethan Portraiture and Pageantry* (London: Thames and Hudson, 1977). For discussions of the tensions between the Crown and the aristocracy during this period, see Lawrence Stone, *The Crisis of the Aristocracy 1558–1641* (Oxford: Clarendon Press, 1965), 250–57; W. T. MacCaffrey, "England: The Crown and the New Aristocracy, 1540–1600," *Past and Present* 30 (1965): 52–64; and Mervyn James, *Society, Politics, and Culture: Studies in Early Modern England* (Cambridge: Cambridge University Press, 1986), 308–415.

11. Eric S. Mallin, "Emulous Factions and the Collapse of Chivalry: *Troilus and Cressida*," *Representations* 29 (1990): 157. In addition to Mallin's fine discussion of the conjunction of court factionalism and an aging queen, see McCoy, *Rites*, who contends that by the end of the century, "the Queen found it much harder to share the stage with her powerful nobles because their aggressive aspirations were increasingly insubordinate" (98).

12. McCoy, *Rites*, 98.

13. Nichols, *Progresses*, 3:44.

14. Thomas Nashe's reference to "brave *Talbot*" in *Pierce Penilesse His Supplication to the Divell* establishes the play's upper limit of 1592. For useful reviews of the problems involved in dating the *Henry VI* plays, and *1 Henry VI* especially, see Hanspeter Born, "The Date of *2, 3 Henry VI*," *Shakespeare Quarterly* 25 (1974): 323–34, and Stanley Wells and Gary Taylor, *William Shakespeare: A Textual Companion* (Oxford: Clarendon Press, 1987), 113.

15. George Peele, *Polyhymnia*, in *The Life and Minor Works of George Peele*, ed. David H. Horne (New Haven: Yale University Press, 1952), 1:232.

16. Nichols, *Progresses*, 3:45, 46, 49–50.

17. Ibid., 3:49, 50.

18. Peele, *Life and Minor Works*, 1:235–36.

19. McCoy, *Rites*, 78. In a radically different reading of the device, Strong sees Essex as "the 'sable sad' penitent making his contrite way across the tiltyard at Whitehall to implore the Queen's forgiveness" (*Cult*, 152).

20. A number of scholars have noted the echoes of court pageantry in this play; see, for example, Edward I. Berry, *Patterns of Decay: Shakespeare's Early Histories* (Charlottesville: Virginia University Press, 1975); and Michael Hattaway, ed., *The First Part of King Henry VI* (Cambridge: Cambridge University Press, 1990), 6.

21. Robert Naunton, *Fragmenta Regalia* (1641), reprinted in *A Collection of Scarce and Valuable Tracts*, ed. Walter Scott (London: T. Cadell and W. Davies, 1809), 253. For a discussion of the decline of the Talbots, see David Starkey, ed., *Rivals in Power: Lives and Letters of the Great Tudor Dynasties* (New York: Grove Weidenfeld, 1990), 230–49.

22. Marcus, *Puzzling Shakespeare*, 51–83. For other discussions of the parallels between Elizabeth and Joan, see Hodgdon, *End Crowns All*, 54–59; and Gabriele

Bernhard Jackson, "Topical Ideology: Witches, Amazons, and Shakespeare's Joan of Arc," *ELR* 18 (1988): 40–65.

23. While most agree that Shakespeare draws on both Hall and Holinshed for the scenes involving Joan, debate continues about which is the principal source. See, for example, Bullough, *Narrative and Dramatic Sources*, 3:25, who argues that Hall is the play's primary source, supplemented perhaps by the chronicles of Richard Grafton, Raphael Holinshed, and Robert Fabyan; and Hattaway, *The First Part of King Henry VI*, 56–57, who argues for *Holinshed's Chronicles*.

24. Edward Hall, *The Union of the Two Noble and Illustre Famelies of Lancastre and Yorke* (1548), ed. H. Ellis (London, 1809), 197.

25. Shakespeare does not, as some apologists have asserted, simply lift his portrait of Joan straight from his sources. See, for example, Andrew S. Cairncross, ed., *The First Part of King Henry VI* (London: Methuen, 1962), xl, who writes: "Shakespeare, it is recognized, took Joan as he found her in Hall and Holinshed, and did no more than reflect the current English attitude"; G. B. Harrison, ed., *Shakespeare: The Complete Works* (1948; reprint, New York: Harcourt, Brace and World, 1968), 106; and David Bevington, ed., *The First Part of King Henry the Sixth*, in *William Shakespeare: The Complete Works* (Baltimore: Penguin, 1969), 438.

26. Leslie A. Fiedler, *The Stranger in Shakespeare* (New York: Stein and Day, 1972), 54. For other considerations of the *Henry VI* plays and the decline of patriarchal power, see Marilyn French, *Shakespeare's Division of Experience* (New York: Summit Books, 1981); Coppélia Kahn, *Man's Estate: Masculine Identity in Shakespeare* (Berkeley: University of California Press, 1981); Norman Rabkin, *Shakespeare and the Problem of Meaning* (Chicago: University of Chicago Press, 1981); and David Sundelson, *Shakespeare's Restorations of the Father* (New Brunswick: Rutgers University Press, 1983).

27. See David M. Bevington, "The Domineering Female in *1 Henry VI*," *Shakespeare Studies* 2 (1966): 51–58.

28. Recent discussions of the classical Amazon myth include Mandy Merck, "The City's Achievements: The Patriotic Amazonomachy and Ancient Athens," in *Tearing the Veil: Essays on Femininity*, ed. Susan Lipshitz (London: Routledge and Kegan Paul, 1978); Page duBois, *Centaurs and Amazons: Women and the Pre-History of the Great Chain of Being* (Ann Arbor: University of Michigan Press, 1982); and Wm. Blake Tyrrell, *Amazons: A Study in Athenian Mythmaking* (Baltimore: Johns Hopkins University Press, 1984).

29. This confrontation is brilliantly illustrated, of course, by the meeting between Belphoebe and Braggadochio in book 2, canto 3 of Spenser's *The Faerie Queene*, published in 1590.

30. The scene of Joan's triumph over the dauphin, resonant with sexual innuendoes and bawdy punning, also bears a resemblance to a "fowle picture" of Elizabeth and Anjou that, according to the report of the English ambassador to France, had been publicly displayed in Paris in 1583:

> The Queen's majesty sett vpp she beinge on horsback her left hande holdinge the brydell of the horse, with her right hande pullynge vpp her clothes shewinge her hindparte . . . vnder ytt was a picture of Monsieur . . . in his best apparell havynge vppon his fiste a hawke which continually bayted and koulde never make her sytt styll. (PRO, SP 78/10, no. 79; cited in Roy Strong, *Gloriana: The Portraits of Queen Elizabeth I* [London: Thames and Hudson, 1987], 168 n.)

31. See the discussion of "the fight for the breeches" by Linda Woodbridge, *Women and the English Renaissance: Literature and the Nature of Womankind, 1540–1620* (Urbana: University of Illinois Press, 1986), 184–223.

32. John Knox, *The First Blast of the Trumpet against the Monstruous Regiment of Women* (1558), facsimile ed. (New York: Da Capo, 1972), sig. B3.

33. Kahn also notes that Joan is "a composite portrait of the ways women are dangerous to men" (*Man's Estate*, 55), but she sees the apparent misogyny as serving to criticize the narrow social categories of the patriarchal society.

34. Hall, *Union*, 148.

35. *Holinshed's Chronicles of England, Scotland and Ireland* (1587), ed. H. Ellis (London, 1808), 3:163.

36. Part of the bawdiness is to turn upside down Joan's claim of chastity: "Pucelle or puzzel"(1.4.107), Talbot calls her, setting up the opposition of "maid" and "whore" that will furnish jokes about Joan through the rest of the play. But while "puzzel" means "whore," it also suggests "pizzle" or "penis," the wordplay again giving voice to anxieties about women who usurp masculine domains of the court or battlefield; see Sundelson, *Shakespeare's Restorations*, 20.

37. Cited in Carole Levin, *"The Heart and Stomach of a King": Elizabeth I and the Politics of Sex and Power* (Philadelphia: University of Pennsylvania Press, 1994), 66.

38. For discussions of the period's fascination with Amazons, see Louis Adrian Montrose, "'Shaping Fantasies': Figurations of Gender and Power in Elizabethan Culture," *Representations* 1 (1983): 61–94; Simon Shepherd, *Amazons and Warrior Women: Varieties of Feminism in Seventeenth-Century Drama* (Sussex: Harvester, 1981); and Celeste Turner Wright, "The Amazons in Elizabethan Literature," *Studies in Philology* 37 (1940): 433–56.

39. William Painter, *The Palace of Pleasure* (1575), ed. Joseph Jacobs (1890; reprint, New York: Dover, 1966).

40. Winfried Schleiner, *"Divina Virago*: Queen Elizabeth as an Amazon," *Studies in Philology* 78 (1978): 163–80.

41. Sir Walter Ralegh, *A Report of the Truth, The Discoverie of Guiana* (1596), facsimile ed. (Menston, England: Scholar, 1967), 101.

42. Montrose writes: "Ralegh's strategy for convincing the queen to advance his colonial enterprise is to insinuate that she is both like and unlike an Amazon; that Elizabethan imperialism threatens not only the Empire of Guiana but the Empire of the Amazons and that Elizabeth can definitively cleanse herself from contamination by the Amazons if she sanctions their subjugation ("Shaping Fantasies," 76). This strategy is also consistent with defenses of Elizabeth earlier in her reign that depict the queen as an exception to her sex; see Allison Heisch, "Queen Elizabeth I and the Persistence of Patriarchy," *Feminist Review* 4 (1980): 45–56.

43. Hall, *Union*, 146. For an interesting discussion of the "economy of exposure and shame" in this scene, see Christopher Pye, "The Theater, the Market, and the Subject of History," *ELH* 61 (1994): 501–22.

44. Hall, *Union*, 178.

45. Ibid., 157. Historically, Bedford was one of Joan's most outspoken critics, and his letters provide some of the earliest English descriptions of Joan. In 1434, three years after Joan's death, in a confidential report to Henry VI, Bedford attributed English losses in France to "a disciple and leme of the fende called the Pucelle that used fals enchantement and sorcerie the whiche stroke and discomfiture not oonly lessened in greet partie the nombre of youre peuple ther but aswel withdrawe the courage of the remenant in

marvaillous wise" (quoted in W. T. Waugh, "Joan of Arc in English Sources of the Fifteenth Century," in *Historical Essays in Honor of James Tait*, ed. J. G. Edwards, V. H. Galbraith, and E. F. Jacob [Manchester, 1933], 390). For a vivid account of the proceedings against Joan, see Marina Warner, *Joan of Arc: The Image of Female Heroism* (New York: Knopf, 1981), 139–46.

46. *The Works of Thomas Nashe*, ed. Ronald B. McKerrow (Oxford: Basil Blackwell, 1958), 1:212. The consensus is that Nashe's mention of a Talbot play refers to *1 Henry VI*; see Cairncross, *The First Part of King Henry VI*, xxx–xxxi. Corroborating Nashe's remarks on the play's popularity, Henslowe records that "harey the vi" was performed fifteen times between March and June of 1592 (Walter W. Greg, ed., *Henslowe's Diary* [London: A. H. Bullen, 1904], 1:13).

47. *Works of Thomas Nashe*, 1:212.

48. Hodgdon writes that Nashe's remarks on Talbot suggest "how empathetic engagement with a particular character, combined with intense patriotic fervor, can not only reshape a play in a spectator's imagination but supply a desired end—in this case, England's triumph" (*End Crowns All*, 54).

49. As most editors point out, the interviews between York and Suffolk in 4.4 and 4.5 are entirely fictitious, designed, in Cairncross's words, "to emphasize the internal dissension of the English" (*The First Part of King Henry VI*, 94 n.). Hall (*Union*, 179) and *Holinshed's Chronicles* (185) both note the animosities between Somerset and York in conjunction with Bedford's death in 1435 and the subsequent appointment of York as the French regent, and both see this rivalry as culminating in the loss of France. But neither sees the quarrel as having an immediate effect on the French campaigns or as contributing to the death of Talbot and his son on the battlefield.

50. For this quotation, I refer to the editions of Cairncross and Hattaway, which emend "my will" to "mine ill" on the basis that "'my will' is probably due to a misreading of the last two letters of 'mine' as 'w'" (Hattaway, *The First Part of King Henry VI*, 118).

51. Bernard Shaw, "Preface," in *Saint Joan: A Chronicle Play in Six Scenes and an Epilogue* (1924; reprint, Baltimore: Penguin Books, 1969), 23, speculates that either Joan's portrait is by a hand other than Shakespeare's or that Shakespeare blackened what began as a sympathetic portrait of Joan to appease the patriotism of his audience. Joan especially troubled eighteenth- and nineteenth-century editors, at odds about how to reconcile "the unforgivable insult" given to the "Maid of France" in act 5 with expectations of the Bard; see Allison Gaw, *The Origin and Development of "1 Henry VI" in Relation to Shakespeare, Marlowe, and Greene* (Los Angeles: University of Southern California Press, 1926), 137; and E. M. W. Tillyard, *Shakespeare's History Plays* (London: Chatto and Windus, 1944), 187, who writes, "The chief reason why people have been hostile to Shakespeare's authorship is the way he treats Joan of Arc."

52. See, for example, Hardin Craig, *An Interpretation of Shakespeare* (New York: Dryden, 1948), 52; and S. C. Sen Gupta, *Shakespeare's Historical Plays* (London: Oxford University Press, 1964), 63.

53. Henry Ellis, ed., *Three Books of Polydore Vergil's English History* (from an early translation) (London: Camden Society, 1844), 38. For discussions of historical and literary representations of Joan of Arc in the fifteenth and sixteenth centuries, see Waugh, "Joan of Arc"; Deborah Fraioli, "The Literary Image of Joan of Arc: Prior Influences," *Speculum* 56 (1981): 811–30; and Richard F. Hardin, "Chronicles and Mythmaking in Shakespeare's Joan of Arc," *Shakespeare Survey* 42 (1989): 25–35.

54. Keith Thomas, *Religion and the Decline of Magic* (New York: Scribner's, 1971), 454; see also Christina Larner, *Witchcraft and Religion: The Politics of Popular Belief* (Oxford: Basil Blackwell, 1984), 69–78.

55. Examining fifteenth-century English sources for mention of Joan, Waugh, in "Joan of Arc," finds a "silence" (392) on matters relating to Joan's trial and execution, particularly in those sources completed before her "rehabilitation." Without taking into account the moral and legal implications of Joan's death for those responsible, Waugh interprets this silence simply as evidence of Joan's minimal effect on the English troops: "Had she really terrified them, more tales about her would have made their way into English writings" (397).

56. The king explains in his letter that rather than prosecuting the rebellious "Puzell" themselves, the English mercifully turned her over to the ecclesiastical judge of the French parish in which she was captured. This judge displayed great leniency in giving Joan several chances to repent "and to returne humbly to the right way," but in the end, Joan refused to submit to the church's authority and so "was delivered to the secular power, the which condempned her to be brent, and consumed her in the fire" (Hall, *Union*, 158–59).

57. Like Hall, the Holinshed chronicler calls attention to Joan's continued immoral and unwomanly behavior but goes further in including the story of Joan's professed pregnancy that had long circulated among the English to impugn the maid's claim of chastity. Less worried than Hall, it seems, about contaminating the English with Joan's death, the Holinshed account is not silent about the details of the execution itself (*Holinshed's Chronicles*, 3:169–70).

58. *Holinshed's Chronicles*, 3:170.

59. Sundelson, *Shakespeare's Restorations*, 20. See also A. L. French, "Joan of Arc and Henry VI," *English Studies* 49 (1968): 427, who writes: "So odd and out of key with what has gone before is the third scene of Act V, when Joan enters and starts raising evil spirits, that we can only wonder whether there was not an abrupt change of intention on Shakespeare's part." Conversely, Hattaway argues that the scene "cannot be taken as an unequivocal manifestation of the diabolic power of Joan . . . and there is no evidence earlier in the text to support the English view that her victories were won through supernatural agency" (*The First Part of King Henry VI*, 24).

60. Waugh, "Joan of Arc," 395.

61. Jackson also suggests that Elizabethan audiences would have been bothered by the "total violation of English custom" ("Topical Ideology," 62) on the part of York and Warwick.

62. See McCoy's discussion of the queen's reaction to the "dangerous image" of Essex on horseback that circulated in 1600, prompting the Privy Council to suppress "anie pictures but of her most excellent Majesty"(*Rites*, 98).

63. J. P. Brockbank, "The Frame of Disorder—*Henry VI*," in *Early Shakespeare*, Stratford-upon-Avon Studies 3, ed. John Russell Brown and Bernard Harris (London: Edward Arnold, 1961), 75. Brockbank goes on to qualify this statement, noting that these plays, like Shakespeare's later histories, "express stresses and ironies, complexities and intricate perspectives beyond the reach of the condescensions usually allowed them."

2. Dangerous Practices: Making History in 2 Henry VI

1. For discussions of the ideological basis of witchcraft accusations, see Deborah Willis, "Shakespeare and the English Witch-Hunts: Enclosing the Maternal Body," in *Enclosure Acts: Sexuality, Property, and Culture in Early Modern England*, ed. Richard Burt and John Michael Archer (Ithaca: Cornell University Press, 1994), 96–120; Christina Larner, *Witchcraft and Religion: The Politics of Popular Belief* (Cambridge: Basil Blackwell, 1984); Catherine Belsey, *The Subject of Tragedy: Identity and Difference in Renaissance Drama* (London: Methuen, 1985), 185–91; and Peter Stallybrass, "*Macbeth* and Witchcraft," in *Focus on "Macbeth,"* ed. John Russell Brown (London: Routledge and Kegan Paul, 1982), 189–209.

2. Critical interest in *2 Henry VI* has significantly increased in the last decade, although it has focused more on issues of class than gender. For recent discussions of gender in the play, see Jean E. Howard, *The Stage and Social Struggle in Early Modern England* (London: Routledge, 1994), 134–39; Barbara Hodgdon, *The End Crowns All: Closure and Contradiction in Shakespeare's History* (Princeton: Princeton University Press, 1991), 60–63; Phyllis Rackin, *Stages of History: Shakespeare's English Chronicles* (Ithaca: Cornell University Press, 1990), 173–74 n.; and Irene G. Dash, *Wooing, Wedding, and Power: Women in Shakespeare's Plays* (New York: Columbia University Press, 1981), 170–74.

3. On the basis of the conjuring scene, Jean Howard, among others, concludes: "There is in this case little doubt that the overreaching woman bears the immediate blame for her husband's fall and, consequently, some of the blame for Henry's" (*Stage and Social Struggle*, 136).

4. For a discussion of "representation" that informs my own use of the term, see Michel Foucault, *The Order of Things: An Archaeology of the Human Sciences* (New York: Vintage Books, 1973).

5. Richard Helgerson, *Forms of Nationhood: The Elizabethan Writing of England* (Chicago: University of Chicago Press, 1992), 214.

6. Warren W. Wooden, *John Foxe* (Boston: Twayne, 1983), 12–13. For discussions of Harpsfield's charges and Foxe's response, see George Townsend, "Life and Defence of John Foxe," in *The Acts and Monuments of John Foxe* (1841; reprint, New York: AMS, 1965), 1:202–25; and J. F. Mozley, *John Foxe and His Book* (1940; reprint, New York: Octagon Books, 1970), 175.

7. Foxe, *Acts and Monuments*, 3:704. Additional references to Foxe are cited parenthetically within the text.

8. Ralph A. Griffiths, "The Trial of Eleanor Cobham: An Episode in the Fall of Duke Humphrey of Gloucester," *Bulletin of the John Rylands Library* 51 (1969): 381.

9. "Lament of the Duchess of Gloucester," in *Political Poems and Songs Relating to English History*, ed. Thomas Wright (1861; reprint, New York: Kraus, 1965), 2:206.

10. According to Keith Thomas, *Religion and the Decline of Magic* (New York: Scribner's, 1971), 454 n., the cases of Roger Bolingbroke and Margery Jourdemain are among the six recorded instances of executions for witchcraft in England between the time of the Norman Conquest and the Reformation.

11. J. G. Bellamy, *The Law of Treason in England in the Later Middle Ages* (Cambridge: Cambridge University Press, 1970), 126; see also A. R. Myers, "The Captivity of a Royal Witch: The Household Accounts of Queen Joan of Navarre, 1419–21," *Bulletin of the John Rylands Library* 24 (1940): 263–84.

12. Bellamy, *Law of Treason*, 127.

13. Griffiths, "Trial," 399; see also S. B. Chrimes and A. L. Brown, eds., *Select Documents of English Constitutional History, 1307–1485* (New York: Barnes and Noble, 1961), 276–77.

14. John Silvester Davies, ed., *An English Chronicle* (London: Camden Society, 1856), 60.

15. "Lament of the Duchess," 205–8.

16. J. G. Nichols, ed., *Chronicle of the Grey Friars of London* (London: Camden Society, 1852), 18–20.

17. Davies, *English Chronicle*, 56.

18. Ibid.

19. Robert Fabyan, *The New Chronicles of England and France*, ed. Henry Ellis (London: Rivington, 1811), 614. Geoffrey Bullough, *Narrative and Dramatic Sources of Shakespeare* (London: Routledge and Kegan Paul, 1960), 3:5, places Fabyan's chronicle in the tradition of the London chronicles whose details "often reveal the City's attitude to great personages, e.g., they favour Humphrey of Gloucester and are hostile to Richard III."

20. Edward Hall, *The Union of the Two Noble and Illustre Famelies of Lancastre and Yorke* (1548), ed. H. Ellis (London, 1809), 202.

21. Ibid. For Fleming's version of the events, see *Holinshed's Chronicles of England, Scotland and Ireland* (1587), ed. H. Ellis (London, 1808), 3:203–4.

22. F. J. Levy, *Tudor Historical Thought* (San Marino: Huntington Library, 1967), 168–201.

23. Annabel Patterson, *Reading Between the Lines* (Madison: University of Wisconsin Press, 1993), 126–27. For a fuller discussion of the *Chronicles*, in which Patterson develops this argument in detail, see *Reading Holinshed's "Chronicles"* (Chicago: University of Chicago Press, 1994), 3–21.

24. *Holinshed's Chronicles*, 2: "Preface to the Reader."

25. Hall, *Union*, 49.

26. Mozley, *John Foxe*, 177.

27. While the debate about Foxe's historical practices continues, most scholars now acknowledge his concern for reliability. See, for example, Mozley, *John Foxe*, 152–74; J. A. F. Thompson, "John Foxe and Some Sources for Lollard History: Notes for a Critical Appraisal," *Studies in Church History* 2 (1965): 251–57; John T. McNeill, "John Foxe: Historiographer, Disciplinarian, Tolerationist," *Church History* 43 (1974): 216–29; and Anne Hudson, *The Premature Reformation: Wycliffite Texts and Lollard History* (Oxford: Clarendon Press, 1988), 40, who concludes of the scholarship on Foxe's reliability: "It would seem that Foxe is generally trustworthy to a fairly high degree."

28. F. J. Levy notes the influence of Foxe's "insistence on the primacy of sources" (*Tudor Historical Thought*, 104). See also Patterson, *Reading Holinshed's "Chronicles,"* 37, who asserts that the Holinshed chroniclers turned to Foxe for methods as well as materials, in "the grand-scale salvage and preservation in print of early documents" and in "the use and privileging, wherever possible, of eyewitness accounts."

29. Donna B. Hamilton, *Shakespeare and the Politics of Protestant England* (Lexington: University of Kentucky Press, 1992), x. See also Robert Weimann, *Authority and Representation in Early Modern Discourse*, ed. David Hillman (Baltimore: Johns Hopkins University Press, 1996).

30. Robert Weimann, "Bifold Authority in Shakespeare's Theatre," *Shakespeare Quarterly* 39 (1988): 409.

31. Ibid., 414.

32. Howard, *Stage and Social Struggle*, 135.

33. Hall, *Union*, 202.

34. Ibid.

35. Lily B. Campbell, ed., *The Mirror for Magistrates* (New York: Barnes and Noble, 1938), 435.

36. Robert Rentoul Reed Jr., *The Occult on the Tudor and Stuart Stage* (Boston: Christopher, 1965), 117, argues for dramatic reasons governing Shakespeare's substitution.

37. Paola Pugliatti, *Shakespeare the Historian* (New York: St. Martin's, 1996), 200.

38. See John G. Bellamy, *The Tudor Law of Treason* (London: Routledge and Kegan Paul, 1979), 61–82.

39. Ibid., 52.

40. For a discussion of the 1581 legislation, see J. E. Neale, *Elizabeth I and Her Parliaments 1559–1581* (London: Jonathan Cape, 1953), 393–406.

41. M. M. Reese, *The Cease of Majesty: A Study of Shakespeare's History Plays* (New York: St. Martin's, 1961), 126. For other discussions of the play's conservative politics, see E. M. W. Tillyard, *Shakespeare's History Plays* (London: Chatto and Windus, 1944); Bullough, *Narrative and Dramatic Sources*, 3:89–100; and Richard Dutton, *Mastering the Revels: The Regulation and Censorship of English Renaissance Drama* (Iowa City: University of Iowa Press, 1991), 84–85. For opposing views, see Michael Hattaway, "Rebellion, Class Consciousness, and Shakespeare's 2 Henry VI," *Cahiers Elisabethains* 33 (1988): 13–22; Annabel Patterson, *Shakespeare and the Popular Voice* (Cambridge: Basil Blackwell, 1989), 32–51; Thomas Cartelli, "Jack Cade in the Garden: Class Consciousness and Class Conflict in 2 Henry VI," in *Enclosure Acts: Sexuality, Property, and Culture in Early Modern England*, ed. Richard Burt and John Michael Archer (Ithaca: Cornell University Press, 1994): 48–67.

42. Richard Wilson, "'A Mingled Yarn': Shakespeare and the Cloth Workers," *Literature and History* 12 (1986): 164–80.

43. Helgerson, *Forms of Nationhood*, 214.

44. Ibid., 234.

45. Stephen Greenblatt, "Invisible Bullets: Renaissance Authority and Its Subversion, *Henry IV* and *Henry V*," in *Political Shakespeare: New Essays in Cultural Materialism*, ed. Jonathan Dollimore and Alan Sinfield (Ithaca: Cornell University Press, 1985), 30.

46. For a discussion of treason in the play, and a review of divergent critical opinion on the outcome of the Horner trial, see Nina Levine, "Lawful Symmetry: The Politics of Treason in 2 Henry VI," *Renaissance Drama* 25 (1994): 197–218.

47. For discussions of the treason-witchcraft trials in Scotland, see Larner, *Witchcraft and Religion*, 3–22; and Helen Stafford, "Notes on Scottish Witchcraft Cases, 1590–91," in *Essays in Honor of Conyers Read*, ed. Norton Downs (Chicago: University of Chicago Press, 1953).

48. G. B. Harrison, ed., *King James, the First: Daemonologie (1597), Newes from Scotland (1591)* (New York: Barnes and Noble, 1966), 29.

3. Ruling Women and the Politics of Gender in *2* and *3 Henry VI*

1. See, for example, David M. Bevington, "The Domineering Female in *1 Henry VI*," *Shakespeare Studies* 2 (1966): 51–58; Leslie A. Fiedler, *The Stranger in Shakespeare*

(New York: Stein and Day, 1972), 73–74; John W. Blanpied, "'Art and Baleful Sorcery': The Counterconsciousness of *Henry VI, Part I*," *Studies in English Literature* 15 (1975): 213–27; Patricia Silber, "The Unnatural Woman and the Disordered State in Shakespeare's Histories," *Proceedings of the PMR Conference* 2 (1977): 87–95; and Patricia-Ann Lee, "Reflections of Power: Margaret of Anjou and the Dark Side of Queenship," *Renaissance Quarterly* 39 (1986): 183–217. Similarly, Michael Hattaway, ed., *The Third Part of King Henry VI* (Cambridge: Cambridge University Press, 1993), 16 n., comments that "Margaret may have served to evoke the sentiments aroused by John Knox against (Catholic) queens at the beginning of Elizabeth's reign."

2. Lee, "Reflections of Power," 217.

3. Leah S. Marcus, *Puzzling Shakespeare: Local Reading and Its Discontents* (Berkeley: University of California Press, 1988), 93. See also Barbara Hodgdon, *The End Crowns All: Closure and Contradiction in Shakespeare's History* (Princeton: Princeton University Press, 1991), 61.

4. J. Aylmer, *An Harborowe for Faithfull and Trewe Subjectes* (1559), facsimile ed. (New York: Da Capo, 1972), sig. D2v, cites an extensive list—from which Margaret is conspicuously absent—that includes such notable women as Deborah, Dido, Semiramis, Artemisia, Judith, Joan of Arc, and even the late Queen Mary to illustrate that "many countreis have bene wel governed by women"; additional references to *An Harborowe* are cited parenthetically within the text. See also Thomas Heywood's *The Exemplary Lives and Memorable Acts of Nine the Most Worthy Women of the World* (London, 1640), published long after Elizabeth's death, which does include both Margaret of Anjou and Elizabeth I (alongside Deborah, Judith, Esther, Bonduca, Penthesilea, Artemisia, and Elphleda). For a catalogue of women worthies, see Celeste Turner Wright, "The Elizabethan Female Worthies," *Studies in Philology* 43 (1946): 628–43.

5. For discussions of history's treatment of Margaret of Anjou, see Lee, "Reflections of Power"; and Antonia Gransden, *Historical Writing in England: c. 1307 to the Early Sixteenth Century*, vol. 2 (London: Routledge and Kegan Paul, 1982).

6. John Silvester Davies, ed., *An English Chronicle* (London: Camden Society, 1856), 79.

7. Thomas Wright, ed., *Political Poems and Songs Relating to English History* (1861; reprint, New York: Kraus, 1965), vol. 2.

8. Henry Ellis, ed., *Three Books of Polydore Vergil's English History* (from an early translation) (London: Camden Society, 1844), 70.

9. Robert Fabyan, *The New Chronicles of England and France*, ed. Henry Ellis (London: Rivington, 1811), 618.

10. Ellis, *Polydore Vergil's English History*, 70.

11. Vergil's innovative historiography may partially explain the shape of his narrative: concerned with ordering the often disjointed details of his fifteenth-century sources into coherent narratives, he typically structured his accounts of individual reigns around thematic and causal explanations. Popular literature warning of the dangers of women who stepped out of their place clearly offered one such thematic narrative. For discussions of Vergil's contribution to sixteenth-century English historiography, see F. J. Levy, *Tudor Historical Thought* (San Marino: Huntington Library, 1967), 57–61.

12. Edward Hall, *The Union of the Two Noble and Illustre Famelies of Lancastre and Yorke* (1548), ed. H. Ellis (London: 1809), 205.

13. Ibid., 208.

14. Levy, *Tudor Historical Thought*, 177.

15. *Holinshed's Chronicles of England, Scotland and Ireland* (1587), ed. H. Ellis (London, 1808), 3:211.

16. Ibid., 3:218.

17. Hall, *Union*, 208.

18. Raphael Holinshed, et al., *The Chronicles of England, Scotlande, and Irelande* (London, 1577), 1256.

19. *Holinshed's Chronicles*, 3:210.

20. For discussions of censorship in Holinshed, see Stephen Booth, *The Book Called "Holinshed's Chronicles"* (San Francisco: Book Club of California, 1968); Elizabeth Story Donno, "Some Aspects of Shakespeare's Holinshed," *Huntington Library Quarterly* 50 (1987): 229–48; and Annabel Patterson, *Reading Holinshed's "Chronicles"* (Chicago: University of Chicago Press, 1994).

21. In addition to the discussion of censorship in *Reading Holinshed's "Chronicles,"* see Patterson's more general study, *Censorship and Interpretation: The Conditions of Writing and Reading in Early Modern England* (Madison: University of Wisconsin Press, 1984).

22. *Statutes of the Realm* (Record Commission, 1831), 4:526.

23. John Knox, *The First Blast of the Trumpet Against the Monstruous Regiment of Women* (1558), facsimile ed. (New York: Da Capo, 1972), sig. 25v.

24. Ibid., sig. BI.

25. For recent discussions of the midcentury debate, see Constance Jordan, "Woman's Rule in Sixteenth-Century British Political Thought," *Renaissance Quarterly* 40 (1987): 421–51; Patricia-Ann Lee, "A Bodye Politique to Governe: Aylmer, Knox and the Debate on Queenship," *The Historian* 52 (1990): 242–61; Pamela Joseph Benson, *The Invention of the Renaissance Woman: The Challenge of Female Independence in the Literature and Thought of Italy and England* (University Park: Pennsylvania State University Press, 1992); Theodora A. Jankowski, *Women in Power in the Early Modern Drama* (Urbana: University of Illinois Press, 1992); and Amanda Shephard, *Gender and Authority in Sixteenth-Century England: The Knox Debate* (Keele, Staffordshire: Ryburn, 1994). Earlier reviews of the sixteenth-century debate include James E. Phillips Jr., "The Background of Spenser's Attitude Toward Women Rulers," *Huntington Library Quarterly* 5 (1941–42): 5–32; Gordon J. Schochet, *Patriarchalism in Political Thought* (New York: Basic Books, 1975), 1–53; and Paula Louise Scalingi, "The Scepter or the Distaff: The Question of Female Sovereignty, 1516–1607," *The Historian* 41 (1978): 59–75.

26. Jordan, "Woman's Rule," 423–24.

27. For a discussion of sixteenth-century theories of resistance, see Quentin Skinner, *The Foundations of Modern Political Thought* (Cambridge: Cambridge University Press, 1978), 2:189–238; and Michael Walzer, *The Revolution of the Saints: A Study in the Origins of Radical Politics* (London: Weidenfeld and Nicholson, 1965).

28. Hastings Robinson, ed. and trans., *The Zurich Letters* (2nd series) (Cambridge: Cambridge University Press, 1845), 34 n.

29. Knox, *First Blast*, sig. A7v.

30. Ibid., sig. G5.

31. David Laing, ed., *The Works of John Knox* (1855; reprint, New York: AMS, 1966), 4:49.

32. Christopher Goodman, *How Superior Powers Oght to Be Obeyd* (1558), facsimile ed. (New York: Da Capo, 1972), 113.

33. John Guy, "The Elizabethan Establishment and the Ecclesiastical Polity," in *The Reign of Elizabeth I: Court and Culture in the Last Decade*, ed. John Guy (Cambridge: Cambridge University Press, 1995), 130. For a discussion of the scholarly debate over Aylmer's description of a mixed government, see also Michael Mendle, *Dangerous Positions: Mixed Government, the Estates of the Realm, and the Making of the "Answer to the*

xix propositions" (University: University of Alabama Press, 1985), 48–51. The argument for mixed government also appears in Sir Thomas Smith's remarks on female rule in *De Republica Anglorum*, ed. Mary Dewar (Cambridge: Cambridge University Press, 1982), 65. Like Aylmer, Smith's standard for good government rests with the preservation of the commonwealth and with the custom of lineal succession: "For the right and honour of the blood, and the quietnes and suertie of the realme, is more to be considred, than either the base age as yet impotent to rule, or the sexe not accustomed (otherwise) to intermeddle with publicke affaires, being by common intendment understood, that such personages never do lacke the counsell of such grave and discreete men as be able to supplie all other defaultes." In making his pitch for law and commonwealth, Smith insists that the monarch's gender, or age, is far less important than matters of the nation's strength.

34. A curious series of errors in act 3, scene 2 (ll. 26, 27, 99, and 119) of the 1623 folio text, in which Eleanor's name appears several times in place of Margaret's, underscores the generic nature of the characterizations. The mistake is Shakespeare's, editors tell us, caused by the proximity of Gloucester's name in the same passage, but it may also offer evidence of the playwright's thinking about the two women. See Andrew S. Cairncross, ed., *The Second Part of King Henry VI* (London: Methuen, 1957), 80; and Michael Hattaway, ed., *The Second Part of King Henry VI* (Cambridge: Cambridge University Press, 1991), 147.

35. See Phyllis Rackin, *Stages of History: Shakespeare's English Chronicles* (Ithaca: Cornell University Press, 1990), 146–200.

36. A. P. Rossiter, ed., *Woodstock: A Moral History* (London: Chatto and Windus, 1946), 66. See also David Riggs, *Shakespeare's Heroical Histories: "Henry VI" and Its Literary Tradition* (Cambridge: Harvard University Press, 1971), 119, who observes that "Gloucester is a type of the Renaissance governor, whom humanists like Ascham and Elyot saw as supplanting such medieval *chevaliers* as Talbot."

37. As Hodgdon points out, the quarto and folio texts of this play invite us to consider *The Contention* as an Elizabethan version of the play and *2 Henry VI*, as it appears in the folio text, as a Jacobean version (*End Crowns All*, 60–68). Although these two texts offer intriguing possibilities for discussions of Margaret in relation to Elizabeth I, given the difficulties involved in speculating about the politics of a bad quarto, this chapter grounds its discussion in the folio text. For another discussion of variants in the portrait of Margaret, see Steven Urkowitz, "Five Women Eleven Ways: Changing Images of Shakespearean Characters in the Earliest Texts," in *Images of Shakespeare: Proceedings of the Third Conference, International Shakespeare Association, 1986,* ed. Werner Habicht, D. J. Palmer and Roger Pringle (Newark: University of Delaware Press, 1988), 292–304.

38. Marilyn L. Williamson, "'When Men Are Rul'd by Women': Shakespeare's First Tetralogy," *Shakespeare Studies* 19 (1987): 48, likewise argues that Shakespeare complicates his sources here by showing how the factions quickly politicize the marriage.

39. Hall, *Union*, 208.

40. Richard Helgerson, *Forms of Nationhood: The Elizabethan Writing of England* (Chicago: University of Chicago Press, 1992), 296–97.

41. Ibid., 214.

42. Ibid., 196.

43. For a discussion of Gloucester in relation to questions of nation and commonwealth, see Peter Womack, "Imagining Communities: Theatres and the English Nation in the Sixteenth Century," in *Culture and History 1350–1600: Essays on English Communities, Identities, and Writing,* ed. David Aers (Detroit: Wayne State University Press, 1992), 134, who writes: "Gloucester is increasingly forced to found his *locus standi* not simply on his loyalty to the king, but on his loyalty to England. . . . The more his less

principled fellow peers spiral into mutually destructive antagonisms, the more his moral uprightness comes to look like a political position, a commitment to the commonwealth."

44. For a discussion of Margaret in relation to the discourse of medieval romance, see Jankowski, who argues that "allying Margaret so closely with the discourse of romance serves to call into question her legitimacy both as a wife and as a political figure" (*Women in Power*, 99).

45. Norman Rabkin, *Shakespeare and the Problem of Meaning* (Chicago: University of Chicago Press, 1981), 90, notes that York is "motivated not by the patriarchal patriotism implicit in his dynastic claims but by a consistently commercial interest in the value of the crown and its real estate."

46. In both Hall and Holinshed, the decision to provide York's heirs with the succession comes not from the king himself but is forced upon him by a compromising parliament. No mention at all is made of a divorce; in fact, according to the chronicles, Margaret is in Scotland, and it is York, rather than Henry's allies, who sends for the queen and her son. For a discussion of the divorce debate that peaked in the 1590s, see Catherine Belsey, *The Subject of Tragedy: Identity and Difference in Renaissance Drama* (London: Methuen, 1985), 137–44.

47. Andrew S. Cairncross, ed., *The Third Part of King Henry VI* (London: Methuen, 1965), 14; Robert B. Pierce, *Shakespeare's History Plays: The Family and the State* (Columbus: Ohio State University Press, 1971), 74; and Edward I. Berry, *Patterns of Decay: Shakespeare's Early Histories* (Charlottesville: University Press of Virginia, 1975), 55.

48. Sir Thomas Elyot, *The Defence of Good Women* (London, 1540), sig. E2. See also Constance Jordan, "Feminism and the Humanists: The Case for Sir Thomas Elyot's *Defence of Good Women*," in *Rewriting the Renaissance: The Discourses of Sexual Difference in Early Modern Europe*, ed. Margaret W. Ferguson, Maureen Quilligan, and Nancy J. Vickers (Chicago: University of Chicago Press, 1986), 255.

49. Allison Heisch, "Queen Elizabeth I: Parliamentary Rhetoric and the Exercise of Power," *Signs* 1 (1975): 35, cites Elizabeth's bold response to a petition from Parliament urging her to marry: "As for my owne parte I care not for deathe, for all men are mortall, and thoughe I be a woman, yet I have as good a corage awnsuerable to my place as evere my fathere hade: I am yor anoynted *Queene* / I wyll never be by vyolence constreyned to doo any thynge."

50. J. P. Brockbank, "The Frame of Disorder—*Henry VI*," *Early Shakespeare*, Stratford-upon-Avon Studies 3, ed. John Russell Brown and Bernard Harris (London: Edward Arnold, 1961), 95.

51. Hall, *Union*, 251. Curiously, few studies point out Shakespeare's radical revision of his sources in making Margaret York's sadistic executioner. Exceptions include Cairncross, *The Third Part of King Henry VI*, 32; and David M. Bergeron, "The Play-within-the-Play in *3 Henry VI*," *Tennessee Studies in Literature* 22 (1977): 37–45.

52. The account in *Holinshed's Chronicles* reads as follows: "Some write that the duke was taken alive, and in derision caused to stand upon a molehill, on whose head they put a garland in steed of a crowne, which they had fashioned and made of sedges or bulrushes; and having so crowned him with that garland, they kneeled downe afore him (as the Jewes did unto Christ) in scorne, saieng to him; 'Haile king without rule, haile king without heritage, haileduke and prince without people or possessions.' And at length having thus scorned him with these and diverse other the like despitefull words, they stroke off his head, which (as yee have heard) they presented to the queene" (3:269).

53. Emrys Jones, *The Origins of Shakespeare* (Oxford: Oxford University Press, 1977), 278.

54. Robert Ornstein, *A Kingdom for a Stage: The Achievement of Shakespeare's History Plays* (Cambridge: Harvard University Press, 1972), 55, offers another, but related, explanation: "By casting the atrocities of *Part III* in ritual form, Shakespeare focuses attention on the moral perversity rather than the physical horror of the crimes. We shudder more at the sadistic deliberateness of Margaret's taunting of York than at the sudden fury of Clifford's murder of Rutland."

55. Hall, *Union*, 250.

56. *Holinshed's Chronicles*, 3:269.

57. A. C. Hamilton, *The Early Shakespeare* (San Marino: Huntington Library, 1967), notes the connection but diminishes the seriousness of York's breaking of his oath, arguing that Margaret's accusation is "only one of many charges, and one of which she is guilty."

58. Hall goes on to explain that the Crown was able to assemble a large army, largely because the subjects were afraid of the queen, "whose countenaunce was so fearfull, and whose looke was so terrible, that to al men, against whom she toke a small displeasure, her frounyng was their undoyng, and her indignacion, was their death" (*Union*, 241).

59. Ibid., 297.

60. Ibid.

61. For contemporary descriptions of Elizabeth's appearance at Tilbury, see James Aske, "Elizabetha Triumphans, 1588," in John Nichols, ed., *The Progresses and Public Processions of Queen Elizabeth* (1823; reprint, New York: AMS, 1966), 2:545–82. See also Susan Frye, "The Myth of Elizabeth at Tilbury," *Sixteenth Century Journal* 23 (1992): 95–114, who persuasively argues that the legendary details of Elizabeth's visit to Tilbury and her reported speech to the troops are not documented by contemporary evidence. For the ruling elite in the late sixteenth century, Frye concludes, the myth of Tilbury contributed to fictions about the power of the queen's virginity.

62. Nichols, *Progresses*, 2:536.

63. Ibid., 536–37.

64. Hodgdon, *End Crowns All*, 71.

65. Edward's "repurchasing" of the Crown, which, as the Arden editor reminds us, is "a legal term for acquisition otherwise than by inheritance or descent," only reiterates the Yorkist attitudes toward the Crown as property (Cairncross, *The Third Part of King Henry VI*, 140–41 n.).

66. Marcus, *Puzzling Shakespeare*, 94. Hodgdon also reads Elizabeth as correcting Margaret's "misrule" with an "image of domestic womankind" (*End Crowns All*, 75).

4. Misogyny, Marriage, and the Succession in *Richard III*

1. *The Works of Thomas Nashe*, ed. Ronald B. McKerrow (Oxford: Basil Blackwell, 1958), 1:212. For a discussion of Nashe's gendered discourse, see chapter 1.

2. See, for example, M. D. Faber, *The Design Within: Psychoanalytic Approaches to Shakespeare* (New York: Science House, 1970); Richard P. Wheeler, "History, Character and Conscience in *Richard III*," *Comparative Drama* 5 (1971–72): 301–21; Michael Neill, "Shakespeare's Halle of Mirrors: Play, Politics, and Psychology in *Richard III*," *Shakespeare Studies* 8 (1975): 99–129; Coppélia Kahn, *Man's Estate: Masculine Identity in Shakespeare* (Berkeley: University of California Press, 1981); C. L. Barber and Richard P. Wheeler, *The Whole Journey: Shakespeare's Power of Development*

(Berkeley: University of California Press, 1986); and Janet Adelman, *Suffocating Mothers: Fantasies of Maternal Origin in Shakespeare's Plays, "Hamlet" to "The Tempest"* (New York: Routledge, 1992). For recent discussions of Richard's inwardness in relation to his role as stage-machiavel, see Linda Charnes, *Notorious Identity: Materializing the Subject in Shakespeare* (Cambridge: Harvard University Press, 1993); and Katharine Eisaman Maus, *Inwardness and Theater in the English Renaissance* (Chicago: University of Chicago Press, 1995).

3. Adelman, *Suffocating Mothers*, 9. See also René Girard, "Hamlet's Dull Revenge," *Stanford Literature Review* 1 (1984): 161, who remarks about the play in general: "Richard, at times, sounds like the only character with an ethical dimension in the entire cast."

4. Much has been written about Richard's place within Henrician histories of Polydore Vergil, Sir Thomas More, and Edward Hall. For reviews of the literature, see A. R. Myers, "Richard III and Historical Tradition,"*History* 53 (1968): 81–202; and Alison Hanham, *Richard III and His Early Historians: 1483–1535* (Oxford: Clarendon Press, 1975). For a discussion of Richard's deformity in terms of Tudor historiography, see Marjorie B. Garber's chapter, "Descanting on Deformity: *Richard III* and the Shape of History," in *Shakespeare's Ghost Writers: Literature as Uncanny Causality* (New York: Methuen, 1987).

5. For a discussion of the "saving stereotypes of female heroism" during this period, see Lisa Jardine, *Still Harping on Daughters: Women and Drama in the Age of Shakespeare* (1983; reprint, New York: Columbia University Press, 1989), 169–98.

6. According to the chronicles, Margaret was sent back to France after the death of Henry VI in 1471. Edward Hall, *The Union of the Two Noble and Illustre Famelies of Lancastre and Yorke* (1548), ed. H. Ellis (London, 1809), 301, writes that following the Lancastrian defeat at Tewkesbury, Margaret was imprisoned in London, "where she remayned tyll kyng Reiner her father raunsomed her with money," a fact which Clarence alludes to at the close of *3 Henry VI*, explaining to King Edward that her father "hath pawn'd the Sicils and Jerusalem, / And hither have they sent it for her ransom" (5.7.39–40). Although the chronicles make no mention of her death, Margaret died in France in 1482, a year before the death of Edward IV. For discussions of history's treatment of Margaret, see Antonia Gransden, *Historical Writing in England: c. 1307 to the Early Sixteenth Century*, vol. 2 (London: Routledge and Kegan Paul, 1982); and Patricia-Ann Lee, "Reflections of Power: Margaret of Anjou and the Dark Side of Queenship," *Renaissance Quarterly* 39 (1986): 183–217.

7. Keith Thomas, *Religion and the Decline of Magic* (New York: Scribner's, 1971), 509. Thomas cites the case of two women, accused in 1536 of cursing the mayor of York for enclosing the commons, and that of the notorious John Story, who was said to have cursed the queen daily before his meals and was subsequently executed for treason in 1471. Story's case, like that of Shakespeare's Margaret, illustrates the ambivalent status of curses, which, on the one hand, were considered the weapon of the marginalized but, on the other, were granted a certain efficacy and often regarded with fear. It is commonplace, however, to regard the fulfillment of Margaret's curses in *Richard III* as evidence not so much of the queen's power but of the play's larger scheme of retributive justice and providence. See, for example, Richard G. Moulton, *Shakespeare as a Dramatic Artist* (1885; reprint, New York: Dover, 1966), 107–24; E. M. W. Tillyard, *Shakespeare's History Plays* (London: Chatto and Windus, 1944), 198–214; and Edward I. Berry, *Patterns of Decay: Shakespeare's Early Histories* (Charlottesville: University of Virginia Press, 1975), 83.

8. Leslie A. Fiedler, *The Stranger in Shakespeare* (New York: Stein and Day, 1972), 49.

9. See Barbara Hodgdon, *The End Crowns All: Closure and Contradiction in Shakespeare's History* (Princeton: Princeton University Press, 1991), 107–8, who likewise points out similarities between Margaret and Richard.

10. Wolfgang Clemen, *A Commentary on Shakespeare's "Richard III,"* trans. Jean Bonheim (London: Methuen, 1968), 36–37, writes that Richard's speech on Anne "embodies Shakespeare's own commentary. Here Richard's comment is unmistakably moral: Anne's capitulation is retrospectively condemned, and the virtues and charms of her murdered husband are reviewed."

11. Geoffrey Bullough, *Narrative and Dramatic Sources of Shakespeare* (London: Routledge and Kegan Paul, 1960), 3:236. Bullough notes that after the death of prince Edward, Clarence tried to hide Anne, his sister-in-law, "with an eye on her inheritance" (241 n.), but Richard found her and placed her in sanctuary until Warwick's estate was settled and the king gave him permission to marry her.

12. Ibid., 3:236. See also Harold F. Brooks, *"Richard III*, Unhistorical Amplifications: The Women's Scenes and Seneca," *Modern Language Review* 75 (1980): 721–37, who cites Seneca's *Hippolytus* as a source for the scene as well.

13. Robert Ornstein, *A Kingdom for a Stage: The Achievement of Shakespeare's History Plays* (Cambridge: Harvard University Press, 1972), 75.

14. Marguerite Waller, "Usurpation, Seduction, and the Problematics of the Proper: A 'Deconstructive,' 'Feminist' Rereading of the Seductions of Richard and Anne in Shakespeare's *Richard III*," in *Rewriting the Renaissance: The Discourses of Sexual Difference in Early Modern Europe*, ed. Margaret W. Ferguson, Maureen Quilligan, and Nancy J. Vickers (Chicago: University of Chicago Press, 1986), 172, argues that it is Anne rather than Richard who establishes the terms of the exchange, by casting herself as powerless, as "poor Anne / Wife to thy Edward, to thy slaughtered son." Dependent upon men for her position and power, Anne succumbs to Richard's tempting offer "to see herself *reflected in him*, as immensely powerful."

15. Charnes, in her insightful discussion of this scene, points out Richard's use of a misogynistic tradition of blaming women for conflicts between men and his simultaneous "awareness of it as a form of *preposterous displacement*, in which the outcome of aggression between men is proleptically installed in the bodies of women as originary cause" (*Notorious Identity*, 46).

16. Camille Wells Slights, *The Casuistical Tradition in Shakespeare, Donne, Herbert, and Milton* (Princeton: Princeton University Press, 1981), 75, writes: "The temptation Richard presents is power over an otherwise invulnerable man. Anne, a woman without husband or father to protect her and hence powerless in a power-mad world, surrenders to the appeal of power in the form of the chance to reform a strong man."

17. By implicating Anne in her own seduction, Shakespeare complicates the audience's response to the scene of confrontation. If critical opinion from the eighteenth century to the twentieth is any indication, the play indeed invites members of the audience to align themselves with Richard in blaming Anne. In 1779, William Richardson, cited in Brian Vickers, ed., *Shakespeare: The Critical Heritage, 1774–1801* (London: Routledge and Kegan Paul, 1981), 209, confesses to a response that will remain typical for the next two hundred years: "We shall find ourselves more interested in the event, and more astonished at the bold ability of *Richard*, than moved with abhorrence of his shameless effrontery or offended with the improbability of the situation." At the close of the nineteenth century, Moulton characterizes Richard as "an artist in villainy" and his

wooing of Anne as a *"tour de force"* (*Shakespeare*, 93), establishing the terms by which critics in the twentieth century admire Richard's success. See, for example, Bernard Spivack, *Shakespeare and the Allegory of Evil: The History of a Métaphor in Relation to His Major Villains* (New York: Columbia University Press, 1958), 404–6; Wilbur Sanders, *The Dramatist and the Received Idea: Studies in the Plays of Marlowe and Shakespeare* (Cambridge: Cambridge University Press, 1968), 84–87; Neill, "Shakespeare's Halle of Mirrors," 103–4; and Antony Hammond, ed., *King Richard III* (London: Methuen, 1981), 105. Critical discussion of Anne, by contrast, centers on her weakness. In the eighteenth and nineteenth centuries, critics tended to see her moral and intellectual failing as an inherent weakness of her sex. Anne is considered to be "of a mind altogether frivolous; incapable of deep affection; guided by no steady principles of virtue, produced or strengthened by reason and reflection; the prey of vanity, which is her ruling passion" (qtd. in Horace Howard Furness Jr., ed., *A New Variorum Edition of Shakespeare: The Tragedy of Richard the Third* [Philadelphia: J. B. Lippincott, 1908], 16:43); W. Oechelhaüser referred to her as "a true daughter of Eve, with the normal weakness, and especially the normal vanity of her sex, no more, no less" (qtd. in *New Variorum,* 16:44). In the twentieth century, critics have tended to see Anne more as a victim than an inherently weak woman. Of course, Anne has also had her defenders. Robert B. Pierce, *Shakespeare's History Plays: The Family and the State* (Columbus: Ohio State University Press, 1971), 110–11, sees her as "representative of traditional values" and an easy mark for Richard's "anarchic power"; Irene G. Dash, *Wooing, Wedding, and Power: Women in Shakespeare's Plays* (New York: Columbia University Press, 1981), 195, explains Anne's failure to resist Richard in cultural terms: "Her training as a woman assures him success." But whether defending or accusing Anne, most critics admit the weakness of her position.

18. Charnes, *Notorious Identity*, 56.

19. Hall, *Union*, 406.

20. Ibid.

21. See Clemen, *Commentary*, 190–92, for a review of critical attitudes toward Elizabeth's capitulation. Samuel Johnson reacted by dismissing the entire scene: "On this dialogue 'tis not necessary to bestow much criticism, part of it is ridiculous, and the whole improbable" (qtd. in Furness, *New Variorum: The Tragedy*, 16:337); whereas Colley Cibber, in his adaptation of the play, eliminated the ambiguity altogether, allowing his Elizabeth to explain in an aside that she only appears to comply with Richard in order to gain time for her daughter to escape to Richmond, an interpretation many have since found attractive. Those who argue that Elizabeth makes no concession include John Palmer, *Political Characters of Shakespeare* (London: MacMillan, 1945), 104–5; Emrys Jones, *The Origins of Shakespeare* (Oxford: Oxford University Press, 1977), 222–26; and Chris R. Hassel, *Songs of Death: Performance, Interpretation, and the Text of "Richard III"* (Lincoln: University of Nebraska Press, 1987), 22–23. A notable exception is Tillyard, who writes in response to E. K. Chambers's suggestion that Elizabeth has outwitted Richard: "A better explanation is that Elizabeth was merely weak and changeable and that Richard's comment on her . . . was truer than he thought, forecasting the second change" (*Shakespeare's History*, 214).

22. For a discussion of the "masculine tradition" of Renaissance historiography in relation to Shakespeare's history plays, see Phyllis Rackin, *Stages of History: Shakespeare's English Chronicles* (Ithaca: Cornell University Press, 1990), 146–200.

23. Hodgdon, *End Crowns All*, 105.

24. For discussions of representations of the queen in the 1590s, see Roy Strong, *Gloriana: The Portraits of Queen Elizabeth I* (London: Thames and Hudson, 1987); and

Susan Frye, *Elizabeth I: The Competition for Representation* (Oxford: Oxford University Press, 1993).

25. For discussions of the misogyny characterizing the final years of Elizabeth's reign, see Christopher Haigh, *Elizabeth I* (London: Longman, 1988), 164–74; and Steven Mullaney, "Mourning and Misogyny: *Hamlet, The Revenger's Tragedy*, and the Final Progress of Elizabeth I, 1600–1607," *Shakespeare Quarterly* 45 (1994): 139–62.

26. John Knox, *The First Blast of the Trumpet Against the Monstruous Regiment of Women* (1558), facsimile ed. (New York: Da Capo, 1972), sig. B1.

27. Ibid., sig. D3–D3v.

28. Qtd. in Carole Levin, *"The Heart and Stomach of a King": Elizabeth I and the Politics of Sex and Power* (Philadelphia: University of Pennsylvania Press, 1994), 81.

29. Richard's accusations of his brother's bastardy, like those of Robert Faulconbridge in *King John*, conform to what was considered acceptable proof of bastardy in sixteenth-century courts. See George W. Keeton, *Shakespeare's Legal and Political Background* (London: Isaac Pitman and Sons, 1967), 118–31.

30. See Louis Adrian Montrose, "The Elizabethan Subject and the Spenserian Text," in *Literary Theory/Renaissance Texts*, ed. Patricia Parker and David Quint (Baltimore: Johns Hopkins University Press, 1986), 303–40.

31. Carole Levin, "Queens and Claimants: Political Insecurity in Sixteenth-Century England," in *Gender, Ideology, and Action: Historical Perspectives on Women's Public Lives*, ed. Janet Sharistanian (New York: Greenwood Press, 1986), 55–61.

32. Judith H. Anderson, *Biographical Truth: The Representation of Historical Persons in Tudor-Stuart Writing* (New Haven: Yale University Press, 1984), 118, 223 n. See also Hammond, *King Richard III*, 295 n., who, following Anderson, also cites *The Faerie Queene* as a source. Earlier editions generally tended to find a source for the "nest of spicery" in the phoenix emblem, a parallel that also underscores Richard's perversion of an image of regeneration, in this case one associated with Elizabeth I herself.

33. Edmund Spenser, *The Faerie Queene*, ed. Thomas P. Roche Jr. (London: Penguin Books, 1978).

34. Kahn, *Man's Estate*, 63–64. See also Neill, "Shakespeare's Halle of Mirrors," 99–129.

35. Adelman, *Suffocating Mothers*, 4. Adelman points out that Renaissance beliefs in the mother's ability to deform the fetus during gestation—"through her excessive imagination, her uncontrollable longings, her unnatural lusts"(6)—give authority to Richard's charges.

36. Allison Heisch, "Queen Elizabeth I and the Persistence of Patriarchy," *Feminist Review* 4 (1980): 50.

37. Qtd. in J. E. Neale, *Elizabeth I and Her Parliaments 1559–1581* (London: Jonathan Cape, 1953), 109.

38. Joel Samaha, "Gleanings from Local Criminal-Court Records: Sedition Amongst the 'Inarticulate' in Elizabethan Essex," *The Journal of Social History* 8 (1975): 69.

39. Levin, "Queens and Claimants," 59.

40. Qtd. in J. E. Neale, "Peter Wentworth," *English Historical Review* 39 (1924): 196–97.

41. Qtd. in J. E. Neale, *Elizabeth I and Her Parliaments 1584–1601* (New York: St. Martin's Press, 1957), 248–49.

42. Ibid., 249.

43. In an insightful reading of the play's close, Hodgdon also notes that even as the play bridges the gap between past and present, it contests that movement (*End Crowns All*, 122–24). My own analysis differs from Hodgdon's in its emphasis on contestation.

44. W. W. Greg, ed., *The True Tragedy of Richard the Third 1594*, Malone Society Reprints (Oxford: Oxford University Press, 1929), sig. I2. For a discussion of the relationship between *Richard III* and *The True Tragedy of Richard III*, see Bullough, *Narrative and Dramatic Sources*, 3:237–39.

45. Robert J. Lordi, *Thomas Legge's "Richardus Tertius": A Critical Edition with a Translation* (New York: Garland, 1979), 461.

46. Hall, *Union*, 425.

47. Ibid., 2–3. York's recitation of genealogy in *2 Henry VI* also includes Philippa and Anne; it is by Anne, in fact, that York "claim[s] the kingdom" (2.2.47).

48. Hodgdon, *End Crowns All*, 113.

49. Tillyard, *Shakespeare's History*, establishes the orthodox reading of the Richmond-Richard opposition in relation to the Tudor myth of history. More recently, Hodgdon has refigured the relation between this structural opposition and Tudor history, arguing that the play "conceives and spatializes history as a theatrical spectacle of opposition that decrees succession by providential fiat, substituting ritual for genealogy" (*End Crowns All*, 114).

50. According to Mortimer Levine, *Tudor Dynastic Problems, 1460–1571* (London: George Allen and Unwin, 1973), the historical Richmond based his title to the throne on his victory at Bosworth, not on his marriage to Elizabeth of York. That the legitimacy of the Crown rested on Henry alone was affirmed by a parliamentary declaration of 1485 and the fact that he did not actually marry Elizabeth of York until 18 January 1486. But if the marriage to Elizabeth was not essential to Richmond's legitimacy, it was essential in ensuring his continued possession of the throne, for as Levine notes, "the dangers involved in anyone but the king gaining possession of Edward IV's eldest daughter must have been only too obvious" (35). See also Ralph A. Griffiths and Roger S. Thomas, *The Making of the Tudor Dynasty* (New York: St. Martin's, 1985), 179–98.

51. *Holinshed's Chronicles*, 4:161.

52. Ibid., 4:162.

53. Ibid., 4:161.

54. See Frye's fine analysis of the "engendered economics" of this interchange between Elizabeth and the London citizens (*Elizabeth I*, 22–55). For other discussions of the procession, see David M. Bergeron, *English Civic Pageantry 1558–1642* (London: Edward Arnold, 1971); Clifford Geertz, *Local Knowledge: Further Essays in Interpretive Anthropology* (New York: Basic Books, 1983); Steven Mullaney, *The Place of the Stage: License, Play, and Power in Renaissance England* (Chicago: University of Chicago Press, 1988); and Jonathan Goldberg, *James I and the Politics of Literature: Jonson, Shakespeare, Donne, and Their Contemporaries* (1983; reprint, Stanford: Stanford University Press, 1989).

55. Levin records the rumors about Edward VI's survival that, she claims, gave voice to the nation's longing for the security of a male monarch: "The pattern of the male monarch as savior echoes through sixteenth-century England, so that the fears caused by female rule manifested themselves in a longing for the safety and tradition of the king" ("Queens and Claimants," 61).

56. Qtd. in Haigh, *Elizabeth I*, 166.

5. Refiguring the Nation: Mothers and Sons in *King John*

1. John Harington, *A Tract on the Succession to the Crown (A.D. 1602)* (New York: Burt Franklin, 1970), 82.

2. J. W. Allen, *A History of Political Thought in the Sixteenth Century* (1928; reprint, London: Methuen, 1941), 249.

3. For an overview of topical approaches to *King John* that extend from Richard Simpson, "The Politics of Shakespere's Historical Plays," *New Shakespere Society Transactions*, 1 (1874), to Lily B. Campbell, *Shakespeare's "Histories": Mirrors of Elizabethan Policy* (San Marino: Huntington Library, 1947), see E. A. J. Honigmann, ed., *King John* (1954; reprint, London: Methuen, 1973), xxvii–xxx.

4. Phyllis Rackin, *Stages of History: Shakespeare's English Chronicles* (Ithaca: Cornell University Press, 1990), 178. Though my own analysis of the play differs from Rackin's, and from her reading of the play's conclusion in particular, it is clearly indebted to her insightful discussion of women's roles within history.

5. Qtd. in Mortimer Levine, *The Early Elizabethan Succession Question 1558–1568* (Stanford: Stanford University Press, 1966), 197. Levine points out that, in the end, Elizabeth had little choice in her handling of the succession because of the precedent her father's succession acts established for settling the matter in Parliament. For other discussions of the Elizabethan succession, see J. Hurstfield, "The Succession Struggle in Late Elizabethan England," in *Elizabethan Government and Society*, ed. S. T. Bindoff, J. Hurstfield, and C. H. Williams (London: Athlone, 1961); Marie Axton, *The Queen's Two Bodies: Drama and the Elizabethan Succession* (London: Royal Historical Society, 1977); A. R. Braunmuller, ed., *The Life and Death of King John* (Oxford: Oxford University Press, 1989), 55–61; and, more generally, Gertrude Catherine Reese, "The Question of the Succession in Elizabethan Drama," *University of Texas Studies in English* 22 (1942): 59–85.

6. *Statutes of the Realm* (Record Commission, 1831), 4:527.

7. Harington, *Tract on the Succession*, 3.

8. Peter Wentworth, *A Pithie Exhortation to Her Majestie for Establishing Her Successor to the Crowne* (1598), facsimile ed. (New York: Da Capo, 1973).

9. J. E. Neale, *Elizabeth I and Her Parliaments 1584–1601* (New York: St. Martin's, 1957), 256–59. See also Neale, "Peter Wentworth," *English Historical Review* 39 (1924): 184–205.

10. Parsons, [R. Doleman], *A Conference about the Next Succession to the Crowne of Ingland* (1594), facsimile ed. (New York: Da Capo, 1972); additional references to Parsons are cited parenthetically within the text. See also Campbell's discussion documenting the enormous amount of attention the book received as well as Elizabeth's anger at Essex over the dedication (*Shakespeare's "Histories,"* 176–80).

11. For a full discussion of Elizabeth's accession and the legal issues raised by Henry VIII's will, see Mortimer Levine, *Early Elizabethan Succession*, 147–62.

12. John R. Elliott Jr., "Shakespeare and the Double Image of King John," *Shakespeare Studies* 1 (1965): 68.

13. Campbell, *Shakespeare's "Histories,"* 139.

14. Polemics like Anthony Munday's *A Watch-woord to England* (1584), for example, attributed "all the mischeefes that fell" during John's reign to "the good workes of Popes and Papistes" (cited in Honigmann, *King John*, xxvii).

15. Mortimer Levine, *Early Elizabethan Succession*, 32.

16. Ibid., 196.

17. *Answer to Allegations against Mary* (Ashmolean MS, 829, fol 34), qtd. in Mortimer Levine, *Early Elizabethan Succession*, 102.

18. Qtd. in Axton, *Queen's Two Bodies*, 32.

19. Harington, *Tract on the Succession*, 59.

20. Parsons argued that because "the lady Mary late Queene of Scotland, mother of this king, was condemned and executed by the authority of the said parlament, it seemeth evident, unto these men, that this king who pretendeth al his right to the crowne of Ingland by his said mother, can have none at al" (*Conference*, sig. I8). For a discussion of this particularly repressive statute, which barred descendants of those conspiring against Elizabeth from the succession, see Neale, *Elizabeth I and Her Parliaments 1584–1601*, 16–18.

21. See, for example, Barbara Hodgdon, *The End Crowns All: Closure and Contradiction in Shakespeare's History* (Princeton: Princeton University Press, 1991), 24, who rightly argues that the parallels between John and Elizabeth and Arthur and Mary, Queen of Scots, were "out of date by the mid-1590s."

22. Braunmuller, *King John*, 61.

23. John Foxe, *Acts and Monuments*, ed. George Townsend (1841; reprint, New York: AMS, 1965), 2:319–21.

24. *Holinshed's Chronicles of England, Scotland, and Ireland*, ed. Henry Ellis (London, 1808), 2:270.

25. Ibid., 2:274.

26. For discussions of the relationship between *King John* and *The Troublesome Raigne*, see Honigmann, *King John*, xviii–xix; Braunmuller, *King John*, 17–19; Geoffrey Bullough, *Narrative and Dramatic Sources of Shakespeare* (London: Routledge and Kegan Paul, 1962), 4:1–24; J. L. Simmons, "Shakespeare's *King John* and Its Source: Coherence, Pattern, and Vision," *Tulane Studies in English* 17 (1969): 53–72; and Guy Hamel, "*King John* and *The Troublesome Raigne*: A Reexamination," in *"King John": New Perspectives*, ed. Deborah T. Curren-Aquino (Newark: University of Delaware Press, 1989), 41–61.

27. *The Troublesome Raigne of King John* (1591), reprinted in Bullough, *Narrative and Dramatic Sources*, 4:73.

28. *Holinshed's Chronicles*, 2:278.

29. See the discussion of will and inheritance law in Braunmuller, *King John*, 54–61; the argument against a death-bed will rested on the fear that it might be "wrung from a man in his agony" (55 n.).

30. Qtd. in Honigmann, *King John*, 10 n.

31. George W. Keeton, *Shakespeare's Legal and Political Background* (London: Isaac Pitman and Sons, 1967), 126. The case of the bastardy of Elizabeth I shows how this law might be abrogated: when the marriage between Henry VIII and Anne Boleyn was nullified, Elizabeth was able to be declared a bastard because, technically, she was born out of wedlock; see T. B. Howell, ed., *A Complete Collection of State Trials* (London: T. C. Hansard, 1816), 1:419.

32. Rackin, *Stages of History*, 189.

33. Bullough, *Narrative and Dramatic Sources*, 4:78.

34. Keeton, *Shakespeare's Legal*, 125. Although bastardy laws were probably more concerned with stemming the economic drain caused by illegitimate children than with curbing the power of adulterous wives, the effect of the law is, nonetheless, to deny that women have any power in matters of inheritance—even if it means allowing another man's child to inherit your lands. For a discussion of the socioeconomic implications of

bastardy, see Martin Ingram, *Church Courts, Sex and Marriage in England, 1570–1640* (Cambridge: Cambridge University Press, 1987), 253–61.

35. For an excellent discussion of this point, see Rackin, *Stages of History*, 191.

36. For discussions of this scene of women scolding, see the commentary in Horace Howard Furness Jr., ed., *A New Variorum Edition of Shakespeare: The Life and Death of King John* (Philadelphia: J. B. Lippincott, 1919), 81–87; and Juliet Dusinberre, "*King John* and Embarrassing Women," *Shakespeare Survey* 42 (1989): 37–52.

37. Howell, *State Trials*, 418. Catholics also considered Elizabeth a bastard, objecting to the marriage with Anne Boleyn on different grounds. Indeed, as Scotland's Maitland bluntly informed Elizabeth at the start of her reign: "All that follow in religion the Kirk of Rome, your Highness knows, think the King your father's marriage with your mother unlawful, and consequently the issue of the marriage siclike" (qtd. in Mortimer Levine, *Early Elizabethan Succession*, 34).

38. Some opponents to James VI of Scotland objected to his succession to the English throne on the basis that his grandmother Lady Margaret Douglas may have been a bastard; see Wentworth, "A Treatise Containing M. Wentworth His Judgement," in *Pithie Exhortation*, 15.

39. By contrast, see Robert Lane, "'The sequence of posterity': Shakespeare's *King John* and the Succession Controversy," *Studies in Philology* 92 (1995): 460–81, who ascribes agency to the play's citizens; published after this chapter was completed, Lane's article also places the play's politics in relation to the succession debates of the 1590s, but in focusing on the common people, and omitting the women altogether, his emphasis, as well as his conclusions, differs significantly from my own.

40. Rackin, *Stages of History*, 184. For other discussions of the "containment" of women in *King John*, see Virginia M. Vaughan, "*King John*: A Study in Subversion and Containment," in *"King John": New Perspectives*, ed. Deborah T. Curren-Aquino (Newark: University of Delaware Press, 1989); and Hodgdon, *End Crowns All*. For a more general assessment of the play's conclusion, see Larry S. Champion, "The 'Un-end' of *King John*: Shakespeare's Demystification of Closure," in *"King John": New Perspectives*.

41. Janet Adelman, *Suffocating Mothers: Fantasies of Maternal Origin in Shakespeare's Plays, "Hamlet" to "The Tempest"* (New York: Routledge, 1992), 10.

42. See Braunmuller, *King John*, 61. For discussions of fathers and sons in the *Henriad*, see Peter Erickson, *Patriarchal Structures in Shakespeare's Drama* (Berkeley: University of California Press, 1985), 39–65; and Adelman, *Suffocating Mothers*, 11–12.

43. Dusinberre, "*King John*," 40.

44. Jonathan Goldberg, *James I and the Politics of Literature: Jonson, Shakespeare, Donne, and Their Contemporaries* (1983; reprint, Baltimore: Johns Hopkins University Press, 1989), 14.

45. Harington, *Tract on the Succession*.

46. G. P. V. Akrigg, ed., *Letters of King James VI and I* (Berkeley: University of California Press, 1984).

47. G. B. Harrison, ed., *The Letters of Queen Elizabeth I* (1935; reprint, New York: Funk and Wagnalls, 1968), 223.

48. Neale, *Elizabeth I and Her Parliaments 1584–1601*, 251–52.

49. Steven Mullaney, "Mourning and Misogyny: *Hamlet, The Revenger's Tragedy,* and the Final Progress of Elizabeth I, 1600–1607," *Shakespeare Quarterly* 45 (1994): 157–58.

50. Adelman, *Suffocating Mothers*, 10.

51. Bullough, *Narrative and Dramatic Sources*, 4:150.

52. Peter Womack, "Imagining Communities: Theatres and the English Nation in the Sixteenth Century," in *Culture and History 1350–1600: Essays on English Communities, Identities, and Writing*, ed. David Aers (Detroit: Wayne State University Press, 1992), 126, writes: "At the very end of the play, standing over another morsel of dead royalty, he asserts the immortality of an England true to itself, appealing from the ruin of John's body to 'the *universitas*' 'which never dies.'"

53. Bullough, *Narrative and Dramatic Sources*, 4:151.

54. Honigmann, *King John*, 147 n.

55. David Scott Kastan, "'To Set a Form upon that Indigest': Shakespeare's Fictions of History," *Comparative Drama* 17 (1983): 14.

Epilogue

1. Benedict Anderson, *Imagined Communities: Reflections on the Origin and Spread of Nationalism* (London: Verso, 1991), 6.

2. See, for example, John Pocock, "England," in *National Consciousness, History, and Political Culture in Early-Modern Europe*, ed. Orest Ranum (Baltimore: Johns Hopkins University Press, 1975), 98–117; Richard Helgerson, *Forms of Nationhood: The Elizabethan Writing of England* (Chicago: University of Chicago Press, 1992); and Andrew Hadfield, *Literature, Politics and National Identity* (Cambridge: Cambridge University Press, 1994).

3. Helgerson, *Forms of Nationhood*, 234.

4. Leah S. Marcus, *Puzzling Shakespeare: Local Reading and Its Discontents* (Berkeley: University of California Press, 1988), 95.

5. For discussions of questions of women and legitimacy in the second tetralogy, see Phyllis Rackin, *Stages of History: Shakespeare's English Chronicles* (Ithaca: Cornell University Press, 1990); and J. L. Simmons, "Masculine Negotiations in Shakespeare's History Plays: Hal, Hotspur, and 'the foolish Mortimer,'" *Shakespeare Quarterly* 44 (1993): 440–63.

6. See the discussions of these women by Jean E. Howard, "Forming the Commonwealth: Including, Excluding, and Criminalizing Women in Heywood's *Edward IV* and Shakespeare's *Henry IV*," in *Privileging Gender in Early Modern England*, ed. Jean R. Brink, vol. 23 of *Sixteenth Century Essays and Studies* (Kirksville, Mo.: Sixteenth Century Journal, 1993), 109–21; and Jyotsna Singh, "The Intervention of History: Narratives of Sexuality," in *The Weyward Sisters: Shakespeare and Feminist Politics*, ed. Dympna C. Callaghan, et al. (Oxford: Blackwell, 1995).

Bibliography

Adelman, Janet. *Suffocating Mothers: Fantasies of Maternal Origin in Shakespeare's Plays, "Hamlet" to "The Tempest."* New York: Routledge, 1992.

Akrigg, G. P. V., ed. *Letters of King James VI and I.* Berkeley: University of California Press, 1984.

Allen, J. W. *A History of Political Thought in the Sixteenth Century.* 1928. Reprint, London: Methuen, 1941.

Anderson, Benedict. *Imagined Communities: Reflections on the Origin and Spread of Nationalism.* London: Verso, 1991.

Anderson, Judith H. *Biographical Truth: The Representation of Historical Persons in Tudor-Stuart Writing.* New Haven: Yale University Press, 1984.

Axton, Marie. *The Queen's Two Bodies: Drama and the Elizabethan Succession.* London: Royal Historical Society, 1977.

Aylmer, J. *An Harborowe for Faithfull and Trewe Subjectes.* 1559. Facsimile ed. New York: Da Capo, 1972.

Barber, C. L. and Richard P. Wheeler. *The Whole Journey: Shakespeare's Power of Development.* Berkeley: University of California Press, 1986.

Bellamy, John G. *The Law of Treason in England in the Later Middle Ages.* Cambridge: Cambridge University Press, 1970.

―――. *The Tudor Law of Treason.* London: Routledge and Kegan Paul, 1979.

Belsey, Catherine. *The Subject of Tragedy: Identity and Difference in Renaissance Drama.* London: Methuen, 1985.

Benson, Pamela Joseph. *The Invention of the Renaissance Woman: The Challenge of Female Independence in the Literature and Thought of Italy and England.* University Park: Pennsylvania State University Press, 1992.

Bergeron, David M. *English Civic Pageantry, 1558–1642.* London: Edward Arnold, 1971.

―――. "The Play-within-the-Play in *3 Henry VI.*" *Tennessee Studies in Literature* 22 (1977): 37–45.

Berry, Edward I. *Patterns of Decay: Shakespeare's Early Histories.* Charlottesville: University Press of Virginia , 1975.

Bevington, David M. "The Domineering Female in *1 Henry VI.*" *Shakespeare Studies* 2 (1966): 51–58.

————. *Tudor Drama and Politics: A Critical Approach to Topical Meaning.* Cambridge: Harvard University Press, 1968.

————, ed. *The First Part of King Henry Sixth.* In *William Shakespeare: The Complete Works.* Baltimore: Penguin, 1969.

Blanpied, John W. "'Art and Baleful Sorcery': The Counterconsciousness of *Henry VI, Part 1.*" *Studies in English Literature* 15 (1975): 213–27.

Booth, Stephen. *The Book Called "Holinshed's Chronicles."* San Francisco: Book Club of California, 1968.

Born, Hanspeter. "The Date of *2, 3 Henry VI.*" *Shakespeare Quarterly* 25 (1974): 323–34.

Boswell, James, ed. *The Plays and Poems of William Shakespeare.* 1821. Reprint, New York: AMS Press, 1966.

Braunmuller, A. R., ed. *The Life and Death of King John.* Oxford: Oxford University Press, 1989.

Brockbank, J. P. "The Frame of Disorder—*Henry VI.*" In *Early Shakespeare.* Stratford-upon-Avon-Studies 3, edited by John Russell Brown and Bernard Harris. London: Edward Arnold, 1961.

Brooks, Harold F. "*Richard III,* Unhistorical Amplifications: The Women's Scenes and Seneca." *Modern Language Review* 75 (1980): 721–37.

Bullough, Geoffrey. *Narrative and Dramatic Sources of Shakespeare.* 8 vols. London: Routledge and Kegan Paul, 1957–75.

Cairncross, Andrew S., ed. *The First Part of King Henry VI.* London: Methuen, 1962.

————. *The Second Part of King Henry VI.* London: Methuen, 1957.

————. *The Third Part of King Henry VI.* London: Methuen, 1965.

Campbell, Lily B. *Shakespeare's "Histories": Mirrors of Elizabethan Policy.* San Marino: Huntington Library, 1947.

————, ed. *The Mirror for Magistrates.* New York: Barnes and Noble, 1938.

Cartelli, Thomas. "Jack Cade in the Garden: Class Consciousness and Class Conflict in *2 Henry VI.*" In *Enclosure Acts: Sexuality, Property, and Culture in Early Modern England,* edited by Richard Burt and John Michael Archer. Ithaca: Cornell University Press, 1994.

Champion, Larry S. "The 'Un-end' of *King John*: Shakespeare's Demystification of Closure." In *"King John": New Perspectives,* edited by Deborah T. Curren-Aquino. Newark: University of Delaware Press, 1989.

Charnes, Linda. *Notorious Identity: Materializing the Subject in Shakespeare.* Cambridge: Harvard University Press, 1993.

Chrimes, S. B. and A. L. Brown, eds. *Select Documents of English Constitutional History, 1307–1485.* New York: Barnes and Noble, 1961.

Clemen, Wolfgang. *A Commentary on Shakespeare's "Richard III."* Translated by Jean Bonheim. London: Methuen, 1968.

Cohen, Walter. *Drama of a Nation: Public Theater in Renaissance England and Spain.* Ithaca: Cornell University Press, 1985.

Craig, Hardin. *An Interpretation of Shakespeare.* New York: Dryden, 1948.

Dash, Irene G. *Wooing, Wedding, and Power: Women in Shakespeare's Plays.* New York: Columbia University Press, 1981.

Davies, John Silvester, ed. *An English Chronicle*. London: Camden Society, 1856.

Donno, Elizabeth Story. "Some Aspects of Shakespeare's Holinshed." *Huntington Library Quarterly* 50 (1987): 229–48.

duBois, Page. *Centaurs and Amazons: Women and the Pre-History of the Great Chain of Being*. Ann Arbor: University of Michigan Press, 1982.

Dusinberre, Juliet. "*King John* and Embarrassing Women." *Shakespeare Survey* 42 (1989): 37–52.

Dutton, Richard. *Mastering the Revels: The Regulation and Censorship of English Renaissance Drama*. Iowa City: University of Iowa Press, 1991.

Eggert, Katherine. "Nostalgia and the Not Yet Late Queen: Refusing Female Rule in *Henry V*." *ELH* 61 (1994): 523–50.

Elliott, John R. Jr. "Shakespeare and the Double Image of King John." *Shakespeare Studies* 1 (1965): 64–84.

Ellis, Henry, ed. *Three Books of Polydore Vergil's English History* (from an early translation). London: Camden Society, 1844.

Elyot, Sir Thomas. *The Defence of Good Women*. London, 1540.

Erdman, David V. and Ephim G. Fogel. *Evidence for Authorship: Essays on Problems of Attribution*. Ithaca: Cornell University Press, 1966.

Erickson, Peter. *Patriarchal Structures in Shakespeare's Drama*. Berkeley: University of California Press, 1985.

Faber, M. D. *The Design Within: Psychoanalytic Approaches to Shakespeare*. New York: Science House, 1970.

Fabyan, Robert. *The New Chronicles of England and France*. Edited by Henry Ellis. London: Rivington, 1811.

Fiedler, Leslie A. *The Stranger in Shakespeare*. New York: Stein and Day, 1972.

Foucault, Michel. *The Order of Things: An Archaeology of the Human Sciences*. New York: Vintage Books, 1973.

Foxe, John. *Acts and Monuments*. 8 vols. Edited by George Townsend. 1841. Reprint, New York: AMS, 1965.

Fraioli, Deborah. "The Literary Image of Joan of Arc: Prior Influences." *Speculum* 56 (1981): 811–30.

French, A. L. "Joan of Arc and Henry VI." *English Studies* 49 (1968): 425–29.

French, Marilyn. *Shakespeare's Division of Experience*. New York: Summit Books, 1981.

Frye, Susan. *Elizabeth I: The Competition for Representation*. Oxford: Oxford University Press, 1993.

———. "The Myth of Elizabeth at Tilbury." *Sixteenth Century Journal* 23 (1992): 95–114.

Furness, Horace Howard Jr., ed. *A New Variorum Edition of Shakespeare: The Life and Death of King John*. Vol. 19. Philadelphia: J. B. Lippincott, 1919.

———. *A New Variorum Edition of Shakespeare: The Tragedy of Richard the Third*. Vol. 16. Philadelphia: J. B. Lippincott, 1908.

Garber, Marjorie. "Descanting on Deformity: *Richard III* and the Shape of History." In *Shakespeare's Ghost Writers: Literature as Uncanny Causality*. New York: Methuen, 1987.

Gaw, Allison. *The Origin and Development of "1 Henry VI" in Relation to Shakespeare, Marlowe, and Greene*. Los Angeles: University of Southern California Press, 1926.

Geertz, Clifford. *Local Knowledge: Further Essays in Interpretive Anthropology*. New York: Basic Books, 1983.

Girard, René. "Hamlet's Dull Revenge." *Stanford Literature Review* 1 (1984): 159–200.

Goldberg, Jonathan. *James I and the Politics of Literature: Jonson, Shakespeare, Donne, and Their Contemporaries*. 1983. Reprint, Stanford: Stanford University Press, 1989.

Goodman, Christopher. *How Superior Powers Oght to Be Obeyd*. 1558. Facsimile ed. New York: Da Capo, 1972.

Gransden, Antonia. *Historical Writing in England: c. 1307 to the Early Sixteenth Century*. Vol. 2. London: Routledge and Kegan Paul, 1982.

Greenblatt, Stephen. Introduction to *The Power of Forms in the English Renaissance*, edited by Stephen Greenblatt. Norman, Okla.: Pilgrim Books, 1982.

———. "Invisible Bullets: Renaissance Authority and Its Subversion, *Henry IV* and *Henry V*." In *Political Shakespeare: New Essays in Cultural Materialism*, edited by Jonathan Dollimore and Alan Sinfield. Ithaca: Cornell University Press, 1985.

Greg, Walter W., ed. *Henslowe's Diary*. 2 vols. London: A. H. Bullen, 1904.

———. *The True Tragedy of Richard the Third 1594*. Malone Society Reprints. Oxford: Oxford University Press, 1929.

Griffiths, Ralph A. "The Trial of Eleanor Cobham: An Episode in the Fall of Duke Humphrey of Gloucester." *Bulletin of the John Rylands Library* 51 (1969): 381–99.

——— and Roger S. Thomas. *The Making of the Tudor Dynasty*. New York: St. Martin's, 1985.

Guy, John, ed. *The Reign of Elizabeth I: Court and Culture in the Last Decade*. Cambridge: Cambridge University Press, 1995.

Hadfield, Andrew. *Literature, Politics and National Identity*. Cambridge: Cambridge University Press, 1994.

Haigh, Christopher. *Elizabeth I*. London: Longman, 1988.

Hall, Edward. *The Union of the Two Noble and Illustre Famelies of Lancastre and Yorke*. Edited by Henry Ellis. London: 1809.

Hamel, Guy. "*King John* and *The Troublesome Raigne*: A Reexamination." In "*King John": New Perspectives*, edited by Deborah T. Curren-Aquino. Newark: University of Delaware Press, 1989.

Hamilton, A. C. *The Early Shakespeare*. San Marino: Huntington Library, 1967.

Hamilton, Donna B. *Shakespeare and the Politics of Protestant England*. Lexington: University of Kentucky Press, 1992.

Hammond, Antony, ed. *King Richard III*. London: Methuen, 1981.

Hanham, Alison. *Richard III and His Early Historians: 1483–1535*. Oxford: Clarendon Press, 1975.

Hardin, Richard F. "Chronicles and Mythmaking in Shakespeare's Joan of Arc." *Shakespeare Survey* 42 (1989): 25–35.

Harington, John. *A Tract on the Succession to the Crown (A.D. 1602)*. New York: Burt Franklin, 1970.

Harrison, G. B., ed. *King James, the First: Daemonologie (1597), Newes from Scotland (1591)*. New York: Barnes and Noble, 1966.

———. *The Letters of Queen Elizabeth I.* 1935. Reprint, New York: Funk and Wagnalls, 1968.

———. *Shakespeare: The Complete Works.* 1948. Reprint, New York: Harcourt, Brace and World, 1968.

Hassel, Chris R. *Songs of Death: Performance, Interpretation and the Text of "Richard III."* Lincoln: University of Nebraska Press, 1987.

Hattaway, Michael. "Rebellion, Class Consciousness, and Shakespeare's *2 Henry VI.*" *Cahiers Elisabethains* 33 (1988): 13–22.

———, ed. *The First Part of King Henry VI.* Cambridge: Cambridge University Press, 1990.

———. *The Second Part of King Henry VI.* Cambridge: Cambridge University Press, 1991.

———. *The Third Part of King Henry VI.* Cambridge: Cambridge University Press, 1993.

Heisch, Allison. "Queen Elizabeth I: Parliamentary Rhetoric and the Exercise of Power." *Signs* 1 (1975): 31–55.

———. "Queen Elizabeth I and the Persistence of Patriarchy." *Feminist Review* 4 (1980): 45–56.

Helgerson, Richard. *Forms of Nationhood: The Elizabethan Writing of England.* Chicago: University of Chicago Press, 1992.

Heywood, Thomas. *The Exemplary Lives and Memorable Acts of Nine the Most Worthy Women of the World.* London, 1640.

Hodgdon, Barbara. *The End Crowns All: Closure and Contradiction in Shakespeare's History.* Princeton: Princeton University Press, 1991.

Holderness, Graham. *Shakespeare's History.* New York: St. Martin's, 1985.

Holinshed, Raphael, et al. *The Chronicles of England, Scotlande, and Irelande.* London, 1587.

———, et al. *Holinshed's Chronicles of England, Scotland, and Ireland.* Edited by Henry Ellis. 6 vols. London, 1808.

Honigmann, E. A. J., ed. *King John.* 1954. Reprint, London: Methuen, 1973.

Howard, Jean E. "Forming the Commonwealth: Including, Excluding, and Criminalizing Women in Heywood's *Edward IV* and Shakespeare's *Henry IV.*" In *Privileging Gender in Early Modern England,* edited by Jean R. Brink. Vol. 23 of *Sixteenth Century Essays and Studies.* Kirksville, Mo.: Sixteenth Century Journal, 1993.

———. *The Stage and Social Struggle in Early Modern England.* London: Routledge, 1994.

Howell, T. B., ed. *A Complete Collection of State Trials.* Vol. 1. London: T. C. Hansard, 1816.

Hudson, Anne. *The Premature Reformation: Wycliffite Texts and Lollard History.* Oxford: Clarendon Press, 1988.

Hurault, André, Sieur de Maisse. *A Journal of All That Was Accomplished by Monsieur de Maisse Ambassador in England from King Henry IV to Queen Elizabeth Anno Domino 1597.* Translated and edited by G. B. Harrison and R. A. Jones. London: Nonesuch, 1931.

Hurstfield, J. "The Succession Struggle in Late Elizabethan England." In *Elizabethan Government and Society*, edited by S. T. Bindoff, J. Hurstfield, and C. H. Williams. London: Athlone, 1961.

Ingram, Martin. *Church Courts, Sex and Marriage in England, 1570–1640*. Cambridge: Cambridge University Press, 1987.

Jackson, Gabriele Bernhard. "Topical Ideology: Witches, Amazons, and Shakespeare's Joan of Arc." *ELR* 18 (1988): 40–65.

James, Mervyn. *Society, Politics, and Culture: Studies in Early Modern England*. Cambridge: Cambridge University Press, 1986.

Jankowski, Theodora. *Women in Power in the Early Modern Drama*. Urbana: University of Illinois Press, 1992.

Jardine, Lisa. *Still Harping on Daughters: Women and Drama in the Age of Shakespeare*. 1989. Reprint, New York: Columbia University Press, 1989.

Jones, Emrys. *The Origins of Shakespeare*. Oxford: Oxford University Press, 1977.

Jordan, Constance. "Feminism and the Humanists: The Case for Sir Thomas Elyot's *Defence of Good Women*." In *Rewriting the Renaissance: The Discourses of Sexual Difference in Early Modern Europe*, edited by Margaret W. Ferguson, Maureen Quilligan, and Nancy J. Vickers. Chicago: University of Chicago Press, 1986.

———. "Representing Political Androgyny: More on the Siena Portrait of Queen Elizabeth I." In *The Renaissance Englishwoman in Print: Counterbalancing the Canon*, edited by Anne M. Haselkorn and Betty S. Travitsky. Amherst: University of Massachusetts Press, 1990.

———. "Woman's Rule in Sixteenth-Century British Political Thought." *Renaissance Quarterly* 40 (1987): 421–51.

Kahn, Coppélia. *Man's Estate: Masculine Identity in Shakespeare*. Berkeley: University of California Press, 1981.

Kastan, David Scott. "Shakespeare and 'The Way of Womenkind.'" *Daedalus* 111 (1982): 115–30.

———. "'To Set a Form upon that Indigest': Shakespeare's Fictions of History." *Comparative Drama* 17 (1983): 1–15.

Keeton, George W. *Shakespeare's Legal and Political Background*. London: Isaac Pitman and Sons, 1967.

King, John N. *Tudor Royal Iconography*. Princeton: Princeton University Press, 1989.

Kittredge, George Lyman, ed. *The Complete Works of Shakespeare*. Boston: Ginn, 1936.

Knox, John. *The First Blast of the Trumpet Against the Monstruous Regiment of Women*. 1558. Facsimile ed. New York: Da Capo, 1972.

Laing, David, ed. *The Works of John Knox*. Vol. 4. 1855. Reprint, New York: AMS, 1966.

Lane, Robert. "'The sequence of posterity': Shakespeare's *King John* and the Succession Controversy." *Studies in Philology* 92 (1995): 460–81.

Larner, Christina. *Witchcraft and Religion: The Politics of Popular Belief*. Oxford: Basil Blackwell, 1984.

Lee, Patricia-Ann. "A Bodye Politique to Governe: Aylmer, Knox and the Debate on Queenship." *The Historian* 52 (1990): 242–61.

———. "Reflections of Power: Margaret of Anjou and the Dark Side of Queenship." *Renaissance Quarterly* 39 (1986): 183–217.

Levin, Carole. *"The Heart and Stomach of a King": Elizabeth I and the Politics of Sex and Power*. Philadelphia: University of Pennsylvania Press, 1994.

———. "Queens and Claimants: Political Insecurity in Sixteenth-Century England." In *Gender, Ideology, and Action: Historical Perspectives on Women's Public Lives*, edited by Janet Sharistanian. New York: Greenwood Press, 1986.

Levine, Mortimer. *The Early Elizabethan Succession Question 1558–1568*. Stanford: Stanford University Press, 1966.

———. *Tudor Dynastic Problems, 1460–1571*. London: Allen and Unwin, 1973.

Levine, Nina. "Lawful Symmetry: The Politics of Treason in *2 Henry VI.*" *Renaissance Drama* 25 (1994): 197–218.

Levy, F. J. *Tudor Historical Thought*. San Marino: Huntington Library, 1967.

Lordi, Robert J. *Thomas Legge's "Richardus Tertius": A Critical Edition with a Translation*. New York: Garland, 1979.

MacCaffrey, W. T. "England: The Crown and the New Aristocracy, 1540–1600." *Past and Present* 30 (1965): 52–64.

Mallin, Eric S. "Emulous Factions and the Collapse of Chivalry: *Troilus and Cressida.*" *Representations* 29 (1990): 145–79.

———. *Inscribing the Time: Shakespeare and the End of Elizabethan England*. Berkeley: University of California Press, 1995.

Malone, Edmond. "A Dissertation on the Three Parts of *Henry IV.*" In *The Plays and Poems of William Shakespeare*, edited by James Boswell, vol. 18. 1821. Reprint, New York: AMS, 1966.

Marcus, Leah S. *Puzzling Shakespeare: Local Reading and Its Discontents*. Berkeley: University of California Press, 1988.

———. "Shakespeare's Comic Heroines, Elizabeth I, and the Political Uses of Androgyny." In *Women in the Middle Ages and the Renaissance: Literary and Historical Perspectives*, edited by Mary Beth Rose. Syracuse: Syracuse University Press, 1986.

Maus, Katharine Eisaman. *Inwardness and Theater in the English Renaissance*. Chicago: University of Chicago Press, 1995.

McCoy, Richard C. *The Rites of Knighthood: The Literature and Politics of Elizabethan Chivalry*. Berkeley: University of California Press, 1989.

McNeill, John T. "John Foxe: Historiographer, Disciplinarian, Tolerationist." *Church History* 43 (1974): 216–29.

Mendle, Michael. *Dangerous Positions: Mixed Government, the Estates of the Realm, and the Making of the "Answer to the xix propositions."* University: University of Alabama Press, 1985.

Merck, Mandy. "The City's Achievements: The Patriotic Amazonomachy and Ancient Athens." In *Tearing the Veil: Essays on Femininity*, edited by Susan Lipshitz. London: Routledge and Kegan Paul, 1978.

Miner, Madonne M. "'Neither mother, wife, nor England's queen': The Roles of Women in *Richard III.*" In *The Woman's Part: Feminist Criticism of Shakespeare*, edited by Carolyn Ruth Swift Lenz, Gayle Greene, and Carol Thomas Neely. Urbana: University of Illinois Press, 1980.

Montrose, Louis Adrian. "The Elizabethan Subject and the Spenserian Text." In *Literary Theory/Renaissance Texts*, edited by Patricia Parker and David Quint. Baltimore: Johns Hopkins University Press, 1986.

———. "'Shaping Fantasies': Figurations of Gender and Power in Elizabethan Culture." *Representations* 1 (1983): 61–94.

Moulton, Richard G. *Shakespeare as a Dramatic Artist*. 1885. Reprint, New York: Dover, 1966.

Mozley, J. F. *John Foxe and His Book*. 1940. Reprint, New York: Octagon Books, 1970.

Mullaney, Steven. "Mourning and Misogyny: *Hamlet, The Revenger's Tragedy*, and the Final Progress of Elizabeth I, 1600–1607." *Shakespeare Quarterly* 45 (1994): 139–62.

———. *The Place of the Stage: License, Play, and Power in Renaissance England*. Chicago: University of Chicago Press, 1988.

Munro, John. "Some Matters Shakespearean—III." *TLS* 11 October 1947: 528.

Myers, A. R. "The Captivity of a Royal Witch: The Household Accounts of Queen Joan of Navarre, 1419–21." *Bulletin of the John Rylands Library* 24 (1940): 263–84.

———. "Richard III and Historical Tradition." *History* 53 (1968): 81–202.

Nashe, Thomas. *The Works of Thomas Nashe*. Edited by Ronald B. McKerrow. Vol. 1. Oxford: Basil Blackwell, 1958.

Naunton, Robert. *Fragmenta Regalia*. In *A Collection of Scarce and Valuable Tracts*, edited by Walter Scott. London: T. Cadell and W. Davies, 1809.

Neale, J. E. *Elizabeth I and Her Parliaments, 1559–1581*. London: Jonathan Cape, 1953.

———. *Elizabeth I and Her Parliaments, 1584–1601*. New York: St. Martin's, 1957.

———. "Peter Wentworth." *English Historical Review* 39 (1924): 184–205.

Neill, Michael. "Shakespeare's Halle of Mirrors: Play, Politics, and Psychology in *Richard III*." *Shakespeare Studies* 8 (1975): 99–129.

Nichols, J. G., ed. *Chronicle of the Grey Friars of London*. London: Camden Society, 1852.

Nichols, John, ed. *The Progresses and Public Processions of Queen Elizabeth*. 3 vols. 1823. Reprint, New York: AMS, 1966.

Ornstein, Robert. *A Kingdom for a Stage: The Achievement of Shakespeare's History Plays*. Cambridge: Harvard University Press, 1972.

Painter, William. *The Palace of Pleasure*. Edited by Joseph Jacobs. 1890. Reprint, New York: Dover, 1966.

Palmer, John. *Political Characters of Shakespeare*. London: MacMillan, 1945.

Parsons, [R. Doleman]. *A Conference about the Next Succession to the Crowne of Ingland*. 1594. Facsimile ed. New York: Da Capo, 1972.

Patterson, Annabel. *Censorship and Interpretation: The Conditions of Writing and Reading in Early Modern England*. Madison: University of Wisconsin Press, 1984.

———. *Reading Between the Lines*. Madison: University of Wisconsin Press, 1993.

———. *Reading Holinshed's "Chronicles."* Chicago: University of Chicago Press, 1994.

———. *Shakespeare and the Popular Voice*. Cambridge: Basil Blackwell, 1989.

Peele, George. *The Life and Minor Works of George Peele*. Vol. 1. Edited by David Horne. New Haven: Yale University Press, 1952.

Phillips, James E. Jr. "The Background of Spenser's Attitude Toward Women Rulers." *Huntington Library Quarterly* 5 (1941–42): 5–32.

Pierce, Robert B. *Shakespeare's History Plays: The Family and the State*. Columbus: Ohio State University Press, 1971.

Pocock, John. "England." In *National Consciousness, History, and Political Culture in Early-Modern Europe*, edited by Orest Ranum. Baltimore: Johns Hopkins University Press, 1975.

Pugliatti, Paola. *Shakespeare the Historian*. New York: St. Martin's, 1996.

Pye, Christopher. "The Theater, the Market, and the Subject of History." *ELH* 61 (1994): 501–22.

Rabkin, Norman. "Rabbits, Ducks, and *Henry V.*" *Shakespeare Quarterly* 28 (1977): 279–96.

———. *Shakespeare and the Problem of Meaning*. Chicago: University of Chicago Press, 1981.

Rackin, Phyllis. *Stages of History: Shakespeare's English Chronicles*. Ithaca: Cornell University Press, 1990.

Ralegh, Sir Walter. *A Report of the Truth, The Discoverie of Guiana*. 1596. Facsimile ed. Menston, England: Scholar, 1967.

Reed, Robert Rentoul Jr. *The Occult on the Tudor and Stuart Stage*. Boston: Christopher, 1965.

Reese, Gertrude Catherine. "The Question of the Succession in Elizabethan Drama." *University of Texas Studies in English* 22 (1942): 59–85.

Reese, M. M. *The Cease of Majesty: A Study of Shakespeare's History Plays*. New York: St. Martin's, 1961.

Ribner, Irving. *The English History Play in the Age of Shakespeare*. Princeton: Princeton University Press, 1957.

Riggs, David. *Shakespeare's Heroical Histories: "Henry VI" and Its Literary Tradition*. Cambridge: Harvard University Press, 1971.

Robinson, Hastings, trans. and ed. *The Zurich Letters*. 2nd series. Cambridge: Cambridge University Press, 1845.

Rossiter, A. P., ed. *Woodstock: A Moral History*. London: Chatto and Windus, 1946.

Samaha, Joel. "Gleanings from Local Criminal-Court Records: Sedition Amongst the 'Inarticulate' in Elizabethan Essex." *The Journal of Social History* 8 (1975): 61–79.

Sanders, Wilbur. *The Dramatist and the Received Idea: Studies in the Plays of Marlowe and Shakespeare*. Cambridge: Cambridge University Press, 1968.

Scalingi, Paula Louise. "The Scepter or the Distaff: The Question of Female Sovereignty, 1516–1607." *The Historian* 41 (1978): 59–75.

Schleiner, Winifred. "*Divina Virago*: Queen Elizabeth as an Amazon." *Studies in Philology* 78 (1978): 163–80.

Schochet, Gordon J. *Patriarchism in Political Thought*. New York: Basic Books, 1975.

Scott, Joan W. "Gender: A Useful Category of Historical Analysis." In *Coming to Terms: Feminism, Theory, Politics*, edited by Elizabeth Weed. London: Routledge, 1989.

Sen Gupta, S. C. *Shakespeare's Historical Plays*. London: Oxford University Press, 1964.

Shakespeare, William. *The Riverside Shakespeare*. Edited by G. Blakemore Evans. Boston: Houghton Mifflin, 1974.

Shaw, Bernard. Preface to *St. Joan: A Chronicle Play in Six Scenes and an Epilogue*. 1924. Reprint, Baltimore: Penguin, 1969.

Shephard, Amanda. *Gender and Authority in Sixteenth-Century England: The Knox Debate.* Keele, Staffordshire: Ryburn, 1994.

Shepherd, Simon. *Amazons and Warrior Women: Varieties of Feminism in Seventeenth-Century Drama.* Sussex: Harvester, 1981.

Silber, Patricia. "The Unnatural Woman and the Disordered State in Shakespeare's Histories." *Proceedings of the PMR Conference* 2 (1977): 87–95.

Simmons, J. L. "Masculine Negotiations in Shakespeare's History Plays: Hal, Hotspur, and 'the foolish Mortimer.'" *Shakespeare Quarterly* 44 (1993): 440–63.

———. "Shakespeare's *King John* and Its Source: Coherence, Pattern, and Vision." *Tulane Studies in English* 17 (1969): 53–72.

Simpson, Richard. "The Politics of Shakespere's Historical Plays." *New Shakespere Society Transactions* 1 (1874).

Sinfield, Alan and Jonathan Dollimore. "History and Ideology, Masculinity and Miscegenation: The Instance of *Henry V*." In *Faultlines: Cultural Materialism and the Politics of Dissident Reading*, edited by Alan Sinfield. Berkeley: University of California Press, 1992.

Singh, Jyotsna. "The Intervention of History: Narratives of Sexuality." In *The Weyward Sisters: Shakespeare and Feminist Politics*, edited by Dympna C. Callaghan, et al. Oxford: Blackwell, 1995.

Skinner, Quentin. *The Foundations of Modern Political Thought.* Vol. 2. Cambridge: Cambridge University Press, 1978.

Slights, Camille Wells. *The Casuistical Tradition in Shakespeare, Donne, Herbert, and Milton.* Princeton: Princeton University Press, 1981.

Smith, Sir Thomas. *De Republica Anglorum.* Edited by Mary Dewar. Cambridge: Cambridge University Press, 1982.

Spenser, Edmund. *The Faerie Queene.* Edited by Thomas P. Roche Jr. London: Penguin Books, 1978.

Spivack, Bernard. *Shakespeare and the Allegory of Evil: The History of a Metaphor in Relation to his Major Villains.* New York: Columbia University Press, 1958.

Stafford, Helen. "Notes on Scottish Witchcraft Cases, 1590–91." In *Essays in Honor of Conyers Read*, edited by Norton Downs. Chicago: University of Chicago Press, 1953.

Stallybrass, Peter. "*Macbeth* and Witchcraft." In *Focus on "Macbeth,"* edited by John Russell Brown. London: Routledge and Kegan Paul, 1982.

Starkey, David, ed. *Rivals in Power: Lives and Letters of the Great Tudor Dynasties.* New York: Grove Weidenfeld, 1990.

Statutes of the Realm. Vol. 4. Record Commission, 1831.

Stone, Lawrence. *The Crisis of the Aristocracy, 1558–1641.* Oxford: Clarendon Press, 1965.

Stow, John. *The Chronicles of England.* London: Ralphe Newberie, 1580.

Strong, Roy. *The Cult of Elizabeth: Elizabethan Portraiture and Pageantry.* London: Thames and Hudson, 1977.

———. *Gloriana: The Portraits of Queen Elizabeth I.* London: Thames and Hudson, 1987.

Sundelson, David. *Shakespeare's Restorations of the Father.* New Brunswick: Rutgers University Press, 1983.

Talbert, Ernest William. *Elizabethan Drama and Shakespeare's Early Plays: An Essay in Historical Criticism.* Chapel Hill: University of North Carolina Press, 1963.

Thomas, Keith. *Religion and the Decline of Magic.* New York: Scribner's, 1971.

Thompson, J. A. F. "John Foxe and Some Sources for Lollard History: Notes for a Critical Appraisal." *Studies in Church History* 2 (1965): 251–57.

Tillyard, E. M. W. *Shakespeare's History Plays.* London: Chatto and Windus, 1944.

Townsend, George. "Life and Defence of John Foxe." In *The Acts and Monuments of John Foxe.* 8 vols. 1841. Reprint, New York: AMS, 1965.

Tyrrell, Wm. Blake. *Amazons: A Study in Athenian Mythmaking.* Baltimore: Johns Hopkins University Press, 1984.

Ure, Peter, ed. *King Richard II.* 1956. Reprint, London: Methuen, 1987.

Urkowitz, Steven. "Five Women Eleven Ways: Changing Images of Shakespearean Characters in the Earliest Texts." In *Images of Shakespeare: Proceedings of the Third Conference, International Shakespeare Association, 1986,* edited by Werner Habicht, D. J. Palmer, and Roger Pringle. Newark: University of Delaware Press, 1988.

Vaughan, Virginia M. "*King John:* A Study in Subversion and Containment." In *"King John": New Perspectives,* edited by Deborah T. Curren-Aquino. Newark: University of Delaware Press, 1989.

Vickers, Brian, ed. *Shakespeare: The Critical Heritage, 1774–1801.* London: Routledge and Kegan Paul, 1981.

Waller, Marguerite. "Usurpation, Seduction, and the Problematics of the Proper: A 'Deconstructive,' 'Feminist' Rereading of the Seductions of Richard and Anne in Shakespeare's *Richard III.*" In *Rewriting the Renaissance: The Discourses of Sexual Difference in Early Modern Europe,* edited by Margaret W. Ferguson, Maureen Quilligan, and Nancy J. Vickers. Chicago: University of Chicago Press, 1986.

Walzer, Michael. *The Revolution of the Saints: A Study in the Origins of Radical Politics.* London: Weidenfeld and Nicholson, 1965.

Warner, Marina. *Joan of Arc: The Image of Female Heroism.* New York: Knopf, 1981.

Waugh, W. T. "Joan of Arc in English Sources of the Fifteenth Century." In *Historical Essays in Honor of James Tait,* edited by J. G. Edwards, V. H. Galbraith, and E. F. Jacob. Manchester, 1933.

Weimann, Robert. *Authority and Representation in Early Modern Discourse.* Edited by David Hillman. Baltimore: Johns Hopkins University Press, 1996.

———. "Bifold Authority in Shakespeare's Theater." *Shakespeare Quarterly* 39 (1988): 401–17.

Wells, Stanley and Gary Taylor. *William Shakespeare: A Textual Companion.* Oxford: Clarendon Press, 1987.

Wentworth, Peter. *A Pithie Exhortation to Her Majestie for Establishing Her Successor to the Crowne.* 1598. Facsimile ed. New York: Da Capo, 1973.

Wheeler, Richard P. "History, Character and Conscience in *Richard III.*" *Comparative Drama* 5 (1971–72): 301–21.

Williamson, Marilyn L. "'When Men Are Rul'd by Women': Shakespeare's First Tetralogy." *Shakespeare Studies* 19 (1987): 41–59.

Willis, Deborah. "Shakespeare and the English Witch-Hunts: Enclosing the Maternal Body." In *Enclosure Acts: Sexuality, Property, and Culture in Early Modern England,* edited by Richard Burt and John Michael Archer. Ithaca: Cornell University Press, 1994.

Wilson, Elkin Calhoun. *England's Eliza*. Cambridge: Harvard University Press, 1939.

Wilson, J. Dover, ed. *The First Part of "King Henry VI."* Cambridge: Cambridge University Press, 1952.

Wilson, Richard. "'A Mingled Yarn': Shakespeare and the Cloth Workers." *Literature and History* 12 (1986): 164–80.

Womack, Peter. "Imagining Communities: Theatres and the English Nation in the Sixteenth Century." In *Culture and History, 1350–1600: Essays on English Communities, Identities, and Writing,* edited by David Aers. Detroit: Wayne State University Press, 1992.

Woodbridge, Linda. *Women and the English Renaissance: Literature and the Nature of Womankind, 1540–1620*. Urbana: University of Illinois Press, 1986.

Wooden, Warren. *John Foxe*. Boston: Twayne, 1983.

Woolf, D. R. "Genre into Artifact: The Decline of the English Chronicle in the Sixteenth Century." *Sixteenth Century Journal* 19 (1988): 321–54.

Wright, Celeste Turner. "The Amazons in Elizabethan Literature." *Studies in Philology* 37 (1940): 433–56.

———. "The Elizabethan Female Worthies." *Studies in Philology* 43 (1946): 628–43.

Wright, Thomas, ed. *Political Poems and Songs Relating to English History*. Vol. 2. 1861. Reprint, New York: Kraus, 1965.

Yates, Frances A. *Astraea: The Imperial Theme in the Sixteenth Century*. London: Routledge and Kegan Paul, 1975.

Index